The Man Who Cycled The World

Mark Beaumont

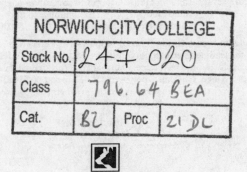

CORGI BOOKS

TRANSWORLD PUBLISHERS
61–63 Uxbridge Road, London W5 5SA
A Random House Group Company
www.rbooks.co.uk

**THE MAN WHO CYCLED THE WORLD
A CORGI BOOK: 9780552158442**

First published in Great Britain
in 2009 by Bantam Press
an imprint of Transworld Publishers
Corgi edition published 2010

Typeset in 11/14pt Times New Roman by
Falcon Oast Graphic Art Ltd.
Printed in the UK by CPI Cox & Wyman, Reading, RG1 8EX.

10 9

for an eight-minute slot) and with Melvyn on *Start the Week*, where Honor had attempted to make herself heard over a lugubrious scientist, a cleric who seemed to be under the impression that he was still in the pulpit, and a novelist with eccentric views about animal welfare.

More recently, there had been the *South Bank Show*. (Melvyn again. Were there no other serious broadcasters left?) She had been assured that the programme would focus exclusively on her work – she had made it clear that her personal life was out of bounds – and she had been stupidly flattered into thinking that it would celebrate her 'place, as a writer, at the heart of twentieth-century history'. Instead, what had it amounted to? A shrivelled old cadaver talking in the gloom about world events that no longer meant anything to anyone; a quavering Miss Havisham recalling the wedding that never was.

They had punctuated the interview with archive footage and stills – of Scotland, Paris, Spain, Germany and Los Angeles, with a procession of artists, poets, politicians and Hollywood panjandrums, and, successively, three husbands – a parodic distillation of her life in six minutes of flickering film. Painstakingly true to their word, the programme makers had refrained from actually mentioning any family, husbands or lovers, but the relentless pictorial parade was less discreet.

The researchers had unearthed a publicity shot of Maxime, waving a cigarette holder like a conductor's baton, dwarfed by his own shadow, flamboyant as Noel Coward, though without the wit or warmth, or indeed the testosterone. Sandor Varga appeared twice: sleek and saturnine as Honor's bridegroom in Basle then, ten years later, plump and smug in Monaco with the cheap little trollop he had left her for. Tad, her third and last husband, had, bizarrely, received less attention in the documentary than the over-praised actress Elizabeth Taylor – the voiceover included an oafish reference to 'Hollywood royalty' – with whom Honor and Tad had been photographed once at some film industry gala. His work was represented by a couple of clips from his films, which proved a mixed curse; out of context, the humour had seemed even more puerile and strained, its nudging sexual references suggesting repression rather than liberation. She had felt for the poor old thing, safely out of it, in St Marylebone Cemetery.

Respect was paid to her working life with some war footage – juddering front-line stuff from Madrid, Poland, Normandy, Buchenwald, Berlin and Incheon. Shadowy figures flitted through the Casbah in Fifties Algiers – more stock footage – and there was a mawkish picture of her cradling a startled infant in a Weimar orphanage in the late Sixties.

Hungarian students dashed themselves against Soviet tanks in 1956 and thirteen years later (three seconds in absurdly concertinaed screen time) their Czech counterparts did the same, while across two borders, in Paris, the privileged sons – it was mostly the sons – of the bourgeoisie, future lawmakers, academics, politicians and pundits, played at revolution, kicked in shop windows and hurled bricks and fire bombs at the proletarian gendarmes.

A shot of Honor in the Fifties in a Korean foxhole, unkempt and besmirched, showed her looking less like a war correspondent at work than a debutante surprised in a face pack. Mostly, though, the clips showed her young self as shiny and groomed, lustrous hair tumbling artfully to her shoulders, her smile an Olympian beacon, defying anyone not to find her beautiful, to desire her, to admire her cleverness and envy her success. The juxtaposition of this luminescent, capering goddess with the palsied pensioner in the filmed interview made for an exquisitely cruel vanitas: an Ozymandia for the modern age. Look on my works, ye mighty, and despair. The friends and lovers momentarily brought to life on screen might all be ghosts now, decomposing slime beneath the soil, or long ago cast to the air as ashes, but the grimmest spectre of them all was Honor Tait, the survivor, condemned to watch, appalled, over her own slow shrivelling.

What a mortifying thing fame was these days. It astonished her that so many people appeared to have little better to do than to sit gape-mouthed before late-night TV arts programmes. She had been recognised everywhere – taxi drivers, maître d's, shopkeepers, strangers at gallery openings, passers-by in the street. One labourer in an orange jerkin, shouldering scaffolding poles near her consultant's clinic in Wimpole Street, had tipped his hard hat at her and called out, 'Keep up the scribbling!'

Then there had been T.P. Kettering, the fawning

academic who had volunteered as 'official biographer' and, when rebutted, attempted to become unofficial snitch. His book, published by an obscure university press with a title of preposterous grandiosity – *Veni Vidi: Honor Tait, History's Witness* – had been a flaccid collage of cuttings, neutered by lawyers and fatally sunk by Honor's unspoken decree that anyone who wished to retain any connection with her should have nothing to do with the proposed book or its author. Martha Gellhorn, Honor had been galled to see, had given Kettering a polite and mendaciously respectful quote. The book had been poorly reviewed. ('There is a compelling biography to be written about the extraordinary Honor Tait, but this vapid volume is not it,' Bobby wrote in the *Telegraph*.) The book had been mercifully forgotten, as had Kettering himself. Honor's pleasure on learning that he had sunk into alcoholic desuetude, and was reduced to ghosting a footballer's autobiography, had verged on indecency.

She could not, however, excise her name from the indices of other people's biographies, or from the press cuttings that had been Kettering's source. Nor could she remove her work from the archives. So much was in the public domain already. At this stage, she needed to preserve the few shreds of dignity and privacy she had left.

She must look around her flat with the eye of a stranger, a malign stranger: a journalist. For her, of all people, this should not be difficult. But she was old and out of practice – she had not published any original reportage for eight years and her last piece, on the plight of Vietnamese boat people in Hong Kong, had been turned down by the *New Statesman* six months ago, with a letter of breathtaking obsequiousness. The 'New Journalism', of which she had once been seen as an exemplar, had been superseded by even newer forms, whose guiding principles baffled her. Like the *nouvelle vague* of French cinema, or the wasp-waisted full skirts of Dior's New Look, Honor Tait's distinct brand of New Journalism – politically informed, veraciously impartial – was as obsolete as an antimacassar in this ironic modern age. Only the wilfully arch, the nostalgia nuts with a taste for 'vintage' style and Bakelite aesthetics, held her approach in any esteem.

She stood in the centre of the room, a fragile, fretful old woman, her hair awry, in a shabby dressing gown of paisley silk. She had recently developed a sporadic tic, a nodding tremor of the head which seemed to become more pronounced when she was agitated, as she was now, and gave the impression of enthusiastic endorsement when the opposite was invariably the case. Her left hand gripped the back of one of Tad's precious wing-back chairs and, steadying herself, she turned slowly, her watery blue eyes narrowing, trying to take in the room as if for the first time, to read it as if she were illicitly scrutinising someone else's intimate journal.

Start with the walls: the pictures and photographs. How long was it since she had actually looked at these things? That watercolour of verdigris waves and muddy mountains – Antrim? The west of Scotland? Not Loch Buidhe, anyway. It was too wild and open for that sheltered glen.

Another of Tad's impulse purchases; blamelessly unbio-graphical and criminally inept. Honor's young interviewer would have difficulty drawing disparaging conclusions from this crude seascape, unless she was a connoisseur of art which, given the calibre of most newspaper people these days, or indeed most young people, was unlikely. For the dealer in swift stereotypes, the picture might reflect a fondness for conventional Sunday painters or Celtic melancholy. Entirely wrong, but a harmless misreading.

The deceptively simple ink and wash of Tristram and Iseult could be more problematic. Tad had found it so. His first inclination had been to destroy the drawing, rip it in two with his meaty hands, or at least to leave it where he had found it, in a stack of Honor's unregarded papers at Glenbuidhe. But the proprietorial husband, furious that his wife, whom he had married in both their middle years, had ever been close to anyone else, lost out to his peculiarly American deference to fame. It was Tad who eventually chose the unwieldy ebony frame, after a degree of contemplation and dialogue that would not have discredited Plato, and placed the picture over the mantelpiece in the flat, where it still hung today. The artist had united the lovers in a single line and, if an interviewer were to examine the drawing closely in an unobserved moment – when, say, Honor was making tea in the kitchen – she might detect his dedication, written vertically in his tiny square print up the line of Iseult's gown: *To Honor from Jean. Je t'embrasse.*

The story of their friendship had been regurgitated

8

several times, in biographies of Cocteau and in the few profiles of her. Most recently, Kettering had attempted to warm it up and serve it again to an apathetic public. And the *South Bank Show* had shown jerky footage of the party for *Le Bel Indifférent* – with Picasso characteristically clowning for the cameras – but, observing her stipulation to the letter, the programme makers had refrained from attribution or comment, using, instead of informative voiceover, a rippling guitar soundtrack from Django Reinhardt and the Hot Club de France. 'Oh, Lady Be Good.' Not an exhortation that was often heard in her circles in those days.

Her brief time with Jean had preceded her marriage to Tad – the last and best of husbands – by many decades, but timing had never been the issue for him. Nor did he need any evidence of intimacy. Tad's jealousy – retrospective, current and prospective – had seemed a manifestation of madness evident nowhere else in his nature. A naughty deed in a good world.

But, really, what interest could such a story of busy couplings and sunderings, opium addiction and wild drinking among artists and bohemians in Paris – what was it? sixty years ago? sixty-five? – possibly hold for readers of a British Sunday newspaper magazine in the dying days of the millennium? Today, art was about smearing your bodily fluids on canvas or parading your personal inadequacies for the benefit of the gawpers. They were all artists now; at it like farm animals, drinking like Bacchae. Opium, or its contemporary equivalent – was it cocaine again? or Ecstasy? – was served at industrialists' dinner parties, shopgirls' suppers and suburban pubs. Yesterday's scandal was today's optional footnote. Who really remembered Jean? And of those few wilful connoisseurs of obscurity who remembered him, who cared? The picture could stay. Besides, it was too heavy for her to move it unassisted.

Opposite the Cocteau, in a frame of unvarnished oak, was a harsh oil portrait of her, painted ten years ago, stiffly coiffed, carmine lipped and glacial. It was unflattering, even menacing, but something about it, its raw candour perhaps, or the timeless impassivity of a Russian icon – The Temptation of St Honor, facing down innumerable unseen demons – had appealed to Tad, despite his constitutional antipathy to the artist. Daniel had painted it in his first and, as it transpired, final term at the Slade. His final year. She wrested the picture from the wall, cursing the effort this simple act required of her. But setting it down against the skirting board, she was dismayed to see that the painting had left a ghostly rectangle of dark wallpaper, like the poignant patch in the Boston museum that awaited the return of the stolen Vermeer. The absence of the portrait might invite more speculation than its presence. Better to leave it. She struggled to replace it on its hook. Her heart began to race uncomfortably, a prick of pain in each beat. She sat down to catch her breath.

Despite Honor's initial refusal, her publisher had persuaded her to meet the interviewer in her flat. For all her earth-mother affectations, Ruth Lavenham, founder and editor-in-chief of Uncumber Press, was a steely operator. The intrusion would be good for sales of Honor's new book, Ruth had said. Good, too, was the implication, a threat sheathed in a smile, for Uncumber Press, a valiant David to the corporate Goliaths of the publishing world. Honor owed her. It was Ruth who had rescued her from insolvency two years ago, just after Tad's death, with a smart new edition of Honor's first collection of journalism, *Truth, Typewriter and Toothbrush*, originally published by Faber in the 1950s and long out of print. The book, in its second incarnation, included her Pulitzer Prize-winning account of the liberation of Buchenwald and became a surprising *succès d'estime*. Honor Tait was 'rediscovered' and, more gratifyingly, she was able to pay off some of her more pressing debts. The hope was that the new book, *Dispatches from a Dark Place: The Collected Honor Tait*, would repeat the trick. And next year, if all went well, there would be a third book, with the title, suggested by Ruth though resisted by Honor, of *The Unflinching Eye*.

'Oh come on,' Ruth had said when they discussed advance publicity for *Dispatches*, 'an interview with the most respected magazine in the land? In the comfort of your own home? Where's the harm in that? And in publicity terms, it's infinitely better than a double-page advert.'

Cheaper, too. So Honor had capitulated. But she knew it was a mistake. On the few occasions in her life that she had consented to be interviewed, she had never admitted any reporter to her home. Even the most well-disposed journalist would regard the flat and its contents as her psyche's porthole, curtainless and illuminated in the dark. The *South Bank Show* conversation with Melvyn had been filmed at the London Library, where she had previously agreed – in a moment of reckless narcissism, justly rewarded by the photograph itself (a Halloween fright mask in Hell's reading room) – to pose for *Vogue*.

Hotels, impersonal no man's lands, stripped of signs and souvenirs, were best for these encounters. The most energetically malevolent reporter would find it hard to take you to task for the blandness of the interior decoration, the stains on the sofa or the musty smell pervading your room. Even then, in a corporate suite of beige leather and chrome, where the only indigenous books were the Gideon Bible and the Yellow Pages, you could be caught out, like poor John Updike. She had written him a note of sympathy after one newspaper interviewer had spotted a discarded pair of underpants under a chair in his hotel room and went on in her article to use the white briefs as a metaphor for what she considered to be the casual, masculine attitude to sex reflected in Updike's fiction. It was the priggishness Honor had abhorred. Here in her flat, at least, thanks to the maid, there would be no underwear on view.

It was an old technique: alight on an apparently insignificant object and use it to construct a catchpenny psychological case history of its owner. How else to sum up a life on the evidence of an hour's conversation and a little legwork in the cuttings library? Honor had resorted to the practice more than once herself, particularly when the interviewee was unforthcoming. Every tchotchke tells a story. Even in the newest New Journalism, some things never change. She recalled her own blood-sport thrill when she had spotted the netsuke mule on MacArthur's bureau in Tokyo; a playbill for a Max Miller burlesque in Beckett's Montparnasse redoubt; the copy of Shakespeare's sonnets by Mme Chiang Kai-shek's hospital bedside, and the signed photograph of Ida Lupino in de Gaulle's austere wartime office in Carlton Gardens.

Could her own photographs, still on the bookcase and on the walls where Tad had first placed them, withstand such scrutiny? One black-and-white shot showed her as a young war reporter, lithe as a lioness and chic in fatigues among the grinning doomed boys before Normandy. Next to it was the iconic image, for *Collier's*, sitting with Franco, newly appointed Commandant General of the Canary Islands. Above the waist she was primly professional, her notebook and pen raised in a posture of exaggerated attentiveness, like a Thirties stenographer. 'Take a letter, Miss Tait.' Below, she was all showgirl. Her long tanned legs, in tailored shorts and high-heeled sandals, looked as if they were on temporary loan from the Ziegfeld Follies. The picture was syndicated all over the world. 'The Newsroom Dietrich', they had called her. All on the record. All part of the myth. Nothing could be done about that now.

The doctored paparazzi shot of the candlelit dinner – a

fund-raiser for the Progressive Party – might be more contentious. In its unexpurgated form, with Sinatra by her side, whispering in her ear, it certainly had been at the time. He was married but openly dating Ava Gardner when the picture was taken and the gossip pages had been exultant, though with the sycophantic tone of those more innocent days; mortals enviously ogling the sport of gods. Now the mortals were in the ascendancy and the gods in the stocks, pelted with rotten vegetables. She lifted the photograph from its hook and held it in her hands, admiring – yes, why not admit it? – the way the light fell across her shoulders, illuminating her gardenia corsage. The blooms were as soft and dewy as her guileless young face, apparently caught in a state of pre-coital deliquescence. How the camera lies, and sometimes in our favour. She had been a matron by the standards of the time; she had hit thirty, with one war, one miserable marriage and several ill-advised romantic liaisons behind her. Two further wars – three, if you counted Algeria – lay just round the corner. She had been in no mood for that kind of evening – her old friend Lois, then working for the Henry Wallace camp, had strong-armed her – and Honor had been irritated to find that the seating plan had twinned her not with Alvin Tilley, a progressive playwright, one of the Hollywood Eleven, but with the kitsch crooner Frank Sinatra. Sinatra, too, clearly had other plans for the evening, though he had been civil. His murmured proposition, as recorded by the camera, was actually a conversation about the Joint Anti-Fascist Refugee Committee.

Two decades later Tad, in another squall of jealousy, had cut the picture in half, removing the singer, with his fallen-seraphim smile, as well as the encircling photographers and fans. The original, unedited picture was still in circulation, owned by one of the big agencies, and had been used in the recent documentary. Posterity, savagely capricious, had kept Sinatra's 40-watt gifts ablaze in the public imagination, while numberless brighter talents had been extinguished. Might Honor's interviewer, the bathetically named Tamara Sim, recognise this version in her hands as bowdlerised and conclude that Honor, a thwarted lover perhaps, had taken the scissors to the photograph herself? Could it set the girl off on a false trail? Honor had no wish to encourage any prurience from *The Monitor*, or its Sunday magazine.

On the brink of a new millennium, and despite their journalists' shambolic private lives, drink problems and drug habits, despite the widespread commodification of the most arcane sexual practices, newspapers faced with any story of the mildest marital impropriety still responded like Edwardian spinsters confronting their first flasher. Honor was permitting this newspaper to invade her privacy only up to a point, and for one purpose only: to sell the wretched book. Or, more precisely, to make money and pay off some bills. Best to be safe. The photograph should go. Clutching it, breathless again, she turned back to her chair. She must sit down.

*

Seven miles away in Hornsey, in a narrow street of sub-divided semis, Tamara Sim sat in the perpetual dusk of her basement flat squinting into a mirror. Lipsticks were scattered like spent bullets on the dressing table and there was an artist's battery of cosmetic brushes at her elbow as she applied her make-up with the infinite care of a girl about to embark on her first date. Which in a way she was.

When the Editor of *The Monitor*'s prestigious *S*nday* magazine had sent a message asking Tamara if she would interview Honor Tait, she had replied instantly.

'Of course! Old-school journalistic heroine!! I'd LOVE to do her!!! . . .' Tamara's response began.

In fact, she had been surprised to learn that the legendary reporter was still alive. Her knowledge of Tait's oeuvre was limited – a piece on the wife of a Chinese dictator from the 1950s had been a set text on Tamara's Media Studies course. According to the lecturer, Tait had borrowed a nurse's uniform, bluffed her way into a hospital where the old woman was being treated and spent an hour at her bedside. The interview itself was as dry and uncompelling as a broadsheet leader, and Tamara got through her finals without actually reading it in its entirety.

Chinese history, or history of any sort, had never much appealed to her. Nor, for that matter, had old-school journalistic heroines. In-depth profiles of elderly writers were not her usual beat and the deadline – three weeks – was tight. But she had been exhilarated by Lyra Moore's terse proposal, sent via the office computer, that she 'write

4,000 words on Honor Tait's life and work, deadline 19 Feb for *S*nday* issue of 30 March, to coincide with Tait's 80th birthday and publication of her new book'.

Tamara worked four days a week on *The Monitor* as a freelance sub editor and occasional writer for *Psst!*, the paper's Saturday celebrity gossip and TV listings magazine – a brash oik to *S*nday*'s snooty metaphysician. The world described in the primary-coloured pages of *Psst!*, peopled by sex-addicted soap stars and feuding boy bands, anorexic footballers' molls and drug-taking TV hosts, was as remote from the intellectual aristocrats of *S*nday* as was Pluto, in both its planetary and Disney incarnations. Lyra Moore's magazine, irreproachably elegant and cerebral, was regarded as the British riposte to the *New Yorker*, with the added appeal of pictures. Its pages, soft and slippery as silk, had most recently hosted a meditation on medieval aesthetics by Umberto Eco, a disquisition on Kierkegaard by George Steiner and an essay by Susan Sontag on the potency of the Polaroid, accompanied by instant photographs – mysterious, personal and touchingly ill-composed – taken on one day last March by the recently besieged citizens of Sarajevo. All three writers were strangers to Tamara and, though she did her best to tackle their contributions to *S*nday*, she felt no compulsion to pursue their acquaintance by reading their books. Never mind the inclination, where would she find the time?

She decided against the vampish slash of red lipstick – it accentuated her incipient cold sore – wiped her mouth with tissue, and opted for frosted pink. She had to look the part today. Groomed but unthreatening. A knee-length navy bias-cut skirt, white cotton blouse, beige trench coat and low-heeled court shoes – the sort of unexceptional outfit Princess Diana might wear on an official visit to a children's hospital.

Tamara knew this commission was going to be a trial of endurance, requiring a long interview and the obligation to write it up, at considerable length and in poly-syllabic words, within a bracingly brief span of time. Four thousand words would, she was aware, be a struggle for someone more used to turning in a two-sentence caption story, a twelve-line list or a two-paragraph column on celebrity mishaps. Her occasional interviews might run to 800 words and she had been called on to produce two pieces of a thousand words each – a cheque-book job with a transsexual lap dancer who claimed to have slept with a children's TV presenter, and an exposé of the drug-taking teenaged son of a senior policeman – for the *Sunday Sphere*. But four times that length? A great deal of typing would be involved, not to mention research.

It was daunting, but a commission from Lyra Moore was the highest compliment any journalist could be paid. Five years after the launch of *S*nday*, its title was still uttered with quiet reverence, despite occasional stumbles over the typographic tic. Snobs admired Lyra Moore's glossy for its intellectual cachet, while pragmatic hacks envied its lavish budget. And as an ambitious journalist with a wide freelance portfolio, no sick pay, holiday or pension provision, no access to a trust fund, and a dependent brother, Tamara could not afford to turn down this opportunity.

She had fretted that her reply, which she'd typed within seconds of seeing Lyra's message flashing on her computer screen, had been perhaps too effusive – '. . . I'd LOVE to do her!!! . . . I SO much admire! . . . I'm THRILLED to be part of!! . . . Amazing magazine!!! . . . Fantastic writers!!! . . .' Did the editor of *S*nday* prefer an aloofness in her contributors that matched her own? Could this explain Lyra's failure to respond to that message, or to reply to any of Tamara's subsequent messages or phone calls? Was it possible that, as with men, one could be *too* enthusiastic?

As a weekly fixture at *Psst!*, Tamara was a 'regular casual', with the job security of a day labourer on a dodgy building site. But as long as she was useful and enjoyed the patronage of *Psst!*'s editor, she had an income and a desk to sit at for four days a week, Monday to Thursday, leaving her three days to find freelance work elsewhere. She had written pieces for *Monitor Extra*, the paper's daily Features section, known as *Me2*, run by the hollow-eyed adrenalin junkie Johnny Malkinson. These pieces were chiefly lists, ring-rounds and vox pops, but she was getting a reputation – extending beyond *The Monitor* to an encouraging number of copy-hungry magazines and papers – as a reliable supplier of humorous, low-cost fillers.

Tamara had done her time – three months – as a junior reporter on the *Sydenham Advertiser*, before moving on to become an adaptable contributor to professional and corporate newsletters, including *Inside the Box: the Voice of the Cardboard Packaging Industry, Glaze: The Chartered Institute of Food Stylists' Quarterly*, and *The Press: Trade Paper of the Laundry and Dry Cleaning Industry*. She had graduated to hobbyists' house journals, addressing weekend mountaineers, ballroom dancers and budgerigar enthusiasts, switched to general consumer magazines – *Glow* and *Chicks' Choice* – and eventually worked and wheedled her way as a freelance into news sections, features pages, diary columns, travel sections and weekend supplements on many national and regional papers, tabloid and broadsheet. The process had equipped her with a diverse knowledge base, giving her a familiarity with the advantages of aluminium ice axes and polypropylene pants, the relative merits of carbon tetrachloride and perchlorethylene, the difference between the Mambo and the Merengue, and the correct spelling of Melopsittacini.

In the course of duty, she had travelled business class and seen the world. In Mexico City, where she had been sent to report on ExpoPack 1995, she enjoyed frozen daiquiris and three days of furtive sex with a big-box retailer from Nebraska; in San Diego, she had fallen in love, painfully unreciprocated, with an Italian photographer while covering a three-day Salad Styling Workshop; and in Mauritius she went deep sea diving for the first – and last – time during an avian veterinarians' conference on the treatment of clinical megabacteriosis. She took pride in her professional versatility and, reflecting on her 'regular casual' role at *Psst!*, saw her working life as a mirror of her love life – she was playing the field, having fun, and felt no pressure to commit until the right publication came along and made an attractive offer. Only then would she be prepared to consider a serious, more monogamous working arrangement. If only Tim Farrow, Editor of the *Sunday Sphere*, had delivered, she would be looking at a satisfactory resolution on both fronts. But he had proved a serious disappointment.

She must not think of Tim. It would ruin her mascara. She had sobbed for a fortnight and needed to move on, and up. The *S*nday* commission was timely. One door closes, another opens. She had served her apprenticeship slogging in the foothills of trade publishing, laboured on to do her share of latrine cleaning in the tabloid base camp and now, at this stage of her career, at the age of twenty-seven, she could aim higher and set her sights on *S*nday*, the Chomolungma of British newspaper publishing. With a little perseverance, a staff job or a fat freelance contract with the most admired publication in the UK would be hers for the taking.

She frowned at herself in the mirror. She wished she could afford a trip to the hairdresser's. Her highlights badly needed retouching, but the cut – a high street approximation of Diana's pageboy, if she tucked her hair behind her ears – was neat enough. She gathered up her notebook, pencil and tape recorder and stowed them in her bag.

Honor Tait was famously tricky. Even her publisher acknowledged as much, warning that any details of her author's private life were off-limits. But Tamara would be prepared. She had *The Monitor*'s cuttings library file on Honor Tait's life and work, printouts from the publishers, an advance copy of the new book, and another unappetising hardback – grim and dense as a sociology text book – of an earlier collection of Tait's journalism, which apparently included a Pulitzer Prize-winning article. Though Tamara had not had a moment to look at any of the research material in depth, she had already jotted down some questions in her notebook. As she walked to the bus stop on her way to the interview, she felt armed and ready for combat.

Two

Honor's energy was fading; the span of alertness between the first cup of coffee and the swooning urge to nap was dwindling daily. But she had to complete this task. Forty-five minutes to go. The picture of Tad on the rosewood side table could stay. As twinkly eyed, white-haired and pink-cheeked as a clean-shaven Selfridges' Santa, a patron saint of goodwill and constancy: the irreproachable, dead, final husband. He had given the photograph to her, in a typical gesture of ingenuous egotism, as a wedding anniversary present. What could be more uxorious?

The one photograph in the flat that she had framed herself, clipping it between two Perspex squares bought from the stationer's, was safely out of range of reportorial eyes, on her bedside table. The summer sun had bleached the boy's untidy thatch of hair and his shirt was coming loose from the woven belt girding his shorts. Honor, wearing a polka-dot frock cinched at the waist with a patent belt, held his hand a little too tightly. Behind them was the solid Georgian bulk of Glenbuidhe Lodge, with dripping candelabras of fuchsia by the front door and, in full sail in the drawing-room window, a ship in a bottle, another appeasement offering from Tad. Daniel's head was tipped on one side, shyly challenging the photographer, and his left eye was closed, as if winking, against the light flaring on the loch. It was Lois who took the picture. She had brought Daniel up on the sleeper for the Easter break. Later, she sent Honor the photo with a presumptious note: 'Look after him Honor. He's more fragile than he seems.' Honor had thrown the note on the fire. In the end, Tad had urged her also to destroy the picture, and she had concealed it for years. She could not get rid of it, though she was ashamed of this maudlin attachment. Now Tad was gone, too, and she could do as she liked.

Propped on the sitting-room mantelpiece above the black maw of the coal-effect gas fire was a postcard, a picture of a graceful coolie-hatted figure in a paddy field. It was a dutiful dispatch from Saigon sent by Tad's god-daughter, who seemed to have spent the last decade on what they called a 'gap year'. Honor's own Saigon gap years had been somewhat different. No blithe backpackers drifting to exotic destinations with the unconscious im-perialism of the young, no pleasure trips on the river, stultifying student bacchanals in ethnic bars, no folkloric dancing or crafts markets. It had been noise, mud, bombs, blood and transcendental terror. There had been comrade-ship, too, and even passion. Watching colleagues die beside you does concentrate the mind, and body, on the pure animal pleasures of being alive. When they were not working, away from the battlefield, it had been one long, orgiastic rout. Back home, she had sometimes felt echoes of that hellish hunger at polite funerals, without the proximate opportunities for satisfaction. The practised poker faces of the undertakers, the whispers and muffled sobs of mourners, the comically slow pace of the cortège, all could trigger inappropriate cravings.

She should have thrown the postcard out months ago; it was only accumulating dust. She tore it up and reminded herself that she should dispose of another, more recent, card, still in its envelope in the hall. It was a crude Donald McGill caricature, of ogling wide boys and oversized mammaries, with a jeering note on the back, part-summons, part-begging letter, that might raise an inquisitive journalistic eyebrow. She would deal with it later. Her attention must not wander from the sitting room. This was to be the only theatre of action.

Coiled around the base of an ormolu clock on the mantelpiece was a string of jade *komboloi*, worry beads, a souvenir from the Cyclades. They could stay, surely, along with Tad's Staffordshire kiltie – it would take a severely inflamed imagination to make anything of either of them. The death mask of Keats, a present from Tad after their reconciliation in Rome, and the little nun in a snowstorm encased in a glass dome – a jokey trifle from Lois – were, surely, also unexceptional. But the winged marble phallus, a replica of a Pompeian household god – a votive offering from Lucio, the skittish Tuscan youth, which Tad had, in a benign moment, found droll

– could be more problematic. She cradled the cool stone in her hand. Was she being overscrupulous? Best to play safe. She scooped up the Little Sister of the Snows, too. Nuns and penises: a desperate journalist might make something of the pairing. Honor might have done so herself in similar circumstances.

She had cleared a space – an oubliette – in the utility cupboard in the hall. What rubbish you can accumulate in a lifetime; vast midden mounds of it, trash troves, even with natural wastage and an abhorrence of bibelots. It seemed that after all, despite her efforts and inclinations, she had ended up as a full-time curator of 'stuff'. A rag and bone woman. That most of it had once been Tad's was irrelevant. It was hers now, this little museum of nostalgic juju, and dismantling it entirely would require an effort of will that was beyond her.

Sometimes, on those days when she left the flat, for a publishing lunch with Ruth, perhaps, or a vernissage with Clemency or Inigo, or an evening of chamber music or theatre with Bobby or Aidan, she had an urge to keep walking, to take a taxi to the airport, fly to a city she had never been to in a country she barely knew, and start again. Rented rooms, few possessions, no damned pictures, books or worthless trinkets. Maybe she would find that, along with the jetsam, she had also discarded the wasted years and the physical shame of old age. She could have another go, and get it right this time.

As she placed her haul on the deep shelf behind the vacuum cleaner, it occurred to her that she might never retrieve this clutter. Only a residual fondness for Tad, who found her periodic purges of possessions physically painful, stopped Honor throwing the lot down the garbage chute.

Now the books. She dragged a footstool to the shelf and sat down to consider them, resisting the urge to close her eyes, even for a second. She had to concentrate. Was she succumbing to paranoia? She was always alert to the possibility of incipient dementia now, having barely noticed the memory lapses and confusions that had signalled the early stages of Alzheimer's in her friend Lois.

Once, when Honor was too young to know better, she had bought the line that old age had its compensations, among them an indifference to the opinions of others. But here she was, scurrying about, fussing, tiring herself out, in the hope of making a good impression on Tamara Sim and her readers. Was this a reasonable defence against ridicule? No one relishes humiliation, whatever their age. Or was she losing her grip? A recent spate of silent phone calls had unsettled her. There had been crank calls in the past and she and Tad had changed their number twice. It was a straightforward matter. But now, instead of taking action, putting in the necessary request to British Telecom, she did nothing and found herself eyeing the phone fearfully, starting whenever it rang.

Only last week she had read in the paper of a condition in the elderly called paraphrenia, whose symptoms – delusions of persecution, the obsessive sense that neighbours, friends, family, strangers, were out to get you –

seemed resonant. She knew that her story was of accelerating decline, even if she was lucky enough to retain her wits. The inexorable dwindling, the grotesque cascade of infirmities, had started years ago. Some days Honor felt like Job, waiting for the next plague of boils. Unlike Job, though, she knew there was no one to blame. She had become resigned to her role as a reluctant archivist of the physical afflictions of age, burdened with the wearisome naming and shaming of parts. But madness? That would be intolerable.

She picked out a handful of books from the shelf, cradling them awkwardly in the crook of her arm. Whenever she was beset by anxieties, she forced herself to step back, to examine her hold on reason. She knew her concerns about allowing the interviewer into her flat were sound; as ghillie-turned-grouse she knew the tricks and could set the traps herself. She had evaluated many men and a few women, personally and professionally, on the basis of their bookshelves. Raoul Salan's incongruous copy of *Le Petit Prince*, for example. Maybe she had made too much of Harold Wilson's Naugahyde-bound set of Catherine Cookson. They had not, he complained after her article was published, belonged to him. More satisfyingly, the Vatican had launched a minor inquisition after her glimpse, reported in *Collier's*, of *The Story of O* alongside *The Cloud of Unknowing* in the Apostolic Library. And the sight of a first edition of *Winnie-the-Pooh* on the bedside table of a Fifties matinée idol had sent her scrambling for her clothes and fleeing into the Santa Monica night.

Today she faced a reckoning of her own. Graham's novels; first-edition hardbacks, signed. There was no point in dissembling, and she was not going to carry all thirty-four volumes to the utility cupboard. But Isadora Talbot's *Snatch the Hour*? How did that get in here? Tamara Sim might assume she subscribed to Talbot's lurid brand of feminism, though Honor had no wish to read any of her books. Why would she choose to spend time in the company of a shrill blowhard who had made a manifesto out of menopausal self-pity?

Honor was constantly sent unsolicited books, which she automatically put in a pile by the front door for disposal, along with old newspapers and magazines. The maid, an uncommunicative refugee from Rwanda, must have thought this hardback had been cast out in error with all those pastel softback proofs. There were few more depressing sounds than that of a weighty jiffy bag squeezing through the letterbox then thudding onto the doormat. Publishers seemed to assume that Honor's remaining years could be usefully occupied reading feather-brained fables and supplying superlatives – free of charge – to be quoted on their jackets.

Now, she scolded herself, where was she? Poetry: Aidan's three collections; Tom Eliot; MacNeice and Larkin. A BFI-sanctioned critical biography of Tad's work, dull as an instruction manual for a washing machine. Some photography books: her own collaborations with Capa and Bown – the Magnum era. Ah! What was this? *The Royal Canadian Air Force Exercise Plans for Physical*

Fitness, an old orange-spined Penguin promising health, beauty and eternal life in exchange for fifteen minutes of boredom and degradation each day. Tad, who had never consciously taken exercise in his life, had said he felt immeasurably leaner and healthier just seeing it on the shelves. There could be few more comic aspirations than fitness in the over-seventies. You were not supposed to care that your body had become a sack of putrefying flesh, and the hope that you could arrest the process and avert imminent extinction with a few daily physical contortions was the highest folly. Out with it, along with R.D. Laing, Alan Watts, Carlos Castaneda – hokum Tad must have picked up in his Haight-Ashbury days.

She slung them on the reject pile. She needed to rationalise her shelves anyway. They could bypass the storage; straight down the chute with them. She would put them in a bag by the front door with a note for the maid, along with the bundle of largely unread Christmas and New Year newspapers – so much television trivia; why would she ever want to read a supplement with a picture of Bing Crosby on the cover? And did they seriously think a free packet of Poinsettia seeds or aspirin would entice new readers?

She had a last look around the room. The maid, sent to buy flowers, had come back with some sinister pink lilies, their inflamed throats exhaling a scent that made Honor's eyes water, and placed them in a vase next to the photograph of Tad. The table now looked like a wayside altar and the copy of her new book, *Dispatches*, lay there like a mockery of a sacred text: *Miserere Mei*. Still, the bouquet might usefully insinuate an element of femininity into the flat. She could not abide cut flowers of any sort herself; they reminded her of funeral parlours. Friends knew better than to bring them but, occasionally, new initiates to her suppers would present an elaborate bunch in an attempt at ingratiation. She would feign enthusiasm and leave the flowers soaking in the sink, saying she would find a container for them later. It was always the maid who rescued them, snipping the stems and arranging them carefully, and throwing them out when the petals shrivelled and the water began to stink like a latrine.

Honor paused by the window, drawn by the sound of an infant's shout, like the call of a seabird, from the communal garden below. A young mother, or possibly a nanny, was pushing a small child on a swing, hitched to the bare lower branches of a plane tree.

The garden was technically owned by the residents of the four mansion blocks in whose back courtyards it lay. The residents' committee, a collection of time-rich busy-bodies, had recently, after energetic lobbying from the young parents who had flooded the neighbourhood, installed the children's swing in the garden, disregarding the hundred-year-old by-law forbidding ball games and amusements.

The scrubby circle of green was ringed by a black wrought-iron fence which gave an imperilled air, like an enclosure of endangered species at the zoo, to its alopecic grass, dormant flowerbeds, sooty shrubs and cluster of threadbare beeches shivering in the shade of two menacing plane trees. There was another yelp from the child, a two-tone klaxon of protest, and he slipped off the swing into his mother's arms and out of Honor's view. Time was running out.

She went into the bathroom to check for stains and smells; she had no wish to confirm stereotypes about elderly incontinence and knew that for an unfriendly reporter, a quick trip to the lavatory mid-interview could be fruitful. Even in featureless hotel suites, *sans* stray underpants, there can be choice pickings for the inquisitive in the bathroom. She remembered the satisfying discovery of a bottle of Grecian 2000 in Saigon, by the sink of Nguyen Van Minh, the monosyllabic Vietnamese army commander. Here, the Lowe cartoon, above the cistern, of Honor as a young Brünnhilde dragging Hitler and Stalin by the hair was inoffensive, but the athlete's foot powder and haemorrhoid cream (more legacies from Tad) by the bath were ripe for ridicule. As was the jar of Youth Dew face cream, an unconsciously cruel present, probably bought in an airport duty free shop, from Tad's beautiful god-daughter.

The bathroom cabinet in particular could yield a hoard of unsavoury truths. Hers contained a miniature pharmacy of prescription pills, ointments and tinctures, each preparation telling its own squalid story. Honor doubted whether Tamara Sim could distinguish between benzodiapenes and nicardipines, but she could not be sure. She swept the lot into a plastic bag to be stowed away, leaving a toothbrush (her teeth were, mostly, her own, though some were brown as shards of sucked toffee), a modest bottle of scent, a packet of aspirins and a box of plasters.

Ten minutes left. She was beginning to feel breathless again and the pain was becoming more insistent. She fetched a glass of water, retrieved her pills and swallowed two. She should sit down, but it was time to turn attention to herself. Clean, kempt and dignified was the best one could hope for these days. She once had, when younger, a weakness for clothes: clever cuts, sensual fabrics, muted colours borrowed from the autumnal Highland landscape, witty details. In her fiftieth year, staring into the brimming chasm of her Glenbuidhe dressing room, a comprehensive museum of mid-twentieth-century fashion gently rotting in the Scottish damp, she realised that, from this point on, even if she were to choose a different ensemble every day, she could never live long enough to wear it all. She was subsequently proved wrong, and had long outlived her wardrobe; the purge, started that afternoon, was decisively completed almost a quarter of a century later by the fire. Now, her single closet in Holmbrook Mansions would not disgrace a nun.

She chose a black jersey dress, recently dry cleaned: a simple draped column, square necked with bell sleeves, worn with black tights to conceal the Stilton marbling of veins, and grey patent pumps, wide enough at the toes to accommodate the bunions. She looked down at her stockinged feet, as unsightly as lepers' stumps. What joker had turned this Miranda into Caliban? Fumbling with the catch, she fastened a necklace of freshwater pearls round her neck then secured a gold watch, its face ringed by marcasite, round her wrist. Even at its tightest notch, the watch hung, loose as a charm bracelet.

She went back into the bathroom and peered into the misted mirror on the cabinet. It was the only looking glass left in her flat since she had the liberating realisation that the best way to combat anguish at one's deteriorating appearance was to stop gazing at it; if she wished, she could look at the monochrome photograph of her Dietrich days and remember. Even then, one had to be careful. In certain lights, the glass in the photo frame could play tricks, superimposing the reflected silhouette of her shrunken self onto the insouciant belle.

She pinned back her hair, grey and insubstantial as cigarette smoke, into an approximation of a chignon. Lipstick? Eyeshadow? She decided against them. Better to face the camera barefaced than with the skewed clowns' daubs conferred by shaky hands and failing eyesight. From the cabinet, she took out the bottle of scent, brought from Budapest by Aidan, and sprayed it behind her ears. Then she sprayed it round the bathroom. She was ready for her interrogator.

*

Sitting in a café opposite Honor Tait's Gothic red-brick mansion block, sipping a lukewarm coffee, Tamara looked through the cuttings. Bucknell was late. When *The*

Monitor's picture desk told her he was the only photographer available for the interview, she had been furious. Why not Snowdon? Or Bown? Once Lyra Moore learned that the lowly Bucknell had been entrusted with a *S*nday* job, she would be livid. Tamara had tried to alert her but Lyra never replied to her electronic messages and, whenever Tamara phoned her, she was always in a meeting. Bucknell was charmless, awkward and surly, a clammy-handed chain smoker whose pictures were flat, straight-to-camera portraits as dreary as police mugshots. He was the worst possible collaborator on a sensitive interview like this.

There was no way of contacting him; Tamara was too junior at *The Monitor*, and Bucknell too unpopular, to be allocated one of the rare company mobile phones. She could try to find a public call box and ring the office. The picture desk could page him (Bucknell at least had a pager – hers had been pickpocketed on the bus before Christmas) and they could also ring Honor Tait's publisher to apologise and warn her of their late arrival. But the chances were that Tamara would spend twenty minutes trying to find a call box, only to discover that the booth had been used as a wino's toilet and the handset had been vandalised. She cursed Bucknell. Then again, the delay would give her time to mug up on her research.

Honor Tait had been prolific. Tamara wondered what an envelope of her own clippings would look like twenty years from now. She was, at this stage, more resourceful than prolific, an expert recycler of her own work. The green lobby might learn from her energy conservation techniques. Sometimes, she would rewrite and re-angle the same story four or even five times, selling it on to different outlets. Her interview with Lucy Hartson, for example, had been commissioned last year by *Psst!*, and set up by the TV public relations company to publicise *Lady of Quality*, the new prime-time costume drama. It was a straightforward puff – "'I've always admired Georgette Heyer's writing," says Lucy ... "It's such a privilege to work with such a talented cast ... Next, I'd really like to get my teeth into a tough modern role, maybe an edgy detective series."' Frustratingly, the actress refused to be drawn on her former boyfriend, Tod Maloney, narcophiliac bass player with the Broken Biscuits, saying only that 'we were very different people', 'it was time to move on' and claiming that the split had been 'entirely amicable' – a wan euphemism belied the previous month by paparazzi pictures of their fist fight outside a Soho nightclub. But Tamara had managed to siphon off a few quotes for an article about the actress's new flat in Islington – 'The bathroom, a cool haven of limestone and brushed steel, aspires to a luxury spa aesthetic' – for the *Telegraph* property pages; wrote the caption story for a picture spread on doomed rock 'n' roll romances for the features pages of *The Courier*; and padded out Hartson's confessional aside about her trips to Los Angeles for injections of a muscle-paralysing toxin – 'everyone in the business out there has had a face-full of the stuff, believe me' – turning it into a full-page exposé in the *Evening Standard*.

Most lucrative of all was the follow-up. Before the interview appeared in *Psst!*, Tamara called Maloney, out on bail following a drugs raid at a recent gig, made a few flattering remarks about his latest album, informed him that Lucy Hartson had 'told us everything' about their break-up, and offered him a chance to tell his side of the story. Usefully, he seemed high, and on uppers rather than downers. His tirade lasted forty-five minutes. Cleaned up, with some of the more rambling and paranoid assertions removed, it made a double-page spread in the *Sunday Sphere*, headlined SLAPPER OF QUALITY: '*Saucy Lucy broke my heart,' says Biscuits' hard man*. It was this interview that first brought her to the attention of Tim, then newly installed as the *Sunday Sphere's* editor. He had been 'on the look-out for new talent', he said on their first night two months later, after her successful TOP COP'S SON sting, when she had gone wired-up to offer cannabis to the police chief's son.

At the thought of Tim, Tamara's eyes filled with tears. Outside, raindrops were hurling against the café windows in sympathy. Or was it mockery? She dabbed at her eyes with a napkin. Her mascara seemed to be intact. She turned back to the cuttings, a long life of ingenuity and striving shrunk to a bundle of paper scraps. Honor Tait had been a beauty, and the early photographs, many taken with soldiers and politicians, showed a starlet's glamour and a dazzling full-lipped smile. She was said, even now, to be a man's woman, who did not suffer other women gladly. Simon, Tamara's editor and ally at *Psst!*, had met

Tait at a charity event a couple of years ago and claimed her interest in him had not been entirely professional.

'She's a randy old goat,' he told Tamara when he heard that she was about to interview Tait. 'Collects men. The younger the better, apparently. But she's not that fussy – she was all over me.'

She was, according to Simon, grander than Martha Gellhorn and so vain that she had commissioned Snowdon to take her passport photo.

'She's known as the Messalina of Maida Vale,' he added. 'They say she pays for sex with younger men.'

Tamara had wrinkled her nose in disgust – at her age? It did not bear thinking about – though his reference to Messalina was puzzling. Wasn't that the Italian resort where they held last year's *Monitor* management junket? Did Honor Tait trawl European seaside towns in search of attractive young men? Tamara decided to ignore the reference – when in doubt, she had always found it best to stay silent. It saved time, and the unadorned facts were interesting enough in their own right.

'No! She actually pays for it? Really?' she had said.

'Really! How else do you think she manages to pull?'

Tamara had laughed uneasily. Simon liked to gossip – who didn't? His stories were always entertaining, but their accuracy could not be guaranteed.

She looked at her watch – still no sign of Bucknell – and flicked through the new book once more. Spanning sixty years, it included reports from papers and magazines that no longer existed – the *News Chronicle*, *Reynold's*

News, Collier's Weekly – and covered the Spanish Civil War in the Thirties, post-war Berlin in the Forties, Korea in the Fifties, Algeria and China in the Sixties, Vietnam in the Seventies . . . Tamara yawned. The cumulative effect of all these dates and place names was deadening, like looking at an obsolete train timetable.

Turning back to the cuttings, she was relieved to see that there were some stories about Honor Tait herself, rather than merely by her. These were briefer, easier to skim and fillet, and helpfully illustrated with photographs. Tait was pictured in the mid-Forties – her curvaceous figure made the demure twinset look almost raunchy – after winning a Pulitzer Prize for her reports on the liberation of a Nazi death camp. She would have been about the same age that Tamara was now. There was an even earlier photograph, taken in a beachside café; she was wearing a clinging halter-neck top and skimpy shorts which showed off her model's legs. Her interviewee, a dapper man in uniform who looked like a minor customs official, was gazing appreciatively at her knees. The caption read: *Press Corps Golden Girl Honor Tait interviewed Commander General of the Canary Islands, Francisco Franco, two weeks before he joined the military revolt which launched the Civil War in Spain.*

Another clipping showed her on a speedboat around the same time, scanning the horizon, shading her eyes, her skin dark against the white of her two-piece bathing suit, perfect teeth displayed in a carefree laugh, fair hair rippling behind her like a pennant, standing at the helm with 'US ambassador's son, Joseph Patrick Kennedy Jr'.

In fawning gossip columns, in cuttings as fragile as papyrus, she featured alongside Ava Gardner, Rita Hayworth and Jane Russell, and was pictured at Hollywood parties and Broadway first nights. One photograph – glittering, flashlit, black and white – showed her emerging from a Bel Air restaurant with 'newlyweds Arthur Miller and Marilyn Monroe'. At first glance you would be hard-pressed to decide which of the two beautiful women was the screen goddess and which was the intrepid reporter.

Tait was said to have dated Sinatra – there was a picture of them, 'enjoying an intimate dinner together', that looked as posed and flawless as a still from a classic Fifties' movie. She was wearing a corsage of white flowers and her moist lips were parted in a smile as he whispered into her ear. Liz Taylor was a friend, thanks to Tait's third marriage to Tad Challis, the American director of once much-loved, now seldom seen, British comedy films. She had holidayed with Nureyev, partied with Picasso, was photographed 'sharing a joke', and a suspiciously fat cigarette, in a Paris jazz club with a group of friends including Louis Armstrong, and huddled, sheathed in clinging satin – *High IQ in low-cut gown*, read the caption – with Orson Welles at a Hollywood shindig.

With Hollywood, Tamara was on home territory. Her grasp of the subject, her degree in Media Studies, and long nights and marathon weekends spent watching black-and-white movies on TV would be invaluable. Even at *Psst!*, an elite academy of TV, pop and movie trivia scholars, she was regarded as a special authority – she had written her dissertation on Hollywood Romantic Comedy and was seen as a repository of arcane show-business lore and a grandmistress of gossip. You could not survive a week at *Psst!* without an extensive knowledge of contemporary popular culture, but Tamara's expertise was extrasensory. She knew more about stars' private lives – about the Spice Girls' rivalry, about Madonna's tempestuous relationship with Carlos Leon and her tantrums on the set of *Evita*, about Michael Jackson's skin disease and his recent marriage to his frumpy nurse – than she did about the biographies of her family and friends.

It seemed that she picked up this information by osmosis, only having to look at a gaudy line of TV and film gossip magazines on a newsstand for their entire contents to migrate instantly to her hippocampus. Who was having an affair with whom? Who was up for which role in what soap opera/film? Who was in rehab? Who should be in rehab? Who'd had plastic surgery? Who should have? Who was secretly gay? Who was secretly straight? This was what animated her conversations with friends and colleagues and made her work entertaining, if not exacting. Her expertise was valued and *Psst!*, more than any other job so far, satisfactorily combined her personal interests with her professional life.

Apart from writing the weekly 'A-List' (Ten Best/Ten Worst) and the What's In/What's Out, Going Up/Going Down, Good Week/Bad Week lists, most of her working day was spent tightening other contributors' copy, composing readers' letters when there were none, or when the genuine letters were too imbecilic to publish, and helping out on the jokey captions that accompanied pictures of drunken stars grimacing outside nightclubs. Simon also threw the occasional interview her way.

Psst!'s relaxed regime also offered expenses, free phone calls and stationery, computer and word processor facilities, an infinite supply of floppy disks, access to a fax and a photocopier, the use of the cuttings library (the journalistic equivalent of an academic's twenty-four-hour pass to the British Library), a subsidised canteen (where Tamara occasionally enjoyed a lone late-night supper under the pretext of doing overtime), the pleasures of comradeship and useful networking possibilities. It was as important to put in face-time in the wine bar after work as it was to be seen behind the desk during the day.

The commission from *S*nday* had proved just how useful it was to maintain a regular presence in a newspaper office. She had received a herogram message from Johnny, the Features editor, for her Ten Best Soap Opera Shags and last month he had asked her to step in and turn round a quick column for *Me2* – an 800-word why-oh-why in forty-five minutes with picture byline – when their regular columnist, Liselotte Selsby, the soap opera cutie with a reputation as an intellectual (she had once claimed that *The Wretched of the Earth* was her favourite book) and a taxing coke habit, had failed to deliver. The invitation to write the Tamara Sim Column, a prominent picture-bylined platform for highly paid, light-hearted, pun-filled musings involving no research, amounted to journalistic apotheosis and Tamara hoped it would become a weekly fixture in *Me2*.

Disappointingly, Johnny had been unable to find space for a follow-up since Selsby, or rather her ghost-writing publicist, had repented of her truancy and become a scrupulous observer of deadlines. But these things do get noticed and Tamara's reputation had clearly radiated upwards at the paper, like a thermal current, beyond the second-floor Features desk and finally reached *S*nday*, way up in *The Monitor*'s penthouse office suite. Lyra Moore would have been looking for someone with a light touch to leaven a potentially deadly subject; for who, in their right minds, was honestly interested in an old biddy's memories of the Vietnam War? Simon must have hymned Tamara's wit in Morning Conference, or at a Features meeting, or maybe Johnny had commended, in Lyra's hearing, her Soap Opera Shags.

There were drawbacks to the job on *Psst!*: it was insecure, it did not stretch her, and the pay was paltry – freelance rates and staff wages on *The Monitor*'s main mid-market broadsheet rival, *The Courier*, were lavish in comparison. Only *S*nday* magazine, and the tabloids – the *Sun*, the *News of the World*, the *Sunday Sphere* and the *Mail* – offered real money. A staff job on any of those titles would be like a lottery win, and, until Lyra Moore's message, just as likely. With regular, well-paid work Tamara's life would be transformed. And so would her brother's. She felt the familiar quiver of panic. She had not heard from him for a fortnight. Silence, in Ross's case, was rarely golden. She would have to make the journey to his grim council estate to check up on him. Her urge to sort him out was not entirely selfless. She did not want to spend any more time worrying about him.

The rain had stopped. If the photographer was much longer there was a danger that the old woman might cancel the interview altogether. Tamara was sure that the picture desk had sent Bucknell because she worked on *Psst!*, which was held in contempt by many of the staff at *The Monitor*. She felt a stubborn loyalty to the magazine, and to its editor, Simon Pettigrew, an ideal boss who had become a good friend. He had started out as a show-business correspondent, where he earned a reputation as a genial fellow who would never stitch anyone up under his own byline. Since then, after an embarrassing incident involving an editor's mistress, he had been fired from every national paper in Britain but had always managed to charm his way into a new sinecure. He had worked, variously, as a diarist, feature writer, columnist, deputy editor, section editor, leader writer, advertising executive, personnel officer and project manager. He was boyish and accident-prone – a stammering, weaker-chinned James Stewart, with wattles and a Bertie Wooster accent – and he made people laugh. Their relationship was chaste – Simon's love life was complicated enough and Tamara had never found him attractive, even when she was catatonic with drink after her first *Monitor* Features party. She was not his type either, she was sure of that. Trouble was his type. Posh trouble.

But he had become a mentor to her, generously over-looking the fact that he had hired her in error, believing *Inside the Box* to be a TV gossip magazine. He had taught her more about journalism, and the demands and intricacies of expenses forms, than she had learned in her three years of Media Studies, or in any of her other jobs. And he had been very kind over the Tim affair, sending her home in a taxi after she had spent a morning weeping in the office. For him, despite her relative youth, Tamara seemed to fulfil the role of agony aunt, a non-judgemental confidante to whom he compulsively described the latest twists and unravellings in his labyrinthine love life.

It was not a demanding role. He did not seek her advice or opinion. All she had to do was listen, and try to avoid yawning, or laughing. And she had another, extra-journalistic skill which he had come to value – a minor talent for forgery. This had more to do with patience than with any gift for calligraphic mimicry. Each month, Tamara would take home a large brown envelope of blank receipts, acquired by Simon from accommodating taxi drivers, restaurateurs and hoteliers, and, using a variety of coloured biros, felt-tips and pencils, she would spend evenings filling them in, writing out bills for fictitious cab journeys, imaginary five-course meals and fancy bottles of wine for invented 'contacts', in extravagant forward-facing loops or in cramped, back-slanting script. She found the process curiously restful and Simon was appreciative and reciprocated, as her immediate boss, by signing her expenses forms without glancing at the figures or the receipts.

She flicked through Tait's file again. There was more gore than glamour, angry reports from the battle front, and not a trace of humour or gossip in her writing. Honor Tait had, in an apparent fit of masochism, left the bountiful comforts of Beverly Hills to sleep rough with the GIs in Quang Tri and Tet. There were stomach-turning accounts of burned children and mortally wounded young soldiers, tedious and unsurprising statistical litanies – literacy in India, infant mortality in Africa – but after that her newspaper articles began to thin and were replaced by longer magazine pieces.

For *Time*, she wrote about a visit to a German orphanage, for *Granta* she fulminated about the changing face of newspaper reporting, and then she was reduced to reviewing, at tedious length, books about the Second World War, Vietnam and Korea for the *New York Review of Books*. In the *New Yorker*, at even greater length, relieved only by apparently random line drawings of gardening implements and small dogs, Tait had written about an American politician with a comb-over called McGovern and had championed the Irish writer Dominic Behan in his plagiarism case against Bob Dylan. Bob Dylan! The singer's name leapt out at Tamara like a friendly face in a rush-hour crowd.

Later clippings which bore Tait's byline came from even worthier, illustration-free magazines, in which long grey slabs of print – reflections on Asia, the Middle East and Latin America – were broken by shorter slabs of unrelated and mystifying verse by obscure poets. Then again, Tamara reflected, all poets were obscure. Would she have to mug up on poetry for the *S*nday* piece? Or pretend to? Honor Tait was said to cultivate an artistic set.

One diary clipping from the 1960s showed her, imperious and elegant in hat and fur coat, with a group of awkwardly grinning men in suits, bland as bank managers, in a publisher's boardroom. One of the men, the caption revealed, was T.S. Eliot. At least Tamara, a fan of West End musicals, had heard of *him*. All the same, the task of familiarising herself to bluffing level with arcane verse and ancient wars was a depressing prospect.

It might be necessary, however. *S*nday* employed some formidable writers and its standards were exacting. She was troubled by what she had heard Johnny refer to, with sombre awe, as the '*S*nday* ethos'. Could she match the magazine's tone, which could be both reverential and haughtily sceptical, its syllable-clotted style, the seasoning of italicised foreign words?

Even *S*nday*'s adverts – stark studio shots of gem-studded watches handcuffed to slender wrists, brooding portraits of tank-sized cars perched like stags on mountain ridges – were intimidating. It was said to be a writers' magazine, written by writers' writers, and was not intended to be taken recreationally. Reading it, Tamara sometimes felt a dress code was required: 'smart casual', at least. Embarked on systematically as a weekly course in self-improvement, even with the promise of a significant salary hike, it was tough going. But Tamara, though she had never seen herself as a writers' writer (more of a readers' writer, really) was not afraid of words. They were important weapons in a reporter's armoury.

She had her mother's two-volume *Oxford English Dictionary*, frequently mined *Roget's Thesaurus* and, as someone who, as a child, had enjoyed fierce games of Scrabble with her brother, she collected words, recording them in her notebook, delighting in the unusual and trying to slip them into a story or, more often, a list, whenever pedestrian sub editors were looking the other way. Only last week she had come across 'transgressive' (in a report of a gruesomely fascinating murder trial), 'crepuscular' (in a pretentious fashion piece on sequins), 'chthonic' (from Tod Maloney's latest album, *Chthonic the Hedgehog*) and 'hermeneutic' (an arresting headline on an arts page piece about the Spice Girls).

A diligent reader of well-crafted detective stories and contemporary romances, as well as countless newspapers and magazines, possessed of a curious mind, respectable vocabulary and a serviceably wide education – solid A-levels in Drama and French (her grasp of both enhanced by six months as an au pair to a flamboyantly self-harming pre-teen in Lyons), and a BA in Media Studies (she narrowly missed an upper second) – known for her nimble humour, cutting comments, encyclopaedic knowledge of the personal peccadilloes of the major cultural icons of the late twentieth century, Tamara was well equipped to join the *S*nday* team. Lyra Moore, a writers' writer's editor, had recognised her promise and her feisty, streetwise touch, so lacking in *S*nday* magazine, and was willing to give her a chance.

At the bottom of the cuttings file was a printout of a profile, ten years old and doggedly respectful, from the long-vanished *Sunday Correspondent*. Tamara did not have time to read it all but at the end, in convenient bullet points, there were some bald biographical details. 'Childhood: stately home in the Scottish Highlands.' A toff then. 'Education: governesses, followed by a Belgian convent school, Swiss finishing college and the Sorbonne.' A French-speaking Catholic toff. 'Employment: Agence France-Presse, the *Herald Tribune*, *L'Espresso*, *Collier's Weekly*, *Der Spiegel*, *Picture Post* . . .' A multi-lingual Catholic toff with good contacts. 'Marriages: three. Marquis Maxime de Cantal, Belgian-born theatre impresario; Sandor Varga, Hungarian publisher; and Tad Challis, American-born film director.' A goer, confirming Simon's claims; for three husbands read thirty lovers, at least.

There were no quotes from Honor Tait at all, apart from a sermonising motto: 'Through patient observation, the meticulous accumulation of detail and a ravening hunger for truth, the bigger picture will emerge. It is the duty of the reporter to champion the weak and to shine a searchlight in the darkest corners of human experience.' Pompous, too.

The peg for the article, a pallid excuse, was the inclusion of one of Tait's dispatches from Korea in a forbiddingly titled anthology, *Classics of World Reportage*. No wonder the *Sunday Correspondent* had disappeared.

There was a more recent news story, seven years old, from *The Monitor*: 'VETERAN JOURNALIST'S HOME GUTTED IN BLAZE'. The house, not the London flat across the road but a former hunting lodge 'on the estate of what had once been her childhood home in the Highlands', had burned to the ground in an electrical fire. One photograph, the older of the two, showed a smug, substantial building – four storeys high, with a narrow fifth-storey tower at each end – painted stark white, apart from black-rimmed window frames and the dark arched door. If that was a 'lodge', what must the main house have been like? Whatever conclusions might be reached about Honor Tait's life, this was not a tale of rags to riches. The second picture, of a single charred wall with a glassless window like a blinded eye, rearing against the sky in a clearing of ashes, sticks and stumps, looked like an image of some blighted post-nuclear landscape.

The story included not a word from Tait herself, though she was said to have been 'comforted by her third husband, Tad Challis, director of cult comedy films including *The Pleasure Seekers* and *Hairdressers' Honeymoon*', and a useful 'friend' had described her as 'devastated'. Tamara gazed across the road at the solid façade of Holmbrook Mansions. She had looked in the estate agents' windows and knew what these flats could cost. Honor Tait may have been devastated by the loss of her holiday home, but she had not been destroyed. This was not a riches-to-rags story either.

Other, briefer, clippings gave a flavour of Honor Tait's

life over the last ten years. She was mentioned in passing in some of the broadsheet news pages as a supporter of pressure groups lobbying for children's rights, against exploitation of third-world labour and against sex trafficking; she had served as a UN goodwill ambassador, campaigned for asylum seekers and, in her spare time, was a regular attendee at book launches, gallery openings and theatre first nights in the company of writers, artists and actors, all of them men, most of them young and highly presentable. There were a number of photographs of Tait at these events, stooped but regal, glowering at the photographer over a glass of champagne, surrounded by handsome acolytes. 'Doyenne of journalists' was the most frequent tag, though the *Mail* preferred 'the darling of the chattering classes'. There had been a TV arts programme about her a year ago (Tamara had been sent the video tape but had not had time to watch it) and one of the trails for it from a listings magazine was included in the publishers' press pack: HONOR BOUND was the headline.

In a piece from *Vogue*, Annie Leibovitz had photographed her in black and white in a book-lined room, looking affronted, as if the old woman had just disturbed an intruder who, if he had any instinct for self-preservation, would have fled the scene at once. The article, on 'salons', also featured a poet who held weekly picnics and poetry readings on Primrose Hill, and a fashion designer who hosted what he called regular 'cake and counselling' sessions for artists in his Thameside warehouse. Honor

Tait was described as a 'modern Madame de Staël' and was said to have gathered round her a group of admirers comprising 'the most exciting young men in Britain's creative industries'. They met on the last Monday of every month and called themselves, in ironic reference to the right-wing think-tank of the same name, the Monday Club. Discussions 'exactingly chaired by Tait, doyenne of British journalism, friend of the Hollywood elite, and one-time muse of some of the greatest artists of the twentieth century', would range from 'Hegelian philosophy and aleatoric music to the single European currency and the future of artificial intelligence'.

Tamara sipped her coffee, by now repellently cold, and hoped that, along with poetry, politics or history, none of these subjects would come up in her interview.

*

The girl was late. Honor fetched a drink, settled in the armchair and picked up the plastic folder that Ruth had couriered over: the interviewer's cuttings. Was their purpose reassurance, indicating that this journalist was not exclusively in the business of character assassination, that she did not habitually ridicule *all* her interviewees? Honor tipped the articles into her lap. Were they originals or colour photocopies? It was hard to tell. Technology had accelerated so fast since the days of the portable Olympia, flimsy carbons and the chunky telephone with its umbilical ringlet of wire.

Her own cuttings, scissored and pasted into large red ledgers by countless secretaries over the years, had amounted to fourteen bound volumes of news stories and features, columns and interviews; almost as large as the complete *OED*. The ledgers, like everything else, had been consumed by the Glenbuidhe flames. In newspaper libraries, the articles, clipped by clerks, were kept in brown envelopes labelled with the writer's name. Shaking out a collection of your work would always be an intimation of mortality; within months of publication the cuttings would be as sere and yellow as a handful of autumn leaves.

And this scant, bright package? From a TV listings supplement, an interview with a young actress, unknown to Honor but, according to the piece, renowned for undressing slowly in a recent TV adaptation of a fatuous historical novel, and for the public break-up of her affair with a tattooed popstar. The photograph showed the actress, a spindly blonde, leaning against a marble fireplace. There was an edge of desperation, a plea for approval, in her effortful smile and the faint spidering of lines around her eyes. She looked tired, wrung out, used up. The article carried a photograph of the interviewer too; a small postage stamp-sized byline picture of a sharp-nosed blonde affecting a frown while chewing a pencil. They were all blonde these days. Was there something of the woodland creature about her? A spiteful creation of Beatrix Potter? Tamara Townmouse? Or was she more of a shrew?

Included in the package of cuttings was a double-page

feature on London's 'café culture', and another on 'flyposting', the practice of illicitly pasting advertisements for nightclubs over lamp posts and hoardings. This was billed as an 'exclusive in-depth investigation by reporter Tamara Sim'. Not quite Watergate. Honor's eyes closed slowly and her head bowed, unresisting, towards sleep.

Minutes later, the amplified whine of a car alarm brought her back into wakefulness. She glanced at the clock. The girl was now insultingly late. Massaging her temples, Honor looked again at the articles in her lap. The same silly byline picture accompanied 'The Tamara Sim Column', 800 words, many of them in capital letters appended by clusters of exclamation marks, reflecting on the plot of a television soap opera, the bad behaviour of Premier League footballers, and 'the modern problem', which was apparently neither third-world poverty nor the spread of Aids but 'the dearth of decent, reliable, sexy, solvent single men in London'. The frivolity of the press no longer surprised Honor. But why this particular girl had been sent to interview her, she could not imagine.

Three

Tamara was startled by a sudden knock on the café window. Bucknell had arrived, out of breath. She glared at him as he walked in.

'Where have you been?' she asked.

'Another job. For the News desk.'

'The News desk? But this is for the magazine! *S*nday*! It's a *much* bigger deal.'

'Try telling that to the News desk.'

She shook her head, picked up the bunch of Barbie-pink lilies she had bought as a peace offering from the supermarket on the corner (expenses would cover it and, if she handed in the doctored receipt for the red roses she had sent last week to Tim's office at the *Sphere*, she would make something on the transaction). They walked in silence up the steps of the mansion block.

She felt a spreading chill of apprehension but reassured herself that this story would require only an extension of those skills she had already used many times in the course of her career. She had to approach it methodically. Talk to the woman, get more on her family background, the love life, the celebrity angle, Sinatra, Liz Taylor, a few key quotes, throw in a handful of cultural references (Picasso, a must for *S*nday* readers, and Marilyn, revered by snobs as well as slobs), a bit of colour – descriptions of her appearance, her flat – coax some soundbites from a few of Tait's friends and top and tail it with a couple of lines on her work. A quick pass-over with *Roget's* would bump up the syllable quotient and she could season it all with some piquant French gleaned from Larousse. It should not be difficult. Once you cracked the intro, you were there. Tamara was working on her first paragraph already.

We were three-quarters of an hour late and out of breath by the time we arrived at Honor Tait's grand mansion flat and the doyenne of British journalism instantly put us at our ease.

Bucknell pushed his way through the revolving glass doors of Holmbrook Mansions and walked towards the reception desk, his leather jacket creaking manfully. A doorman, liveried like a down-at-heel South American military dictator, directed them to the lift.

'Thanks, mate,' the photographer said, giving a condescending thumbs-up.

Tamara followed several paces behind, a resentful squaw, hoping the doorman did not think they were a couple in the conjugal sense. They ascended in hostile silence to the fourth floor. In the confinement of the lift she held her breath, but there was no defence against the acrid scent of distilled tobacco which seemed to ooze from Bucknell's pores. As they walked along the corridor to the flat, her heels echoed portentously on the tiled floor. At the door, her finger beat his to the doorbell. Waiting for the old woman to answer, Tamara mentally reworked her intro.

We're fifteen minutes late and flustered by the time we arrive at Honor Tait's lavishly appointed apartment and the doyenne of British journalism greets us with a welcoming smile.

There was a jingle and clank of chains and bolts before the door opened and Honor Tait, smaller and more frail than she appeared in her most recent photographs, stood before them.

'You're late,' she said.

Tamara looked reproachfully at the photographer but he turned away, attending to the clasps and buckles of his bag.

'So sorry,' Tamara said, addressing the old woman with an apologetic smile. 'The traffic in St John's Wood was horrendous. We tried to ring . . .'

She held out the bouquet of flowers and Honor Tait accepted them, sighing.

'You're here now. You might as well come in.'

They followed her stooped back into the hallway, stepping over a stack of old newspapers and a supermarket carrier bag filled with books. Under her Mediterranean widow's drab, her spine jutted like the vertebrae of an ancient sea creature.

By the time we arrive panting at Honor Tait's faded mansion flat, we're five minutes late and the doyenne of British journalism fixes us with a spooky glare.
'Do you realise how late you are?' she growls.

The old woman showed them into the sitting room and left them standing there while she disappeared into the kitchen with the flowers. It was an old person's flat, unmistakably – shabby, cluttered, faintly grimy, and reeking of the past. Or was it the stench of death? Tamara, on the job already and alert for details, walked towards the bookshelf and looked at the photographs. Not the standard family snaps. No gap-toothed children in school uniform, or dizzy graduates balancing mortars on ana-chronistic hairdos. These were mostly pictures of Honor Tait herself, and taken a very long time ago. The old woman returned and brusquely indicated a flock-covered chair. Tamara smoothed the back of her skirt and sat down with a demure half-smile that she fancied called to mind the biddable charm of the pre-divorce Princess Diana. Honor Tait gripped the scuffed wooden arms of the chair opposite – her hands were as thin and twisted as chicken's feet – and carefully lowered herself into it.

Behind the old woman a tall sash window, hung with green velvet curtains that were coming adrift from their hooks, framed a view of windows in an identical mansion block opposite and, just visible in the gulf between the two buildings, the topmost branches of wintry trees.

The leafless boughs of the oaks in the garden below flail in the wind like the arms of orphaned children once described so vividly by the doyenne of British journalism.

Tamara had to get it all down. She reached into her handbag and, after a spell of noisy rummaging, drew out a pencil, a notebook and a miniature tape recorder.

Honor watched intently, a glint of scepticism in her narrowed eyes. Such a big bag, as capacious as a doctor's Gladstone, and such a small girl. So many tools and devices. Miss Sim was not unattractive, though she would be prone to dumpiness later, perhaps, and her chemically flaxened hair was scored with a black fault line at the parting. But she had a pinched prettiness, and her perky breasts strained against her blouse in a way that many men with a taste for the obvious would find appealing.

A faint cough drew Honor's attention upwards. The photographer was still standing there, looming over the two women, demanding attention without meriting it, a spear-carrier with doomed ambitions to play the lead. Honor looked at him with irritation.

'Yes?'

He shifted his weight nervously from foot to foot as if surreptitiously scraping dog mess from his shoes.

'I'll just set up and fire away, while you two are talking, if that's okay.'

'No. It's not *okay*,' the old woman said.

Tamara opened her notebook and stared at Bucknell, incensed. If it was a question of cost and the picture desk insisted on using a staff photographer, why not good-humoured, obliging Tom, whose easy Irish flattery fooled no one but charmed everyone? Or bashful Milly, dim daughter of a titled brewing family, who treated everybody, including Tamara, with a whispered servility? Tom would not have given a thumbs-up to the doorman, and Honor Tait would not be ready to chuck the interview before she had started if little Milly were here, blushing, apologising and dancing deferentially around her.

'We can get it over with now,' Honor Tait continued. 'Then you can go.'

Bucknell bared his bisque teeth in an abject smile, unfolded his tripod and snapped open the umbrella reflector.

'Don't make such a business of it,' Honor said. 'All these accoutrements. They're just fetish objects. Completely unnecessary. You're not Cartier-Bresson. Just point and shoot.'

Relaxed and emboldened by her colleague's discomfort, Tamara made surreptitious notes.

'What time do you call this?' snaps Honor Tait, the doyenne of British journalism, former femme fatale and friend of the stars, with a menacing growl, when she answers the door of her sumptuously gloomy apartment.

The photographer rubbed his hands and grinned, broad shoulders hunched, frozen in the act of ingratiation. His ill-shaven face looked damp and grubby, more mildewed than bearded. Looking at him, Honor found herself struck by a rare urge for housekeeping; she must get the maid to clean out the back of her fridge. He avoided her eyes, only looking at her directly from behind the safety of his viewfinder.

Once, Honor had liked to draw men in with her gaze. Their eyes would lock on to hers, startled, and then they would be disarmed. She had first become aware of this power as a young girl in Glenbuidhe, home from the convent for the holidays. The timorous estate manager, the stuttering cousin from Aberdeenshire, the over-affectionate uncle visiting from London – it amused her to disconcert them with lingering looks and careless gestures. Later, sprung from Belgian cloisters and Highland fastness, launched in the racy world of work in Paris, where men were unabashed and insatiable, she perfected this skill. And as a journalist, in filthy dugouts and elegant hotels, during political conferences and at Hollywood parties, in the hush of libraries and the crush of airports, it was sport to her, like deer stalking – a stag cull without the carnage.

When did she start to lose that power? In her late fifties? her sixties? First they failed to return her stare, dropping their eyes and turning away, and the averted gaze had the force of a deliberate affront. Later, most men stopped seeing her at all. She was obsolete, and not just sexually. She could still summon lovers of a sort – the drunk, the inadequate, the kinky masochists and gerontophiles – but it was more an act of reciprocal degradation than of carnal pleasure.

'Mrs Tait, if I could just have you standing in the corner by the window.'

How objectionable, to be patronised by such an unprepossessing simpleton.

'Mrs Challis. *Miss* Tait,' she said. 'You can take me here, as I am. No flash. Natural light will be quite sufficient.'

If necessary, she could always pay, she knew. Any service could be summoned by a simple exchange of cash. There was no cause for shame; economic independence meant that, in the latter half of the century, women could enjoy a useful expedient that had been available to men for millennia. But one had to be discreet. Social mores had yet to catch up. The wealthy old man with the glorious girl on his arm might be an acceptable stereotype, perhaps inspiring male envy and defensive female ridicule; one only had to reverse the genders to provoke unanimous disgust.

The photographer crouched, a troglodyte supplicant, and his knees creaked arthritically.

'Lovely, that's lovely,' he said to her as his shutter clicked.

Free from the taint of money, Honor had had no shortage of 'admirers', though for her that term, once a euphemism for licentious petitioners, had largely reverted to its literal meaning. The exhilaration of boundless physical profligacy, the delicious sense that one could seduce the world if one wished, had vanished. All part of time's cruel process of de-pleasuring.

'No need to humour me,' she said.

Bucknell worked swiftly, with the cold-eyed hostility of a sniper.

It must be a chemical signal, or its absence – the musk of fertility had evaporated long ago – that now rendered her invisible to most men. On occasions, though, she had felt that she was not invisible enough; once or twice, she had found herself watching an attractive young man, a stranger, imagining his smooth body unclothed, the swells and hollows of his musculature, the silky tuber stirring in its nest, willing the warmth of his breath on her cheek and his cupped hands at her breasts, when the focus of her idle yearning, sensing that he was being observed, had looked up and, at the sight of her, shrunk back, unable to conceal his horror. Did they fear that old age might be contagious? She had news for them: it was. Early death was the only way to avoid it.

At least in the case of this dolt kneeling by her chair, the revulsion was mutual.

Tamara watched as Honor Tait faced the lens with an enigmatic smile, like a fossilised Mona Lisa. Was that a smile of self-satisfaction or contempt?

The photographer, a man of few words at the best of times, asks if he can snap away while we chat by the hearth.

'No,' says Miss Tait firmly. 'You can do me now.'
As he unpacks his equipment her impatience grows.
'And don't make such a business of it. It's a fetish. Just
fire away.'

Bucknell, back on his feet, made several tentative suggestions with the air of someone, arms aloft, attempting to reason with an armed assailant. Would Miss Tait consider, perhaps, resting her cheek on her hand? Might she see her way to holding up her book? Would she possibly, for a second, contemplate posing with the deerstalker hat hanging on a peg by the door?

'Do you expect me to make a total fool of myself?'

He took a few more token pictures and sullenly began packing his cameras away.

The doyenne of British journalism greets us at the door
of her £200,000 apartment, eyes flashing wildly . . .

'The trouble is,' Honor said, talking over him conspiratorially as he crouched by his bags, 'they all think they're artists these days.'

Tamara smiled. The difficult business with Bucknell was over and Honor Tait was acknowledging her, woman to woman, as a fellow professional. Tamara allowed herself a certain pride. Her status had soared because of her association with Britain's most respectable glossy magazine.

Beneath her steely exterior, Honor Tait, fearless news-hound and former femme fatale, has a 50-carat heart.

The old woman looked at Tamara with a wily smile.

'I hope you don't think you're an artist too, dear. There's nothing more absurd than a reporter who thinks she's an artist.'

Was Bucknell sniggering? Tamara murmured a denial, bent over her notebook and worried her pencil across the lined pages. *Face lift?* she wrote. There was an unnatural silvery sheen across Honor Tait's cheeks, and she appeared to have difficulty smiling. But that could be down to temperament.

'A voice recorder *and* a notebook?' Honor asked, arching her sparse eyebrows at the tiny machine.

The old woman could raise her eyebrows anyway, which was more than Lucy Hartson could do.

'Belt and braces. If one fails, the other won't let me down,' Tamara said.

Honor leaned towards her, as if she was about to share a confidence.

'Very wise, dear,' she said. 'It would be disastrous if one of your stories were to be lost to the reading public. Like Alexandria's Library all over again.'

Tamara caught the hostility but not the reference and smiled – a jaunty, dishonest grin – right back. Okay. She got the picture. Honor Tait was not going to make it easy, or pleasant. But Tamara was a professional. She had come here to get a story, to advance her career, not to make a friend.

'Yes. I suppose so,' she said, with a light laugh intended to suggest that she got the joke but was generous enough to let it pass.

In her notebook she wrote: *Chk: who is Alexandria? What happened to her library?*

'We'd better get this over with,' Honor said. Her gloating smile contracted into a pucker of displeasure and she drew back into her chair.

Tamara summoned a TV weather girl's brightness.

'Congratulations!' she said. 'It's a terrific book.'

The girl's accent, Honor noted, had a trace of John Major's estuary whine, and her insincerity was almost heroic.

'A book? You think so? It's not what I'd call a book,' she said. '*If This is a Man* is a book. *Ulysses* is a book. *The Death of Ivan Ilyich* is a book. What you're referring to is a collection of miscellaneous articles culled from many years' work in the journalistic trade – a small block of granite representing a stonemason's lifetime toil.'

'Oh no,' Tamara insisted. 'It stands up very well as a book. A truly great read. A classic.'

'So you've read it?'

'Of course. Marvellous.'

'Well then, you know everything about me that you need to know.'

'Not quite everything, no. Your book raises questions, too.'

Tamara instantly rued her clumsiness. She was setting a trap for herself. Sure enough, Honor Tait tugged the wire.

'What questions might they be?'

'Oh, general questions . . . Global politics. History. The nature of journalism. It was very thought-provoking.'

'And which elements of the book, precisely, provoked these *thoughts* of yours?'

'Difficult to say. All of it, really.'

Tamara was keen to steer the subject away from the book, or, more specifically, from her opinion of it. She had agonised over the best way to start this interview; the first question often set the tone and determined the outcome. Should she go in hard, cut out the foreplay and interrogate the old curmudgeon about the only really interesting aspects of her life – the famous love affairs? The Hollywood parties? Her privileged childhood should provide some anecdotes, too. Dusty details about her work could be woven in from the cuttings later. This method, Tamara knew, often threw naïve interviewees off guard: taken aback by the interviewer's boldness, even rudeness, they would overcompensate with a politeness that had the same result as a truth serum. The more blunt and ill-mannered the question, the more frank and self-damning the answer. But Honor Tait was a cunning old pro, and not overburdened with courtesy. She would show Tamara the door within the first minute.

As if to prove the point, the old woman replied with a viperish smile: 'All of it? Really? The highest praise.'

'I'm your greatest admirer,' Tamara said.

Honor's smile shrank to a fleeting wince.

'I'll be the judge of that.'

'No, honestly. I'm your biggest fan. I've been following your career and reading your work forever.'

'Really! How old are you exactly?'

'Twenty-seven.'

'You were born in nineteen seventy?'

Tamara nodded cautiously.

'Let's see,' Honor said. 'I was covering the aftermath of the Kent State killings in Ohio that year. I suppose, between nappy changes, you were following my reports on the anti-Vietnam War movement? Reading me in your cradle, were you? Cheering me on with your rattle?'

Tamara's cheeks reddened, with suppressed rage rather than embarrassment. Was the old woman trying to provoke her? This was simple antagonism.

'No. No. I mean I read your work when I was at Poly. They're set texts in Media Studies.'

'I always thought that was a contradiction in terms: Media. Studies . . .'

Tamara's throat tightened and she coughed nervously. The old woman was psychotically irritable. How long had they been sitting here? She had not yet managed to ask a single question. But how to begin? Tait would clearly not be seduced easily into conversation. Especially by a woman. If Tamara had been an attractive young male reporter, or even a louche middle-aged toff like Simon, she might have been in with a chance. Best to play it straight.

'I wonder, what was the most memorable story you ever covered?'

Honor gave her a crooked smile. She knew she was being perversely obstructive, but the girl was such a little dunderhead, and so cheerfully dishonest, it was irresistible.

'Memorable? I like to think that they were *all* worth committing to memory.'

'Well, you know . . . historic. Your Pulitzer Prize, for instance. That must have been amazing, winning something like that in your twenties.'

'Considering the subject, what I'd seen, the prize seemed ridiculously unimportant. A frivolity.'

'Yes, of course.'

Tamara nodded, trying to remember the subject of the award-winning piece. She wished she'd had time to read it. Was it Korea? Vietnam?

'But I suppose,' Honor continued, picking at a loose thread near the hem of her dress, 'if it meant that more people read the article than might otherwise have done, it was worthwhile. And now it's been reprinted, so you've read it too, and a new generation can learn lessons from the mistakes of the old.'

'Yes. Right . . . But, apart from that, I mean, what were the biggest historic events you covered?'

Honor sighed.

'Nuremberg? Poland? Berlin? Korea? Was that the sort of thing you had in mind?'

Tamara feared the worst. She had interviewed old people before. While they might forget what they had said five minutes ago, their long-term memories could be horribly intact. The last thing Tamara needed now was a sustained historical soliloquy; a torrent of words and dates without a single usable quote. Her eyes widened and she nodded again in feigned enthusiasm.

'Or were you thinking more of Madrid?' Honor asked. 'Or Vietnam? The Cultural Revolution?'

'Madrid . . . The Vietnamese Cultural Revolution. Great. You choose.'

The pleasure Honor had derived from taunting the girl was beginning to drain away. She was reminded of those absurd games that had been imposed on her and her brothers at Christmas. A dull word contest perhaps: agony for the children, hilarious for the adults. Or Charades. An opportunity for drunken grown-ups to show off to each other.

'You could always pick something from the book,' Honor said.

'I don't want to just lift whole passages from it,' Tamara replied, though that was precisely what she intended to do. 'It would be useful to convey a sense of you in conversation, relaxed, at home . . .'

That she was at home, Honor could not deny. But relaxed? And in conversation? With this girl?

'An interview is not my idea of a conversation. Perhaps you should just get on and ask your questions.'

Tamara bit her pencil and glanced over at the Sony. The red light was still glowing; the machine dutifully recording her humiliation. Bucknell, who was taking an unusually long time to pack away his equipment, was back on his knees, fussing over his bag. This would be all round *The Monitor* in hours.

'What was it *really* like to be a woman journalist in the Nineteen Forties and Fifties?' asked Tamara with a sudden briskness.

'Much the same as it was to be a male journalist,' Honor said. 'Though the scarcity of sanitary napkins in war zones was less of an issue for them.'

There was another cough – a smoker's gurgling hawk – and Honor and Tamara looked over to the photographer, who was now standing, apparently chastened but impatient.

'When this young man picks up his handbag and leaves,' Honor said, 'we can have a cup of tea. Perhaps it will help you get your thoughts in order.'

Bucknell glanced at Tamara and raised his eyebrows in an unwelcome expression of solidarity before turning to go.

'You can let yourself out, can't you?' Honor said, rising stiffly from her chair.

She went into the kitchen and Tamara caught a glimpse of cream vinyl and fluorescent strip lighting. Bucknell, keeping an eye on the door, gingerly pulled a smaller camera from his pocket, took some general shots of the room, then moved in for close-ups of the photographs on the bookcase and wall, as well as one of a smiling elderly man on a side table by Honor Tait's chair. The magazine was bound to need additional material to illustrate the piece and this legitimate pilfering of a few extra images would save time, and costly hours of picture research. As

Honor filled the kettle and clattered crockery, he looked at Tamara and winked – a gesture even more repulsive than his thumbs-up. Pausing to peek into the bedroom down the hall and take one last picture, he left the flat, shutting the door quietly behind him.

'Milk and sugar?' Honor called from the kitchen.

'Just milk, please,' Tamara said, pressing the pause button on her tape recorder and getting up to take a closer look at the photographs. She recognised the Golden Girl picture from the cuttings. Was that really her, Honor Tait, pert and voluptuous in shorts, smiling at the mustachioed soldier? With Franco. Or was it Castro? Hard to believe that the crooked hag filling the kettle in the kitchen was once this soft-eyed beauty who, according to the cuttings, had outfoxed and bewitched some of the most famous men of the past century.

Tamara shuddered. She wanted to get old – it was better than the alternative. Her mother's breast cancer had inoculated Tamara against the romantic view, expressed by flippant friends, that early death with smooth complexion and toned physique was preferable to life post-menopause as a slack-skinned frump. Her mother, who had died at forty-six, would have chosen life at any price. But looking at the radiant girl in the photograph, and hearing her decrepit counterpart shuffle around the kitchen, Tamara knew she did not want to get *that* old. There were limits.

Looking at the photographs of Honor Tait in resplendent youth displayed so proudly in her £250,000 London flat

and turning to her now, is like watching that scene in Last
Horizon *(or was it* Lost*?) the movie masterpiece, when
the chthonically beautiful (chk name) flees the protection of
the magically hermetic valley only to wither horribly, ageing
a thousand years in minutes before her lover's terrified eyes.*

The crockery rattled as Honor Tait carried in a tray bearing
a pot of Darjeeling, two vividly patterned gold-rimmed
cups, a jug of milk and a saucer of sliced lemon, and lowered
it shakily on to a leather stool between the chairs. Tamara
knew that an offer of assistance might cause offence. She
watched apprehensively as the old woman poured the tea
and the brown stream wavered dangerously over the cups.

Using a pair of tongs, Honor dropped a sliver of lemon
into one cup and passed the milk to Tamara. The girl
could serve herself.

'Well? Where were we?' Honor asked, raising her cup
to her lips.

Tamara's gaudy cup rocked in its flooded saucer. For a
reckless moment she was tempted to suggest that Tait
had been in the middle of a detailed appraisal of Frank
Sinatra's performance in bed, but she held back and
flipped through her notebook, looking at some of the
questions she had prepared earlier, buying time.

'You were telling me about the difficulties of being a
woman in journalism when you started out.'

Honor pursed her lips over the tea then drew them
back sharply, recoiling from the heat.

'Was I? Well, I suppose journalism, like much else in

those days, was a male domain. The newsroom was pungent with testosterone.'

Was this what had attracted her to the job in the first place? Honor had sometimes wondered. It had provided an escape route, obviously, from family, from the limited roles available to women at that time, from the silken straitjacket of her class, offering freedom, purpose, adventure. Her parents had wanted nothing more for her than marriage to a member of their caste – landed, wealthy and philistine – and the nuns had groomed her for a life of modesty and self-abnegation. Both options were perfectly compatible, she knew. They were also abhorrent, denying curiosity, passion and ambition. She wanted to make her own way, forge a new kind of life, devour the world. Was there also an exhibitionist's pleasure in storming the grim gentlemen's clubs – part barracks, part monastery – that were the newspaper offices of the Thirties and Forties? Was it like breaching Mount Athos in a bathing costume? As she crossed the newsroom floor in her neat crêpe suit, her heels tapping counterpoint to the thrumming wires and the clattering typewriters with their musical pings, had she enjoyed the sense that her colleagues were watching her, craning their necks, hungrily following her progress, mesmerised by the kinetic retreat of her stocking seams? Perhaps she had relished, more than the story itself, the moues of surprise from taciturn newsmen when they learned that it was a woman, and an attractive woman, who had turned in such an exemplary piece of work. There had also been the singular rigours and, it could not be denied, the pleasures, of work in the field – fighting with them, eating with them, sleeping with them – the sole woman among men of action and men of war.

'That must have been tough,' Tamara said.

'I imagine it's all lipstick and cheap scent at *The Monitor* these days,' Honor said.

Tamara ignored the slight and looked again at her list of questions.

'I wonder if you could tell me in your own words about some of the real-life incidents that inspired the book.'

The old woman's eyes narrowed to two sparks of spite. She had been prepared, for a moment, to give the girl the benefit of the doubt, but this was ridiculous.

'Real life? In my own words? Do you think I made the whole thing up? And whose words are you suggesting that I used? Are you accusing me of plagiarism?'

'Absolutely not. Of course not.' Tamara's laugh, meant to be hearty, sounded panicky. 'I just wanted to get some quotes from you that aren't directly drawn from your book.'

'So you'd like me to paraphrase my own words?'

Tamara nodded.

Honor stared into her cup for a full minute, as if reading her tea leaves, then leaned over to the side table, picked up her book and opened it at random.

'Chapter Seven. The Hotel Deutscher Hof. Nineteen Thirty-eight.'

She snapped the book shut and gave Tamara a challenging look.

'Tea with Hitler? How would that suit you?'

'Great!' Tamara said.

It would do for starters, she supposed. Hitler was not Sinatra, but he was a celebrity, of sorts. At least everyone had heard of him. She leaned over her notebook and wrote: *Chk chapter seven.*

Honor sat back in her chair and spoke in a weary monotone.

'The German army had mobilised in Czechoslovakia and Hitler was refusing to meet the foreign statesmen who had assembled in Nuremberg. The world's press were there, too, and suddenly Ribbentrop announced that tea was to be held in Hitler's honour at 4 p.m. We were all invited.' She paused. 'Is that the sort of thing you wanted?'

Tamara's eager nod was encouraging, and entirely insincere.

'I was sharing a table with Unity Mitford and Robert Byron. Unity was making sheep's eyes at the Führer, who was sitting next to Lord Brocket on the next table; the two men were chuckling over some joke but Hitler kept looking across at Unity, seeking her out.' Honor's voice gradually became more animated; by naming these long-dead phantoms she was calling them, and herself, to life. 'I went over to his table with her,' she continued, 'and when Brocket got up, presumably to smoke a cigar outside – Hitler abhorred smoking – I slipped in beside him . . .'

Apart from Hitler, Byron was the only name Tamara recognised, and poets, living or dead, were of no interest. Occupying her time until Honor Tait said something useful, Tamara continued to redraft her story.

I'm ten minutes late, which, as any Londoner will tell you, given the state of traffic in the capital, amounts to being early. But Honor Tait, doyenne of British journalism and vieille terrible *of Maida Vale, is not happy. 'What time do you call this?' she snarls, as she grudgingly admits me to her cluttered flat, filled with decaying mementoes of her glamorous youth.*

Was the girl actually getting this down? Honor wondered.

'But of course you've read all this already,' she said.

Tamara looked up, startled.

'In the book,' Honor added tartly.

'Yes. Yes. Of course.'

Tamara needed to deflect the old woman's scrutiny with another question.

'And what did you have?' she asked.

'Have?'

'For tea. Cake? Sandwiches?'

Honor's lip curled in tremulous disbelief then she closed her eyes and gripped the arms of her chair.

'Let's see . . . Unity had, if I remember rightly, scones with cream and raspberry jam. No. It was plum. She couldn't abide the pips. And Hitler had sachertorte, chocolate and marzipan, two slices, but he declined the *crème anglaise . . .*'

She was nodding now – her involuntary tremor had taken hold – and she opened her eyes to see Tamara conscientiously taking notes.

'Oh for goodness' sake!' Honor said. 'Of course I don't

remember. This was a moment of historic importance. Europe was on the brink of war. Everyone, except the Nazis, was hoping desperately to avert it. The last thing on anyone's mind was tea.'

Tamara sat up, rigid.

'Yes. Absolutely. Your interview with Hitler . . .'

'You *have* read this?'

The girl's face was as expressionless as a doll's. She did seem very stupid indeed.

'Of *course*,' Tamara said with unpersuasive emphasis. She shifted in her chair. There seemed to be an ortho-paedic cushion at her back, grubby and pink as an old Elastoplast. There was something faintly insanitary about the elderly. She felt a surge of nausea.

'I suppose you've done your homework too, gone through the archives, studied the cuttings?'

'I read as much as I could, yes,' Tamara protested. 'I was only assigned the interview this week and I've been doing other stories in between. Could we get back to your tea with Hitler?' She looked over at her Sony: still recording.

Honor chided herself for lowering her guard for a moment. The girl was a hostile presence, professional in her scepticism if in nothing else, not some neophyte sitting rapt at her feet, revelling in her recollections.

'I've said all I need to say on the subject. You can read – you can reread – the episode in the book. Next ques-tion . . . ?'

'Could you tell me something about your childhood?'

Honor rolled her eyes.

'Is that really necessary?'

The last time Tamara had encountered anything approaching this degree of obstructiveness was when she interviewed a third-rate American TV star who was taking over the lead in a long-running West End musical. He had agreed to open a new shopping centre in Sydenham. After queuing for twenty minutes in the corridor outside his hotel suite with half a dozen other journalists, Tamara had been ushered into his presence by flunkies and given exactly five minutes to wring out 300 words for the *Sydenham Advertiser*'s In Town show business column. He lay sprawled on a sofa, his hair a lacquered bonnet, his tan so florid it could have been a symptom of advanced liver failure, puffing on a cigar and chugging champagne. He had sniggered malevolently at all her questions. But she had persevered.

Now she gathered her resolve and gave Honor Tait a challenging look.

'Childhood. That's usually the starting point in these in-depth interviews,' Tamara said.

Honor shook her head.

'I'm sorry, Tara. We're here to talk about the book. I'm a journalist, not some attention-seeking actress. And you are not hosting a television talk show.'

Tamara wondered if the old woman was deliberately getting her name wrong. She lowered her head, scribbling randomly in her notebook to allow herself time to collect her thoughts.

'But it *is* relevant,' she said, looking up at last. 'Your

past. What made you take off like that? Break with tradition, the expectations of your class at that time?'

'Goodness! A Marxist! How recherché.'

'I mean your mother. Wasn't she an aristocrat or something? She wouldn't have . . . in those days . . . Did it
affect your relationship?'

'The psychoanalytic approach, too?'

Honor laughed. She had often marvelled at the resilience
of the twentieth century's greatest pseudo-science. She
remembered the ascetic room with its Buddhist memora-
bilia, like the vestibule of a Thai restaurant, where she had
visited Dr Kohler five days a week during a tricky patch in
the Sixties. They had talked about her childlessness, her
mother, and her father, and her governesses, and the nuns,
and her dreams; all a stupendous waste of money and energy.
And time. She could forgive Dr Kohler, a kindly old humbug
merchant, not a charlatan, but what had *she* been doing? A
grown woman whining and mewling like an infant about
her barrenness – a choice made in her twenties that became
inescapable biological fact in her thirties – and her long-
dead mother? And her dreams? Since then, Honor had
thought that advances in neuroscience had seen off that
canard. But no, the horoscope-reading class continued to
look for portents and insights in the random electrical
impulses generated by the brain at rest. And this little
nobody, clearly, was a member of that class.

'They're just the standard interview questions. The
questions we ask everyone,' the girl said, with unexpected
firmness.

'Standard questions? As in one-size-fits-all? Don't you ever wonder why your interviews are so bland and devoid of substance?'

Tamara stiffened. She was not going to be defeated. What Honor Tait had not accounted for was the core of steel in her heart.

'It's a formula, yes. But it's a formula that works. You must have asked the same questions, now and again, of your soldiers and politicians, your actors and artists, your writers. The questions might be the same but the answers are always different. It's the answers that make the story.'

She had a point. But Honor was not going to concede it and, perversely, it spurred her to attack.

'In that case, why did you bother coming here at all? Why not send me a multiple-choice questionnaire? How would it go, your "standard interview" questionnaire? "One: As a child were you – a) abused? b) happy? c) witness to an unspeakable family tragedy? Two: As an adult did you have – a) ten lovers or fewer? b) twenty lovers or fewer? c) numberless hordes?"'

Tamara's face coloured. She thought again of her interview with the psychopathically arrogant American TV star.

'I loathe your TV show,' she had wanted to tell him. 'And above all I loathe you, you ridiculous, bloated has-been.'

But she had thought of her salary, clenched her fists and, instead, asked him: 'What are your impressions of Sydenham? Do you have any plans to see more of the area?'

Now she was fighting the urge to tell Honor Tait that

she had no interest in her, her work, her family or her so-called book.

'I'm sorry,' Tamara mumbled. 'I know the really important stuff is about your work . . . politics, history and all that. But we need the human angle too, to bring all this to life. Our readers need to get an impression of you as a person.'

An existential fatigue began to settle over Honor like an autumn mist.

'As a person? What I look like now, as opposed to then? Whether I'm kindly or crotchety? Fragrant or malodorous? Whether I'm a fascinating raconteur or a tedious old bore?'

Tamara wrote: *malodorous, tedious old bore*. She compressed her lips in a grim smile.

'No. No. We just need something about your life outside of work. Your parents – what were they like? A few sentences, that's all. What kind of child were you? Your love life, home life, hopes, dreams, fears . . . Then we can get down to the real story.'

'I'm afraid, Tara,' Honor said, her voice strained with the effort of patience, 'that, like most journalists of my generation, I have an allergy to the first person singular. You wouldn't understand this, of course. You believe in "letting it all hang out", don't you? That's still the phrase, isn't it? Well, my view is, "Put it away. It's neither interesting nor decent. No one else wants to see it."'

'But they *do* want to know! You've seen a lot. You're wise. We could learn from you.'

Honor wondered what possible 'wisdom' might be imparted in an account of her 'love life', past and present. Her love affairs had been another subject for the analyst's parlour, but her agonised monologues, occasionally punctuated by Dr Kohler's neutral yet encouraging murmurs, had yielded no insights, or pleasures. She could have more usefully spent the fees retaining the services of a full-time gigolo.

'The man with insight enough to accept his limitations comes nearest to perfection,' Honor said. 'Goethe. That's wisdom for you. But it requires a certain intelligence, which may be beyond you, to learn from it.'

Tamara's eyes were smarting. She should get up and leave right now. How much did she really want this contract?

'A few simple questions, that's all,' she pleaded. 'What did you do when you filed your pieces and headed for home? When and where were you happiest? And who with? Hobbies. Family. Pet peeves. Most embarrassing moment. Your husbands, lovers. Just a word or two. Name checking, really. That sort of thing.'

'Really? Look around you at the state of the world, the injustice, the suffering.' Honor gestured, with trembling arms, as if her room contained the sum of the world's miseries. 'And you want to exercise your talents, such as they are, by describing the emotional landscape of a vanished childhood, or the extinct love affairs of an elderly woman in one minuscule, privileged corner of a vast and suffering world? What interest is this to anyone?'

'Our readers are interested,' Tamara said weakly.

The possessive pronoun would convince no one, she knew. She could not care less about *S*nday*'s readers, with their superior attitudes, worthy causes, expensive homes and exotic holidays. But she knew she could not work at *Psst!* for ever. She could not afford to.

'If their chief concern is this sort of trivia, then your readers aren't worthy of consideration,' Honor said, reaching for her cup.

Tamara turned to her notebook and wondered if the price of success could ever be too high. She bowed her head to her work once more and, for a moment, Honor imagined that they had swapped places; Honor was the young reporter again, nervous but determined, braving the inhospitality of a grand and grudging interviewee.

'I just wanted some background,' Tamara said, and her voice had the falling pitch of defeat.

'If it's biography you want,' Honor said, 'you'll find everything you need on the inside back flap of the book jacket.'

She picked up her book again and read aloud: '"Honor Tait was born in Scotland and educated in Brussels and Geneva. She worked at a news agency in Paris, before going to Spain to cover the Civil War. She was with the American troops at the Normandy landings, covered the liberation of Buchenwald, the Nuremberg trials," etc. Are you writing this down or are you leaving it to your recording machine?'

Tamara wrote on, furiously: *My interview with the famously frosty Miss Tait has turned her gloomy, antiques-filled flat into a deep freeze.* She despised the old woman.

And she would not be beaten by her. On the other hand, did she really want a job where her days would be spent fawning on egomaniacs? She thought again of Tim with a pang. On the *Sphere*, her job would have been to scythe these people down.

'Any brothers and sisters?' Tamara asked.

'You?' the old lady countered.

Tamara clenched her fists with anger.

'My siblings aren't relevant to this story,' she said.

'Nor mine. Now Tara, that's a good Irish name. "*The Harp that once through Tara's halls/ The soul of music shed,/ Now hangs as mute on Tara's walls/ As if that soul were fled.*" I suppose people quote that to you all the time.'

'No, actually. It's Tamara. Which is Russian. But I'm not.'

'Russian-Irish,' mused Honor, seized by another wild urge to provoke. 'A heady combination. Do you have the Gaelic? *A chailín mo chroí*? Or was Russian your first language? *Dorogaya Moya*?'

'No. Neither. I'm not Irish. Not Russian either. Now if we can—'

'So where are you from?' taunted the old woman. 'Tell me about your background. Isn't that what all you young journalists want to talk about these days? Yourselves, your pasts, your feelings, your *relationships*.'

Honor watched as the girl lowered her head again. Was she fighting tears? Honor had sometimes wondered what it would have been like to have had a daughter. She was sure she would have been singularly ill equipped –

the soft toys and fairy talk, the pastel frocks and glitter, the grooming and hair care, the histrionics . . .

The girl looked up and there was a flare of what could have been hatred in her eyes. Well, Honor thought, that was more interesting.

'I'm not the subject of this interview. You are,' Tamara said in a dull whisper.

She could see her *S*nday* contract slipping away. As if the double blow she had recently suffered – dumped by her lover and a prize job on the *Sphere* snatched from her grasp – was not painful enough.

'Really? This isn't about you?' Honor tilted her head and gave Tamara a penetrating look. 'I thought the papers liked nothing better than interviews with nonentities, by nonentities, these days.'

It was the wrong moment and entirely the wrong place, but Tamara could hold back no longer. The awful truth struck her like a whip across the face – her escape route was barred, she would have to go on compiling cheery lists for *Psst!* and grubbing for work in ever more abstruse regions of the trade press, she would be unable to help her brother and he would sink further, out of sight, and she would end her days, alone and broke, in a shabby rented flat. It was unprofessional, she knew, but she could do nothing about it as the tears seeped from her eyes, spilled down her cheeks and dripped onto her notebook, where they trembled in little quicksilver pools.

Honor was alarmed. Faced by tears, she had always felt revulsion. Tad had been comically lachrymose. He would weep over television adverts – haiku biopics for building societies or insurance companies, in which implausibly handsome young families romped through life to graceful maturity and silvery senescence in soft focus. Maybe she was deficient. She had sometimes wondered whether her apparent lack of tear ducts represented weakness rather than strength. Did it indicate a kind of emotional colour blindness?

The girl was shuddering softly now as she tried to compose herself. What exactly had prompted this fit of weeping? Was something else troubling her? Honor felt embarrassed on her behalf; to be so reduced, in the course of one's work, too, amounted to a kind of incontinence. Whatever the cause of this display, Honor wanted it to cease at once.

'What would you like to know?' she asked gently.

Tamara looked up, wiping her eyes on the cuffs of her blouse.

'Sorry?'

'Shall I just talk?' Honor asked. 'And you can tell me if it's the kind of thing you want . . .'

Tamara sniffed. Had she gained some advantage here?

'Could we start with your Hollywood experiences?' she tried tentatively. She saw Tait's sudden scowl and her voice grew more faint with every syllable: 'Marilyn? Or Sinatra?'

Honor Tait put her hand to her brow.

'Liz Taylor?' Tamara hazarded, pulling a pack of tissues from her bag and dabbing at her notebook.

The old woman's gorgon stare was unnerving, but she was also nodding vigorously.

Encouraged, Tamara added, 'Any reminiscences of the stars would do, really.'

Though the old woman continued to signal her apparent approval of Tamara's questions, she remained silent.

'Your circle of young male friends?' Tamara asked.

Honor was relieved to see that the girl had finally composed herself. Only two panda patches of pink around her eyes betrayed her lapse. But her questions? If this had not been so intrusive, and such a waste of precious time, it might have been comic.

'You're a bit of a role model, for younger women journalists,' Tamara said, trying another tack.

'A crowded field, I'm sure.'

Tamara pulled back. She had to be more cautious. Play the old woman at her own game. Appeal to her intellectual snobbery and then, when she was relaxed and singing like a linnet, go in for the kill. Sinatra. Picasso. Liz Taylor. Marilyn. She looked over at the photograph of the young Honor with Castro. Or was it Franco?

'What about Spain?' she asked suddenly. There had been a module on the Spanish Civil War at Brighton Poly. Though Tamara had chosen the Hollywood option instead, she had looked at the syllabus, seen the photographs.

'What about it?'

Tamara chewed her pencil as she reached for an answer. Then she remembered, and her voice had a bright ring of certainty.

'Your time as a war correspondent with Ernest Hemingway, for instance!'

Tamara congratulated herself. Yes. The boozy, bearded big-game hunter, who wrote the screenplay for the Spencer Tracy vehicle, *The Old Man and the Sea*. They must have made quite a couple, Hemingway and Tait.

Honor screwed up her eyes as if in pain. She did not know how much more of this she could stand.

'I think you'll find that was Martha Gellhorn,' she said.

'I wonder—' Tamara faltered.

The old woman interrupted her.

'I'm sorry. I should never have agreed to this. We've been wasting each other's time. You had better leave.'

Honor walked down the hallway towards the door. Tamara needed to think fast, retrace her steps. She was not going to let this one go without a fight.

'Tell me,' she said, twisting in her chair to address Honor Tait's back, 'what questions would you *like* me to ask?'

'I'm sorry?'

She had to hand it to the girl, she did not give up easily. Her stupidity was impregnable.

'I just wondered what questions you'd be happy to answer,' Tamara said.

Honor paused by the door. She knew she could proceed in two ways: throw the girl out and be done with it – incurring a poisonous paragraph or two in *The Monitor* and an institutional hostility from the paper for the rest of her days, and beyond – or sit down and interview herself, using this little goose as an amanuensis. That way, there would at least be no awkward or painful questions. She could hear Ruth telling her that, if she wanted to sell any books, she only had one option. So what questions would she like to answer? Liking did not come into it. What questions would she be *prepared* to answer? If she had been in a polemical mood, if she had not been so tired and sickened by this whole stupid process, she might have seen it as an opportunity to intercede on behalf of the flood victims of Bangladesh, say, or the exploited Dalits, or the street children of Brazil.

'Questions about the book?' Honor said, checking the terms of the deal.

'The book. Your life, your family, famous friends. Whatever you'd like to say.'

Honor looked up towards the ceiling, as if pleading for intercession. She knew the list of inappropriate questions that she herself had asked was long. She had blundered unfeelingly across human tragedies, large and small, in search of a story: the mother with the dead child in her arms in Madrid; the bereaved father in Algiers; the rape victims in Calcutta; the camp survivors. Had she not exacerbated misery, too? She had welcomed and encouraged expressions of distress, knowing they brought her nearer to a story's nucleus and she had pressed on, pushing the victims further. The spectacle of human grief became part of the narrative. That each story was important did not lessen the offence.

'The book, then,' she offered.

'I wondered, of your many stories, which are you most proud of?'

Honor turned and walked slowly, as if in a trance, back to her chair. She feared her sense of moral certainty had begun to fade, like so much else. She liked to watch it in her friend Paul; his righteous wrath as he tore around the world seeking out injustice, facing down powerful liars, championing the weak, could make her nostalgic. Had she lost her fighting spirit, too?

'Pride?' the old woman said, easing herself back into her seat. Her voice was weak, drained of strength and colour. 'One must always mistrust pride.'

Tamara felt a new determination, as if she had shed, along with her tears, her ineffectual, defeated, third-class self and in her place sat a confident, wily star reporter, a keen-eyed contributor to an illustrious journal, an astute seeker of truths and wrester of insights.

'Which was your *riskiest* story then? The one that placed you in most personal danger?'

Honor looked at the girl with distaste, but the irritable spirit of Ruth was hovering. At last, with a heavy sigh of resignation, she bent to the task. Her answer was long and detailed and involved Berlin, Tokyo, Korea, the 38th Parallel. (Parallel to what? Tamara wondered.) But there were no personal revelations or worthwhile quotes. Even Lyra's most erudite readers would be dozing over their cappuccinos by the second paragraph. Honor Tait's tight little mouth pursed and stretched with surprising vigour and Tamara, hearing the ebb and flow of her voice, felt she had accidentally tuned into a cheerless current affairs discussion on Radio 4.

In the fading light of Honor Tait's flat, Tamara smiled, nodded and shook her head where appropriate, prompted by the rise and fall of the old woman's voice, and pretended to take notes.

Honor Tait, doyenne of war reporters, high priestess of journalists, is far from happy. At eighty, still in possession of her faculties, though with an octogenarian's tendresse for reminiscence, there are few traces of her once-famed chthonic beauty. Staring at Honor Tait is like looking at the horrifyingly shrivelled former beauty (fill in name) played by (name) in the movie classic Last Horizon.

'You have to understand that one was working in a vacuum,' Honor said. 'There was no reliable information network, there were no other news sources one could draw on. The fear was palpable. One had to truly *see*, to rely on the evidence of one's eyes, and record with precision exactly what one was seeing.'

Tamara, cued by the cracked music of Tait's voice, uttered exclamations of surprise or admiration, concern or disapproval.

'Of course!'

'All around us, mortar shells were exploding as I ran to the jeep.'

'Terrifying!'

Most women of her age are doting grandparents and devoted widows, only too happy to pore over photographs of their loved ones with hapless visitors. But for Honor Tait, the indulgent anecdotes, les moments brilliants of her life, her rhapsodies of remembrance, concern not her family or lovers — on the subject of which she is sternly silent — but her work.

Tara was, Honor observed, a scrupulous note-taker. Could she have been too hard on her? The girl was the product of an age in which history had been jettisoned along with seriousness. The young were all gunslingers now, each one a little Goebbels, reaching for their revolvers whenever they heard the word culture. And truth had been reduced to the subjective. This is *my* truth; what's yours? At least Tara seemed to have some measure of the gulf between them, an instinctive sense of what had been lost, and she showed signs of an ability, or at any rate a willingness, to listen.

Honor continued: 'There was widespread panic. Fleeing South Koreans were pushing past, hoping to get across the river, and the artillery fire started. I grabbed my type-writer and set it up on the hood of the radio truck . . .'

'No!'

Interviewees are warned in advance not to mention her famous amours. Her personal life is strictly off limits. Honor Tait's response to questions about her upbringing in a chateau in Scotland is silence.

'The only option was to walk the fifteen-mile mountain trail to Suwon, further south.'

'No!'

Doubled over her notes, Tamara seemed fired up, her hand working frantically to keep pace, inspired by an account of a different, more authentic and vital age. Honor found it almost touching to watch this ignorant child, raised on the intellectual pabulum of the modern media and groomed for mediocrity, respond to the stimulus of real experience, living history. Buried somewhere beneath that commonplace exterior, Honor thought, there were the makings of a decent newspaperwoman who, in a less otiose age, might have been a perfectly efficient reporter of, say, court proceedings.

On the subject of her three husbands, she is mute. On the subject of her many lovers, her lips are sealed. But when it comes to her work as a frontline journalist, covering the century's big stories, les contes grandes, you can't shut her up.

Tamara covered page after page as the soliloquy continued. She was caught out only once.

'Really? Fantastic!' she enthused, before realising, too late, that she had misread Honor Tait's voice; she had been giving an account of the deaths of the first American troops in Korea.

'They were teenagers, barely out of high school, and had arrived at the front only hours before. One horribly wounded boy kept begging his comrade to shoot him—' Honor said, before breaking off.

Had the girl really said 'fantastic'?

It was touch and go. Honor gave her interviewer a beady look and struggled to her feet to fetch a glass of water from the kitchen. Alone in the sitting room, Tamara stood to look around for some tangible leads to the real Honor Tait, not the grandiose soapbox orator. There was a pile of recently opened post by the vase of flowers. She picked up one card, a child's garish drawing of a tree, and turned it over. It was a flyer about a meeting on 'child exploitation' that was taking place next Wednesday to launch a new charity, Kids' Crusaders. Honor Tait was listed as one of the speakers. Not exactly revelatory, but it could be useful. Tamara was noting the details when she heard the old woman coming back into the room.

The monologue resumed. Honor had come too far to stop now. She sipped from her glass and was swept on by the tide of her narrative and a sense of the epic arc of her own life.

'It was Lieutenant General Walker, Commander of the Eighth Army, who ordered me out of Korea, saying the battlefield was no place for a woman. MacArthur refused to get involved at first, saying it was Walker's decision. But after I secured an interview with MacArthur in Tokyo, the ban on women reporters was lifted.'

The task of extricating a lively article from this self-congratulatory litany would have defeated even one of S*nday's Nobel Prize-winners, Tamara thought. What chance did she stand?

*

It was getting dark and Honor Tait did not let up. She was describing the liberation of a concentration camp now.

'Four days later, the surviving prisoners assembled to celebrate their freedom and mourn their dead. They had each fashioned their national flags from rags or scraps of paper they had somehow procured.'

Tamara watched as the lights went on, a window at a time, in the building opposite, turning it into an illuminated Advent calendar of domestic interiors. But Honor Tait seemed indifferent to the gathering gloom.

'You have to understand the chaos of war. Everything we had witnessed. We were all, press corps included, fired up by a monumental anger.'

Tamara was finding all this bragging exhausting and the cessation of hostilities between them had left more room for other anxieties. Without a mention of Hollywood, or husbands or lovers, not a hint of indiscretion or a shred of human interest, how on earth was she going to write 4,000 words? And she had two freelance features to file this week before she could even make a start on the *S*nday* piece.

'I'm really sorry, Miss Tait,' she said, glancing at her watch which, despite its luminous dial, she could barely read in the dusk. 'I was so absorbed I completely lost track of the time. I have to go.'

She closed her notebook.

Honor felt a tug of disappointment. She had not talked about all this – even thought about it in any depth – for so long. It had been too painful. Under pressure from Ruth, she had rashly agreed to return to the subject and write a coda to her original Pulitzer Prize-winning report on Buchenwald for the next book. The prospect filled her with dread. She had not known where to start and had rehearsed several desperate excuses to get herself off the hook. But somehow the blank-faced ignorance of this girl had drawn her out and Honor was beginning to see a way of attempting the piece she had avoided writing for half a century. Was Tara really leaving now, just when they were getting into their stride?

'Already?' Honor said, her hands fluttering. 'I was just going to make another pot of tea. I might even have some biscuits somewhere.'

Tamara slipped her notebook and tape recorder in her bag.

'I'd love to,' she said, springing to her feet. 'Can't think of anything nicer. But I do have to be off. I've got two stories to hand in. The deadlines are tomorrow.'

Honor, rebuffed, felt a familiar prickle of scepticism.

'Stories? So what else are you writing about?'

'Oh, one's a piece about culture, a festival really. And the other's more of a feminist feature.'

Feminism. That clapped-out old jade. Of course. But Honor would not have had Tara, with her shop girl packaging, her proffered cleavage, down as a natural Sister, one of Isadora Talbot's monstrous regiment. Perhaps it was a pose: the ninny wanted to be 'taken seriously'.

'Well, of course. I wouldn't like to stand in the way of The Cause,' Honor said, prising herself from her chair.

'It's been amazing,' Tamara said. 'Thank you so much.'

She could not wait to leave this cranky old woman and her gloomy flat.

'I'll see you out,' Honor said coolly. The girl's sudden departure felt like an insult.

Tamara walked briskly to the door, keen to step out of the suffocating fug of the flat into the purer air of the high street below, to hear the reassuring hum of London traffic instead of the old woman's self-satisfied drone. But she knew her work was unfinished.

'I wondered, though, since we've run out of time, if we might maybe meet again for another chat?'

'I don't think that will be possible.'

'Just another half-hour some time? I've learned an awful lot today but I know we've only scratched the surface, and it would be a pity to leave it there. A drink somewhere?'

'I don't think so, no,' Honor said.

'But I found your conversation so instructive, and inspiring. You really are a heroine for young women journalists. For young people who want to make a difference. And I loved the new book so much,' Tamara said.

'All of it?'

'Every last word. I don't know how you do it.'

Tamara reached for the door handle.

Honor was smiling again, her falsely modest gaze directed downwards to the bundle of newspapers on the floor by the door.

'I did wonder about the Bing Crosby story,' she said with a shrug.

'Oh really?' Tamara was surprised by this outbreak of

humility and the tantalising offer of new information – had Bing been a lover too?

'Why was that?'

'Didn't it all seem just a little baroque?' Honor asked.

This was dangerous ground. Tamara was unfamiliar with architectural terminology and could not think how it might apply to the immortal crooner, beloved of generations of viewers of prime-time Christmas TV classics. She hadn't seen any reference to Crosby in the cuttings and once more she wished that she'd had time to look at Tait's book more closely.

'How do you mean? I thought it worked brilliantly.'

'That's kind of you. But I thought it, you know, was a little *de trop*, you know – too much.'

'Oh no. So vivid. So *vrai!*'

Tamara knew she should be inveigling her way back into the flat, switching on her Sony again and encouraging the old woman's eleventh-hour indiscretions, but right now, all she wanted to do was to run from this cramped mausoleum with its musty smell of neglect.

Honor leaned towards her and whispered girlishly, 'I worried that perhaps I'd said more than I should. Overstepped the mark. With Bing, I mean.'

'Absolutely not. Pioneering stuff,' Tamara said, shaking her head. 'A revelation. One of the best parts of the entire book. By far.' Then, as an afterthought, she added, 'What was he *really* like, Bing?'

'Divine! Just divine!' Honor Tait's laugh was a surprisingly merry tinkle.

Tamara released her grip on the door handle.

'Did he sing to you? When you were together? Alone?'

'Oh, all the time. He was a real songbird. Forever trilling. And he loved to dance!'

Damn, thought Tamara. The first words of any real interest and she had packed her tape recorder and notebook away.

'Did he?'

'Did I tell you what a marvellous, fleet dancer he was?' the old woman said, her focus suddenly distant, apparently enchanted by memories.

Damn, damn.

'Really?'

'One felt like a column of gossamer in his arms.'

Tamara reached into her bag, blindly searching for her notebook. No luck. She leaned against the door and balanced the bag on her knee in an effort to search more thoroughly. She had to get this down. But it was too late; Honor Tait had already lit off in a different direction, bewitched by another apparition beckoning from her scintillating past.

'Elizabeth Taylor? What about her? Do you think I went too far there in the book?'

'Oh no, no,' Tamara said, putting down the bag and grasping the door handle again. 'Amazing.'

Another story that she'd missed. Again, the cuttings had given no clue, apart from a photo of them together at some Hollywood bash. But now, Honor Tait was finally opening up and if she carried on like this, they could be standing here all night. She seemed as reluctant to let

Tamara leave her flat as she had been to admit her. This was a kind of progress, thought Tamara. But she had endured enough geriatric simpering for one afternoon.

'It would be amazing if we could meet up again. It would be so good to learn how you did that, held all that together, pulled it off. I'd really love to go through it with you, break it down – the whole Bing Crosby, Liz Taylor thing. And Berlin, too. Korea . . . It would be like a master class. I'm sure our readers would be interested, too.'

Honor hesitated.

'Phone my publisher. We'll see what can be arranged.'

As she closed the door on her visitor, securing the chain and sliding the bolts, Honor sighed. A Pyrrhic victory. They had parted on good terms. Ruth would be pleased. And Honor had betrayed no confidences, given nothing away. She had, though, come perilously close – a lonely, foolish old woman blethering away to anyone who listened, or gave the appearance of listening. Such an idiotic girl, too. Tara Sim had not read the book. That much was clear. Elizabeth Taylor's name had not been taken in vain in *Dispatches*; it had never been cited. Honor glanced down again at the Christmas newspapers, piled up for the rubbish chute. And references to Bing Crosby, the oleaginous Republican tenor pictured on the cover of the TV supplement at her feet, were far from baroque; they were non-existent, which was unsurprising, since Honor Tait had never met him, or written about him, in her life.

Four

The Monitor was a broad-church broadsheet, a daily and Sunday operation embracing a tabloid robustness in its gossip and celebrity coverage and a rigorously cerebral approach in its Opinion Pages and its *S*nday* colour magazine. While other newspapers, as the new millennium approached, might cling to old-fashioned, monocultural notions of their readership, the pioneering *Monitor* swung both ways.

It was founded in the nineteenth century by an aristocratic Whig who hoped the enterprise would make him a rapid fortune. He went bankrupt within a decade and the newspaper, in keeping with its tradition, had been losing money ever since. In the early years of the twentieth century, in the hands of a social-climbing northern industrialist, it had restyled itself as a 'paper of record', hoping to woo the Establishment readers of *The Times* and *The Courier*. But in its most recent incarnation, under a new proprietor from the former Soviet Union, *The Monitor* had energetically set about broadening its appeal in an effort to boost dwindling circulation. Politically, too, though its current editor's personal inclination was rightwards, the paper hedged its bets, judging that if the tired Tory government was defeated by fresh-faced New Labour – or vice versa – in the coming elections, *The Monitor* should not be too closely identified with the losing side. In this spirit, it attacked MPs on both sides of the house with a high-minded even-handedness. Its aim was to be all things to all men and women and, like a twentieth-century Tower of Babel, the paper accommodated many competing voices in its five-storey ramshackle block of dun concrete.

The precise structure of *The Monitor*'s intellectual hierarchy was reflected in the layout of its office, a poorly converted former printworks a mile up the road from its old Fleet Street base – now the opulent, marble-pillared headquarters of a firm of libel lawyers. *The Monitor*'s basement bunker which accommodated *Psst!*, its gossip and TV listings magazine, edited by the affable Old Etonian waster Simon Pettigrew, was a windowless corridor, comprising the largest portion, the long vertical stroke, of an L-shaped arrangement of desks which had been carved out of a segment of the canteen, and was separated on the left side by a partition wall from a suite of chronically malfunctioning lavatories.

Psst!'s neighbouring office, the short horizontal stroke of the L, was occupied by the paper's website, a fledgling, experimental operation run on a twenty-four-hour basis by tireless teenagers, their faces studded with piercings, and edited by Tania Singh, an Oxford graduate with tiny fairy features and the incandescent ambition of a young Bonaparte.

Above them, on the ground floor, with windows opening onto the thrum of gridlocked traffic shimmering in a haze of fumes, were the ashen-faced toilers of *The Monitor*'s News room. Here, against the background blare and flicker of half a dozen TV sets, the Home desk rewrote the wire stories and worked the phones and fax machines, searching for news of political scandals, serial killers and freak weather incidents in London and the remote regions of the UK.

The Foreign desk inhabited the same floor, against a phalanx of clocks which displayed the time in New York, Los Angeles, Sydney and – after the efforts of one joker, on the day he received his redundancy cheque – Stoke Newington. In this corner of the office, telephones and fax machines rang and squealed in pursuit of stories of war, political scandals, serial killers and freak weather incidents in regions beyond the English Channel and the Irish Sea (with the exception of Northern Ireland, classified as a remote region of the UK and therefore Home's responsibility).

Around the corner on the ground floor – separated from News by the Reception desk, where importuning members of the public were kept at bay by bouncers in business suits – was the mailroom. Here ex-printers, redeployed as messengers by the advent of new technology, shared cigarettes, tea and sporting gossip between genial forays into the building's further reaches with sacks of post. On the same floor was Advertising, whose staff were distinguished from their News-room colleagues by the fastidiousness of their dress and the bright-eyed, undifferentiated enthusiasm usually associated with Revivalist sects of the American south.

Above them, on the first floor, was Sport, edited by Ricky Clegg, whose recent hiring from the *Sunday Sphere* had provoked the tabloid's retaliatory poaching of *The Monitor*'s eminent Political editor, Bernice Bullingdon. Sport shared a third of an acre of soiled grey carpet tiles, and an occasionally rewarding view into the bathroom windows of the flats opposite, with Human Resources, and with Circulation and Marketing. Here, too, was located Miles Denbigh, the managing editor, a haunted figure rarely seen outside his office, a glass box like a see-through confessional marooned in the centre of the open-plan Sports Department. He was responsible for expenses, budgets, adminstration and staffing matters – he was currently meant to be addressing demands for a multi-faith prayer room, which the new Politics editor, a recent convert to Catholicism, insisted should replace the third-floor smoking room. Instead, Denbigh was reputed to sit all day in his cubicle, his telephone switched off, translating the plays of Aristophanes into unperformable contemporary dramas. In conversation, he was a man of few words, most of them synonyms for sorry. He was said to have had a catheter fitted to avoid inconvenient encounters in the men's room with expenses claimants, smokers and recent converts to Catholicism.

The second floor accommodated the Features desk, run by the quixotic Johnny Malkinson. The prevailing atmosphere here was a grudging hush – as in a sixth-form crammer the week before exams – but the team's youth and native high spirits would occasionally find madcap release in the pursuit of work. Then, unwary visitors to this floor could be forgiven for thinking they had wandered into the company crèche, or an outreach course for teenage sufferers of Attention Deficit Disorder. Visitors might have to negotiate nodding thickets of red balloons, say, or shout to make themselves heard over a fusillade of Mardi Gras whistles, on the day *Monitor Extra* was producing a special issue on power-broking party organisers. Or they might have to address Malkinson as he held a parasol aloft while gingerly attempting to negotiate a tightrope strung between the subs' desks, for a double-page spread on the democratisation of circus skills.

Occasionally, a representative from Human Resources would be sent upstairs to ask Features to keep the noise down. In the midst of these jamborees, Vida Waldman, Johnny's grouchy deputy, would sit frowning at her keyboard in the corner, her workstation an islet of quiet disapproval as the party raged around her.

A more persistently serene atmosphere prevailed on the third floor, with its view of the topmost branches of a row of blighted sycamores. Here the scholarly denizens of the Arts and Books pages co-existed peacefully, if uncomprehendingly, with the bizarrely costumed members of the Fashion department. This floor was the main staging post for the messengers who, when not sharing cigarettes, tea and sporting gossip, spent most of their day in convoy from the ground-floor mailroom, like an endless column of ants, bringing sacks of books to the Books editor and bags of frocks to the Fashion editor. Twitters of pleasure, like spring birdsong, greeted every new delivery to Fashion. In Books, each fresh sack would generate sighs and groans and once, in the case of a distressed temp who was finally escorted from the building, the rending of garments.

On this floor, too, was the Library, also known as the Morgue, the busiest department in the building, a maze of tightly packed, floor-to-ceiling metal shelves crammed with hanging files containing envelopes of photographs and wads of cuttings on everyone who had ever appeared in a newspaper.

'Here is the compost,' Simon had said when he showed Tamara around the building on her first day at *The Monitor*, 'which nourishes our freshest blooms; the poop behind the scoop.'

The turbine hum of great minds at work on momentous matters was almost audible as you stepped out of the lift onto the fourth floor, where the windows gave on to views of a multi-storey car park, whose interlinking ramps and walkways resembled an etching by Cornelius Escher. On this floor, men and women in their serious middle years, their days of Mardi Gras and circus skills long behind them, were said to live by the broadsheet journalists' Law of Gravitas: 'Every article in the Opinion Pages attacks every other article therein with a force that is directly proportional to the product of their masses and inversely proportional to the square of the distance between them . . .' Only those who fully understood this law, and could write its algebraic formula from memory, it was claimed, were permitted to work on the Opinion Pages.

They shared their suite with Politics, a team with a more diverse age range than Opinion, encompassing youthful prodigies with a passion for the statistics, form and league tables of party politics, and august greyheads – like the recently departed Bullingdon, and her successor, Toby Gadge – with failing memories and bulging contacts books, who only truly felt alive in Westminster (in Gadge's case, the purlieu now extended southwards, to encompass Cathedral as well as Palace). On this floor, too, behind superfluous soundproof screens, was located the Obituaries and Crossword department, whose venerable members operated in such silence, and paid so little heed to directives from other departments, that they were widely believed to be deaf mutes employed under one of Denbigh's equal opportunities schemes.

Above Opinion, Obits, Politics and Crosswords, and high above the traffic, the flats, the shrivelled trees and the multi-storey car park, on the fifth floor, the view was of untrammelled skies and cloudscapes. Here the elegant Lyra Moore presided over the *S*nday* team, screened from her staff by constantly replenished urns of flowers, discreetly soliciting the finest prose from the world's most renowned writers, teasing and titivating those words to even greater perfection, and matching them with photographs of such beauty and economy that they demanded to be scissored from the magazine's pages, framed in limed oak and mounted on the wall of a docklands loft.

Here, too, behind a portcullis of polished chrome, through a double door of reinforced glass, beyond the searchlight glare of his secretary Hazel, sat *The Monitor*'s Editor-in-Chief, Austin Wedderburn, when he was in residence. Hazel controlled Wedderburn's diary and could delineate his daily trajectory through London and the Home Counties, minute by minute, more efficiently than any military satellite tracking system. This was no mean task, since Wedderburn was a man for whom the vexations of office life were an inconvenient interruption in an abundant social calendar. *The Monitor* was read, as it had always been read, by captains of industry and politicians, cultural grandees, senior figures in the judiciary, arch-bishops, and the rackety remnants of the English aristoc-racy – in short, the people-of-influence whom Wedderburn liked to meet at dinner parties. That the paper was now also read by hairdressers and shop assistants, taxi drivers and policemen, cleaners and canteen workers was a source of quiet satisfaction to Circulation and Marketing, but it was unwise to remind Wedderburn of the fact.

For his personal use, he had commandeered an old service lift, which had once conveyed pallets of paper from the print-plant basement to the upper-floor presses. Its utilitarian aluminium walls were covered with suede-effect vinyl, and the lift now served as an insulated capsule which propelled Wedderburn straight from his chauffeur's parking space to his fifth-floor office, so that he could arrive at his desk uncontaminated by chance sightings of the rabble from *Psst!*, or the drudges from News, or the thugs from Sport, or the excitable children from Features. Thus, he was able to spend his time at the office in exclusive contiguity with the cerebral labourers of *S*nday* and, if he was feeling expansive, engage in Socratic dialogue on the weightier issues of the day – London's draconian parking restrictions, for instance, or the iniquities of capital gains tax – with deputations from Opinion and Politics. Those from other floors who did manage to secure an audience with Wedderburn – and there were only a handful – attested that he was very like an Eskimo: he had fifty words for no.

Most employees of *The Monitor*, except for those already comfortably seated on the fifth floor, aspired upward. But some, like Simon Pettigrew and Miles Denbigh, were downwardly mobile. As former Head of Magazine Project Development, Simon had once been Lyra Moore's boss, until an unfortunate incident with the newly appointed Agriculture Correspondent, Aurora Witherspoon, a snooty beauty from the shires. Simon had propositioned her on the office's new computer messaging system, and pressed 'send' before he had realised that, thanks to the predictive text programme, which filled in 'best fit' addresses as the sender began to type the recipient's name, it was Austin Wedderburn who had received the eulogy to his impressive chest and spectacular legs, and the suggestion that he might like to 'get down and dirty with some farmyard action' and 'play bulls and heifers all night long'. 'Go on.

You know you want to, Gorgeous!' had been Simon's sign-off, which had signed off his career in Magazine Project Development for the foreseeable future.

Miles Denbigh, who had enjoyed a view of the car park from Opinion for fifteen years, had been rusticated to the first floor when it became clear that, while he was happy to express his views on politics and social issues in Ancient Greece, offering any analysis of more contemporary matters caused him acute anxiety.

Until the unexpected message from Lyra Moore, Tamara had set her sights no higher than the second floor. She had given up long ago on the Stakhanovite sourpuss Vida, who had responded to all her proposals for Features with disdainful silence. Johnny had been more amenable. He ran regular articles in his daily *Me2* pages on pop music and film, to the irritation of the paper's *Fr!day* pop and film section, which he regularly scooped; fashion, to the chagrin of the frequently gazumped Thursday *L(oo!)k* pages; and cookery, which the furious editor of the Wednesday *F<oo>d* supplement was increasingly convinced Johnny had lifted directly from his computerised planning schedule. Simon had refused to speak to Johnny since he pre-empted *Psst!*'s special issue on Child Stars' Drug Habits, by running a four-page spoiler in *Me2* on Little Micky's crack bust, augmented by a comprehensive history of the juvenile junkies of stage and screen.

Tamara remained diplomatically neutral on the issue. Her first loyalty was to Simon and *Psst!*, but Johnny's magpie borrowings were always supplemented by the sparky fact boxes and celebrity vox pops which were her speciality. She had hoped that, after proving her abilities on *Psst!* with Soap Opera Shags, providing three vox pops for Johnny's pages (Stars' Top Breakfasts; Me and My Chair – Furnishing Secrets of the Rich and Famous; and My Favourite Celebrity Questionnaire) as well as a pugnacious, pun-packed Tamara Sim Column, he might offer her a regular berth. But instead, Tamara had been fast-tracked. She had stepped into the suede-effect lined lift, figuratively speaking, the doors had shut, the LED display was flashing, the green arrow was pointing skywards and she was on her way up; up beyond *Psst!* and TV listings and celebrity chatter, up, past News on the ground floor, past Features on the second. Up, up, up.

But first, Tamara had some work to do. The basement office was in semi-darkness and pleasingly deserted, apart from a buck-toothed geek – one of Tania's website drones – gawping at a screen at the far end of the room. Tamara bought a cheese sandwich from the canteen, whose only customers were two refugees from the News room late shift, conspiring over coffee. At her desk, she lined up her pens on a north–south axis, alongside her notebook and tape recorder.

She had all she needed for an extended bout of work – solitude, sustenance, stationery and, above all, uninterrupted silence, a necessity so often denied her at home by the upstairs neighbours, two trainee solicitors, weekend Goths with a taste for heavy metal.

Tamara had spent many productive nights at work in the office, not always for *The Monitor*. She had even, when racing to meet a deadline for the *Sphere*, slept here, perfectly comfortably, pushing aside her keyboard and resting her cheek on a plump A4 envelope of Simon's receipts.

But she was going to need more than ideal working conditions to pull this story off. Determination, energy and flair would also be required, as well as a few decent quotes. And this was what was worrying her. Tamara turned to her notes, the written record of the fractious interview, which would serve as her mother lode.

What exactly had the old woman said? Nothing of any value, until the last minute, with her admission of an affair with Bing Crosby, which none of the cuttings had referred to. It would be an exclusive. But what was the quote? Tamara checked the note she had made when she left the mansion block. *Marvellous feet. I felt like a gossip columnist when he held me.* It did not make much sense. But it almost did. And it was original. Apart from that, and the passing reference to Liz Taylor, there was not a single usable line. She would need a further conversation with the old bat, and other interviews would be required, with friends (though it was difficult to imagine that Honor Tait had any) and associates. Then there was the reading – the cuttings and the books – to fall back on, for framework and padding.

At least she had her impressions, rich with detail, telling, and very much her own, to enliven the piece. That was a start. She opened her thesaurus. The substance – facts, quotes – could be filled in later.

We arrived a dilatory fifteen minutes late and flustered at Honor Tait's elegant mansion flat and the doyenne of British journalism received us with glacial formality.
'You're late,' she said as she directed us into the bijou, memento-filled sitting room.

Tamara knew she needed to loosen up and find her *S*nday* voice; a cultivated but breezy charm was the aim. A few jokes, some of the self-deprecating humour that was always appreciated at *Psst!*, would help too.

My anxieties about meeting the legendary Miss Tait were already running high. My boyfriend had dumped me the week before, I was late with my council tax, I'd developed a hideous cold sore that made me look like a Medieval plague victim and now, the morning I'm due to meet my all-time heroine, the doyenne of British journalism, we get stranded in traffic backed up all the way to Regent's Park. It couldn't get worse. It did.

She winced at the memory of her unprofessional weeping fit. It might have given her a temporary advantage – the old woman had not chucked her out, after all – but Tamara did not like this feeling of helplessness, this sense that she was at the mercy of her emotions, that even her work could be jeopardised by her lover's callousness. It had been more than a week now, and she still wasn't over it. She felt a renewed anger towards Tim. No word from him. Love conquers all, except cowardice. His wife was getting suspicious; he could not face the expense of another divorce and the wearying possibility of a third batch of children. (Not that Tamara wanted children. Not yet, anyway.) Naturally, he had not put it like that. They needed space, he had said.

'I've got all the space I need,' she had retorted. 'I see you once a week for a couple of hours at my place, and the occasional Saturday afternoon, while your wife takes the twins to ballet lessons, if you're not heading into the office to deal with a late-breaking story, or playing village cricket, or relaxing with the family by an Andalucian pool. In between, I've got plenty of space. Gobi bloody deserts of space.'

She should have seen it coming. Nearly a month ago, Christmas – the singleton's annual Armageddon – had loomed. He had promised a snatched Boxing Day night in a country house hotel to sweeten the miserable prospect of two days holed up in suburban Leicestershire with her father and stepmother, ludicrous Ludmilla, and their six-year-old son, Tamara's half-brother, the podgy, pampered little prodigy Boris.

Her first Christmas with her father since her mother's death had been the nightmare she had anticipated – Boris playing exhibition games of chess; Boris reciting Russian verse, in Russian; Boris giving timed displays of Rubik cube dexterity; Boris working through his Grade 2 clarinet repertoire, all to rapturous parental applause in a wasteland of discarded giftwrap. Somewhere beneath the torn and crumpled paper, the twinkling heaps of golden ribbons and silver bows, lay the very latest electronic toy, a Tamagotchi pet that Tamara had gone to some trouble to buy, tossed there by Boris as soon as he'd opened it, with a cursory 'fanks'. Ross, her full brother, her father's troubled eldest child, had been banned from the house after some grisly bender. No phone call from Tim, no country house hotel, no escape.

The New Year had been a fiasco, too. She had decided against her friend Gemma's party, choosing instead to wait at home for another promised phone call, another promised night of passion. Neither materialised.

In El Vino last week, Tim had tried to soothe her, stroking her hand and whispering. It had been so intense, he said. They needed time to think.

'Think? What's thinking got to do with it? When have you ever spared a thought for anyone but yourself?'

It had not helped that she was already one bottle up by the time he had arrived, late again, for their date. Tears, she knew, never helped in these situations, but she had found herself blubbing like a smacked child. Did anyone weep picturesquely? She could tell, even as he handed her a paper napkin and sighed sympathetically, that he was repelled by her pink, puffy eyes and the bubbles of phlegm at her nostrils, and he wanted to get out of there as quickly as possible. Was it an intentional irony that his *coup de grâce* was delivered in El Vino, the bar where, six months earlier, after her big TOP COP'S SON IN DRUG SHAME splash, it had all started? It had taken two 'dates', a fumble in the car park and a promise of oral sex to persuade the strapping sixteen-year-old to part with his pocket money.

'Okay,' the boy had groaned. 'Here's the money. Give me the dope. Then can you do that thing again with your tongue?'

The last sentence was excised from the tape transcript published in the *Sphere*.

Tim had invited Tamara to celebrate her triumph at a boozy working lunch with three of his henchmen and when she felt his hand creep under the table to stroke her thigh, with a jolt of intoxicated rapture she knew that their tentative flirtation – the sly smiles over the subs' desk, his hand brushing hers as they looked through the snatched photos – would be consummated that afternoon.

It was fun. And more than fun, she had persuaded herself. It had the makings of an iconic romance. He was a late-twentieth-century Bogie to her Bacall – Hugh Grant to her Liz Hurley, Rod to her Rachel. Didn't he feel the melancholy undertow, the separation pangs, after the euphoria of their long weekend in Paris? He had gone there on a management trip and managed to wangle her fare, first class on Eurostar, as a business expense. They might have been in Scunthorpe for all they saw of the City of Light as, sustained by champagne, cocaine, Ecstasy, the minibar and room service, they feasted on each other for forty-eight luxuriant hours.

She had packed a black velvet sheath dress and

borrowed a diamanté necklace from Gemma for a night in a fabled restaurant, where dinner for two cost three times Tamara's monthly income, but she need not have bothered. Her transparent lilac nightdress, with satin ties and thigh-length slits, also turned out to be superfluous. They did not wear a thing all weekend, startling the timid waiter when he first wheeled in their room service trolley. After that, whenever he reappeared, they lay rigid as corpses, fighting the urge to laugh, with the duvet pulled up tight under their chins.

They talked, too. Tim had told her (at some length – cocaine can have that effect) about his unhappy time at boarding school, the bullying, the sadistic gym master. She described her parents' divorce, the succession of ridiculous stepmothers, her own mother's illness and Ross's decline. She had never talked like that to anyone. And when the moment came to part at Waterloo Station, as she watched him walk away, his touchingly bulky figure shrinking into the distance, she was overcome by a sadness that seemed very like love.

But it was always a mistake to sleep with editors. That much she should have learned in a media career spanning six years. Initially, apart from any physical and emotional satisfactions, there were obvious professional advantages. After their affair started, Tim commissioned three big pieces from her for the *Sphere*'s features section. She had spent a hilarious weekend in a hotel with a lap dancing transsexual who claimed to have slept with a Cabinet minister, she had done a fortnight's undercover work in a rubber suit for the paper's in-depth investigation into the kinky tastes of an elderly soap star, and interviewed a junkie masseur who claimed he had once been the gay lover of a Second Division goalkeeper. When one of the *Sphere*'s reporters was drying out in a South London clinic, she had been called into the office to do a couple of shifts on the paper's News desk. And then there had been the promise of a staff job.

'I've just got to square it with the managing editor,' Tim had said.

Now that, along with their romance, was all off. When an affair with an editor ended, your job was on the line too. Tim had muttered about 'head counts' and 'budget squeezes', but he had managed to find outrageous sums of money to poach *The Monitor*'s Politics editor, a tweedy matron with the accent of a pre-war BBC announcer. Bernice Bullingdon would be as out of place in the office of the *Sunday Sphere* as Margaret Rutherford in a porn movie.

Why would Tim want to make Tamara a permanent fixture in his office when he was ejecting her from his bed? Or, rather, ejecting himself from her bed? Her final freelance feature for the *Sunday Sphere*, on the killer handbag epidemic – 'the fashion for oversized bags that is endangering the posture, and the lives, of a generation of young women' – was to be delivered next week to *BioSphere*, the tabloid's Health and Beauty section. She knew it would never be published now. She would get a generous kill fee, brokered by Tim's secretary, and she would never write for the paper again, until Tim himself was purged from his job in one of the periodic newspaper putsches. She prayed nightly, with a fervour unusual in an agnostic, for a putsch.

Before it all went wrong, the *Sphere* office had seemed to her a twenty-four-hour carnival of mischief, where the gleeful staff did not so much report for work as cartwheel into the party. It was hard to imagine how the pompous Bullingdon, whose idea of a night off was a hand of bridge with a couple of Cabinet ministers, would fare at a newspaper whose greatest contribution to contemporary journalism was its Readers' Husbands page, a weekly feast of coy Quasimodos in string vests and grubby Y-fronts. In comparison with the *Sphere*, *The Monitor*, even in its most playful manifestations, such as *Psst!*, or Johnny's Features desk, was as dull, subdued and rigidly hierarchical as a building society branch office.

She wiped away unwelcome tears and noticed that the geek in the corner was no longer looking at his screen. He appeared to be staring at her. She scowled at him and he bowed his head, tapping intensely at his keyboard once more. There was always work, Tamara consoled herself. Lovers came, and they unfailingly went, but the need to make money was constant. She had her brother to think of, too. Feckless, vulnerable Ross. She dreaded speaking to him on the phone – gauging his mood, his intoxicant intake, from the timbre of his voice, his relative incoherence – yet whenever she couldn't reach him she lay awake all night, sleepless with anxiety. Where was he? What was he doing? Who with?

The last she had heard from him was an answering machine message left a fortnight ago. His voice was slurred and it was hard to make out what he was saying but he sounded happy, and Tamara had tried to cheer herself with the thought that he might be merely drunk. She had called him back but his landline had been cut off. She would end up paying the bill again, and the reconnection fee; it was cheaper in the long run, less time-consuming and far less agonising than the bleak journey through the urban wilderness of King's Cross to track him down.

By supporting Ross was she subsidising his decline? Or was she saving him from going under completely? She could not turn her back on him, as the self-help books advised. She would rather have her brother's dealer on her payroll than risk the consequences of walking away. If anything happened to Ross, she could not bear the guilt. Work, her work, was the only way out for both of them.

She picked up *Dispatches* and scanned the index – nothing on Crosby or Taylor. Would she have to read through the entire book to glean any salty stories? Life was short, and deadlines imminent. She turned to Tait's first book, *Truth, Typewriter and Toothbrush*, which apparently contained the Pulitzer Prize-winning piece. Here it was. April 1945. 'On Goethe's Oak'. What kind of headline was that? She sighed heavily and began to read.

On 27 September 1827, Johann Wolfgang von Goethe, the great renaissance genius of German letters, then in his late seventies, took a morning stroll with a friend

*in the forest on the flanks of Ettersberg mountain above
the town of Weimar. They stopped on a hillock to breakfast on roast partridge, white bread and 'a very good
wine out of a cup of pure gold'. Sitting with their backs
against the trunk of a sturdy oak they looked out over
the broad valley of the Unstrut, its villages sparkling in
the clear autumn sunlight. Beyond it, to the south and
west, ranged the magnificent Thüringer Wald mountains, to the north, the violet peaks and ridges of the
distant Harz.*

The woodland hike of a nineteenth-century poet? This
surely didn't qualify as news, even in 1945.

*'I have often been in this spot,' said Goethe, 'and of late I
have often thought it would be the last time that I should
look down hence on the kingdoms of the world, and their
glories; but it has happened once again, and I hope that
even this is not the last time we shall both spend a pleasant
day here . . . Man shrinks in the narrow confinement of
the house. Here he feels great and free – great and free as
the scene he has before his eyes, and as he ought properly
always to be.'*

Such stuffy, sermonising prose. This was rambling on an
exorbitant scale. No journalist would get away with that
now. It was arduous reading for this time of night. Across
the office the geek had switched off his screen and was
stuffing his belongings into what appeared to be a school

satchel. He left without a word. Tamara was on her own. She returned to her writing with a sense of relief and opened her thesaurus. She might not be in the running for a Pulitzer, but this had to be the best piece she had ever written.

I arrive late, red-faced and out of breath at the soigné *mansion block in Maida Vale. Honor Tait, the formidable doyenne of journalism, opens the creaking door of her crepuscular apartment and fixes me with an icy stare.*

'You're late!' she rasps.

She seems reluctant to let me in.

Is this the delectable siren who once charmed and harried world leaders from Franco and Castro to Kennedy, who was seen on the arm of some of the twentieth century's greatest icons of entertainment – playboy painter Pablo Picasso, crooning golfer Bing Crosby, actor and mobsters' friend Frank Sinatra and Cats' author T.S. Eliot? I name-check the plate under the doorbell. Tait. This little old lady is indeed her: the reporter who covered some of the greatest news stories of the past century – the outbreak of World War Two, the Korean War, (fill in later . . .) – and doorstepped some of the most notorious and celebrated figures of recent history. But would she let this humble reporter past her own doorstep? And if she did, what stories would she share with her?

Tamara's confidence was returning. She might actually enjoy this. But there were more pressing demands. She had already missed her deadlines for two pieces, commissioned last month by her regular freelance outlets. *Mile High*, the inflight magazine for Prêt-à-Jet airline, was pressing her for the travel piece on their new destination in Holland, while *Oestrus*, the glossy monthly 'for the discerning older woman', was still waiting for her consumer report on vibrators. She would honour these obligations, then she would concentrate on the real prize. And Tim Farrow, by that time, with luck, permanently exiled from newspapers and churning out press releases for a plumbing supplies company, would regret the day he ever passed up the chance to share his life with a star writer like Tamara Sim, a twenty-first-century Press Corps Golden Girl.

First work – then vengeance.

Unwary visitors to Alkmaar are confronted by a curious spectacle each September – the sight of giant portions of Edam and Gouda cheese rolling down the steep cobbled streets of the ancient Dutch town. And not a cream cracker in sight!

*

Honor looked up at the clock garlanded with worry beads. Almost midnight. The interview, absurd though it had been, haunted her, and the girl's inane questions had forced her to pose more pertinent ones of her own. Even as she had struggled to make sense of her life, to give it a simple, clear – and, yes, honourable – shape for the benefit of *The Monitor*'s readers, unwanted fragments of her past had floated up, ugly motes in her inner eye, to desecrate the picture and torment her. And how near she had come to unburdening herself before that little vulgarian. Not quite a case of casting pearls before swine; more of strewing facts before fools. But who else was there to talk this through with?

Honor did not mind solitude. Loneliness was another matter. In the two years since Tad had died, she had amassed her group of young friends, her Boys, the Monday Club. And why not? The old friends were dead, if not physically then, like poor Lois, in every other sense. Honor had first met her in post-war Berlin, where Lois was working as an interpreter. She was a brilliant linguist, on secondment from Bryn Mawr, with the dark, slanted eyes and long neck of a Modigliani and the limber body of a dancer. When Honor moved to Los Angeles and Lois, by then a Progressive Party activist, was living in Brentwood, their friendship strengthened and it was sustained over the ensuing decades by rare and punishingly expensive phone calls, rarer but lengthy letters – all lost in the fire – and reunions, at least one a year, usually in Italy, where they would visit museums and churches, eat at neighbourhood trattorias, drink prosecco and talk into the night. Lois finally moved to London in 1970 to work for the American Embassy in Grosvenor Square and bought a little flat in Mayfair. They had seen each other regularly – galleries, concerts, lunches, suppers – and every spring Lois would take the sleeper to Scotland and they would hike the hills around Glenbuidhe.

Lois's romantic life was decorous and comparatively chaste but she had seen Honor through two marriages and countless *crises d'amour*. And then, after the collapse of Honor's marriage to Sandor, there was the spell of depression that Lois, in a classic display of projection, had put down to childlessness. Whatever its cause, Lois had seen her through. When Honor met Tad, he had been threatened by the closeness of her friendship with Lois. He did not believe a relationship of such intensity could be innocent of desire. He would call Lois, with leaden sarcasm, 'The Darling Girl', and Honor wondered if Tad had secretly rejoiced when Lois began to lose her mind seven years ago.

Today, a few of Honor's contemporaries might be reasonably intact neurally and breathing unassisted, but they had become body bores, obsessed by their infirmities, competitive about challenging new symptoms and excruciating medical procedures. Her Boys, though often glib and ignorant, had more to talk about than colonoscopies and CAT scans.

She switched on a lamp and walked to the window. The garden was empty, a shadowy stage-set poised expectantly between the infants' matinee and the teenagers' evening performance. She closed the curtains to discourage curiosity from the flats opposite. Not that there was anything to see here. An old woman, head bowed, sitting alone, waiting. Waiting: the chief business of the old.

She glanced at the page proofs of *The Unflinching Eye*, resting reproachfully on the coffee table. She needed to read through this third – and final, Honor had insisted to her publisher – collection of her journalism. For now, though, she did not have the stomach to revisit old work, casting a jaundiced eye over past triumphs. Instead, she picked up her notebook. New work. The coda to her Pulitzer Prize-winning article about the liberation of Buchenwald would be the last chapter of this final book. Here, with a new and expanded version of the original report, was a chance for reparation. Whether she would be able to write it, she did not know. But she had to try. She had resisted a return to Goethe's Oak for too long.

Buchenwald, 14 April 1945. Liberation Day Four. The survivors, still in their ragged prison uniforms, assembled by the shattered stump of Goethe's Oak to celebrate their freedom. Each held a national flag. As they waved them, in a show of defiant national pride, many silently wept for their comrades who did not live to see this day.

The phone rang early the next morning, jolting Honor out of a pill-induced sleep. She lifted the receiver, expecting another silent call, but this time he spoke. His voice hit her like a shock of iced water. Her questions, banal, essential, tumbled out: 'Where have you been?' 'How are you?' 'What have you been doing?' 'Where are you?'

As he hedged and side-stepped at the end of the line, all that had stood between them shrank away.

'Who else would it be? Another lover?' he said. 'I've been around, you know . . . Pretty good . . . Bit of this, bit of that . . . Hard to say, right now . . .'

She felt the sweet low timbre of his voice reverberate inside her, as if a string had been plucked on an instrument that had not been played for years and was still perfectly in tune. He was pulling her back and, against all reason, she wanted to bind him tightly to her with her questions.

'But are you well? Where have you been living? How have you managed?'

She feared that she would drive him away with her questions and yet she could not stop. She wanted more of that voice, more of him. What he said, or did not say, was irrelevant, just as long as he kept on talking.

'I got by.'

She had dreamed of him, in fitful playlets of separation and reconciliation. His voice had also provided a sound-track for many of her nightmares. She paused to check, passing her hand across her brow, that, no, she was awake, this was really happening and it was him at the end of the line.

'I got your card,' she said. 'You said you needed to see me.'

'Did I say that? Need? I thought need was more *your* game.'

He sounded so close, near enough to touch.

'And where are you now?' she asked, anxious not to provoke him.

'I'm around. Back in circulation.'

'In London?'

She heard him sigh, a long exhalation of exaggerated weariness.

'Not a million miles away,' he said.

'Any plans?' she asked, with a lightness she knew he would detect as fraudulent.

'You read my card. I thought we might get together.'

Get together – the awful slanginess of the phrase. He was mocking her.

'Yes . . . Why not?'

The tentativeness of her reply suggested exactly why not. And yet, at some level only he knew, though Dr Kohler and his colleagues might guess at it, she wanted it, craved it, this 'getting together'.

'Only it's difficult,' he said.

Naturally, it would be difficult. Dangerous, too. He had drawn her in, gained her admission that she wished to see him, and now he was withdrawing. She was feeling light-headed, whether dazed from the effects of the sleeping pill she had taken only two hours ago, or by palpitations brought on by the shock of his call she was not sure.

'I'm sure there is no difficulty that can't be overcome,' she said.

'I'm not so sure. It's been a bit tricky.'

She felt a sudden debilitating warmth steal over her; an ambush of tenderness.

'We can forget all that, surely. Start again,' she said. Could he hear the pathetic note of pleading in her voice?

'My finances. They're a bit compromised right now,' he said.

Finances? Of course. That was what it was all about. How could she forget?

'Money?' she said, with a blustering laugh. 'Look, that's not a concern. Let me know how much you need, where to send it.'

He had to go, he said. He would be in touch again, soon.

'Really?'

'Really!'

Was there a bass note of menace in his voice? He was still angry with her.

And then he was gone.

Honor pushed aside the bedcovers and walked unsteadily into the kitchen. She poured herself a vodka with trembling hands and pulled back the curtains. Outside, the post-dawn sky was grey as an army blanket and the trees were restless, anticipating a storm. A few lights were already on in the flats across the way and she watched as a young woman brought a baby to the window and looked out, pointing down at the garden. Honor turned away and sank into a chair, overwhelmed by a sense of dread. Sometimes, an idle longing for intimacy could become an unseemly hunger, and for her it had always been a hunger that could never be fully satisfied.

She drained her glass and put it on the table next to Tad's photograph. Did she miss her husband? Even though their marriage, outwardly successful, had been something of a sham? One could be as lonely in the corporate bustle of coupledom as in a spinster's bedsit. But intimacy, that was what she missed. The comforting banality of companionship requiring no effort or examination. His body lying next to hers, night after night. Mostly. And sex, not necessarily with Tad – she missed that, too.

There was a time, in her early fifties, as her body began to undergo The Change – a term that could also do useful service as a euphemism for death – when she hoped that her body's fluctuating thermostat, the internal wildfires, would burn out her remaining reserves of libido. Lois had always been comparatively sexually continent and the menopause for her had been merely the dying note of a long diminuendo. How Honor had longed for a sudden, permanent arctic winter of passion, for the time that would be saved, the mental energy spared, to devote herself to contemplation and decisive execution of useful projects: to work, without distraction. The Change that would be as good as a rest. No such luck. John G appeared, twenty-two years her junior, dark, intense and not in the least displeased by her ageing body. She had seen him as her Last Hurrah, her terminal tarantella before the deathbed. And then he was followed by Lucio, and then Bernard ... There had been little dimming of desire since, only diminishing opportunity.

Now this phone call mocked her with a reminder of real, perilous intimacy. He was back, within reach. He had phoned and he would come to see her. She knew he would. He was angry, yes, but perhaps, even now, it was not too late.

Five

Tamara's desk was already occupied when she arrived at *The Monitor* on Monday morning. Tania Singh sat there, her face illuminated, like a spotlit Bollywood princess, by the glow from the computer screen. Her child-sized fingers flickered over Tamara's keyboard and her books and papers were heaped on the desk.

'Excuse me?' Tamara said, dropping her bag on the floor by Tania's feet, which looked preternaturally tiny in their kitten-heel boots.

'Hi!' Tania looked up and smiled. 'I didn't think you'd be in till later. My computer's down. I knew you wouldn't mind.'

'Well, actually . . .'

'Won't be a moment.'

Tania gathered up her possessions and exited, her long hair swishing defiantly behind her like a black silk cape. Tamara noticed with irritation that Tania had left a pile of books behind. There would be nothing remotely readable in there; no ghosted popstar biographies, no paperback fiction about a modern woman's search for love, no quirky detective stories, no jokes. Tania was famously pretentious and was said to spend her waking hours – when not consolidating her position at *The Monitor* – reading educational tracts and going to art galleries, the theatre or the opera.

She wrote a diary for the website and Simon had seen it. 'Waste of time,' he said. 'Don't know why she bothers. The internet is for losers. Citizens' Band radio for pseuds and geeks.' Last week, apparently, Tania was 're-evaluating Lévi-Strauss' – not, as Tamara first thought, a reflection on the disappearance of blue jeans from the wardrobes of the fashion-conscious young (a piece Tamara herself had offered to commissioning editors several times without success) but an extended essay on the founder of structural anthropology.

'I don't know who she thinks she's writing for,' Simon said. 'The small online community, so-called, seems to be a loose fraternity of lonely masturbators. And I'm not talking intellectual onanism here. On the other hand, as it were, her byline picture is *very* fetching.'

In an effort to disseminate that byline photo as widely as possible, Tania wooed commissioning editors in other sections of the paper with a frightening single-mindedness.

Vida, who stood in for Johnny as Features editor when he was away from the office, had commissioned and published two pieces by her – one on a women's refuge in Baluchistan, the other on an artist who painted 'painfully intimate' abstracts using brushes made of her own body hair. Neither would have got past Johnny himself,

133

if he had not been marooned in a Surrey hotel at the time, role-playing trades union negotiation scenarios with other senior editors under the tutelage of a management consultant.

Johnny had fallen foul of Tania directly when he enthusiastically agreed to commission a piece she had apparently offered on the semiotics of the Simpsons, only to be presented, two weeks later, with a 2,000-word essay on someone called Barthes. Roland Barthes. Johnny had been avoiding her ever since, taking imaginary calls on his phone whenever she approached. She had written reviews of Eastern European theatre for Arts and of new Scandinavian fiction for Books, covered a curling competition in Blairgowrie for Sports, expounded on flood relief in Benin for Opinion and was said to have petitioned the unassailable Lyra every day for a month, with messages on the office computer, in a desperate bid to break into *S*nday*.

How satisfying, thought Tamara, that it should be her – modest, unpretentious, straight-talking, street-savvy, down-to-earth Tamara Sim – rather than the flagrant intellectual snob Tania, who had been invited to join Lyra's team. Among *The Monitor*'s senior editors, only Simon remained unsolicited by Tania, who was coolly dismissive of the central subject, the bantering style and debunking japes of *Psst!*. She rarely lunched and never joined the basement team after work in the Beaded Bubbles, the cellar wine bar that served as an external office canteen, with the additional advantages of alcohol and receipts.

Tania was always too busy working, or heading off to some grim poetry reading, or sitting through a new playwrights' season at the Royal Court.

'If she's so brilliant, what's she doing working on the website?' Tamara had asked Simon one evening in the Bubbles.

'Ambition,' he said. 'The new frontier. She wants to be there, planting her flag.'

'She really believes that?'

'Definitely. It's the pioneering spirit, the spirit that saw her choosing to spend her summer holidays in Bosnia a couple of years ago, trying her hand as a war correspondent. She's omnivorous; she wants to write about the future of feminism, economic crisis in South Korea, vote-rigging in Serbia, and the exquisite agonies of literary life.'

'Not much scope for that here.'

'Not on *Psst!*, anyway. Or on the website. But she must have judged that it's better to be queen of the cyber kingdom than a serf in the twilight realm of print.'

Tamara scooped up Tania's books from her desk. Just as she had thought. A novel whose drab cover matched its unalluring title, a Booker Prize-winner according to the sticker on the front. A two-volume biography of Picasso – really, how much more was there to say about the old lecher? A memoir by a nerdy-looking playwright in Buddy Holly glasses. And, for light relief, a book on the history of British film. There was also a copy of Honor Tait's *Truth, Typewriter and Toothbrush*. Tamara opened it. Tania had gone through it, underlining passages and pencilling notes in the margins as if she was cramming for an exam on the subject. So here was Honor Tait's natural constituency. A perfect match – the bland reading the bland. Tamara scooped up the books and dropped them in the nearest waste bin.

She had been asked to write the A-List again. This week, it was to be Top Ten TV Bad Hair Days. She would also, discreetly – she did not want to take too much advantage of her friendship with Simon – put in another call to Honor Tait's publisher, and press on with her *S*nday* piece.

This little old lady is indeed her: the reporter who broke some of the great exclusives of the past century – the outbreak of World War Two, the Korean War (fill in later) . . . and doorstepped some of the most notorious and celebrated figures of recent history.

Disapproval is etched on her face but she opens the door a little wider.

'You'd better come in,' she growls.

Tamara was ringing Uncumber Press when Simon arrived at his desk bearing two pint-sized coffees from the canteen. She cupped her hand over the phone's mouthpiece. The answering machine again.

She dialled another number, this time conspicuously, smiling and rolling her eyes in comradely good humour at Simon, who brought over one of the cups and left it on her desk. In her most efficient voice, delivered at broadcast-level pitch, she spoke to a publicity-addicted West End hairdresser who was always good for a quote, and asked him for some pointers on Bad Hair. She took detailed notes, thanked him loudly, replaced the receiver and began to type in a few of his suggestions. She would visit the Morgue later and see what pictures they could come up with.

'Lunch?' Simon called out to her.

He must have been reading her mind.

'Sure. Half an hour? Just doing Bad Hair.'

'Great. Bubbles?'

'Where else?'

'Fantastic. Still on for the Press Awards next week?'

'You bet.'

She sensed a sudden swell of resentment in the office. Some of her *Psst!* colleagues, she knew, envied her friendship with Simon, didn't rate him as an editor and would undermine them both if they had the chance. A seat at the annual Press Awards dinner was a prized ticket – the biggest social event in the newspaper calendar. Courtney, the embittered administrator, who had worked on *Psst!* longer than any of them and had a hopeless ambition to be a journalist, was staring at the fax machine with an unusual degree of concentration and Jim Frost, chief sub and trade union stalwart, was sucking forcefully at his unlit briar pipe and glowering at Simon.

Well, Tamara had no need to be defensive. Could she help it if Simon preferred her company? She returned to her work. Johnny sent an electronic message asking for a celebrity vox pop. The shadow chancellor had been spotted eating rabbit stew in a fashionable Islington restaurant and had left his broccoli and carrots untouched on the plate. An hour of phone calls to the usual ring-round tarts – former newsreaders, fading popstars, media-savvy actors, an outspoken Tory backbencher with a fondness for drink, a ubiquitous agony aunt, a high-profile hedge fund manager and a publicity-hungry novelist – all happy to name their favourite, and least favourite, vegetables in exchange for a mention in *The Monitor* – produced some serviceable copy, leaving Tamara free to get back to her real work.

It is then that I produce the bouquet of flowers, pink lilies, and she visibly softens. How many bunches of flowers must she have received in her long lifetime of loving? And where, one is tempted to ask, looking at the withered face of this former intimate of folk rock legend Bob Dylan, have all the flowers gone?

By the time they arrived at the Beaded Bubbles the place was as full as a Northern Line tube. Courtney had sulkily rung in advance and reserved the centre booth. They sank into their seats, savouring their first glass of Chardonnay in silence, like communicants draining a chalice.

'So Lucinda found out about Serena,' Simon said as he refilled their glasses.

'No! How?'

'Serena told her.'

'No!'

Tamara sometimes felt she needed a flow chart to keep track of Simon's adventures. Lucinda was his barrister mistress, who shared a flat with Serena, who worked in an auction house. Lucinda had been at a conference last week when Serena had phoned to suggest that Simon might meet her for a drink. The drink became dinner at Claridge's (on his expenses, naturally). The following day Tamara had received a thorough debriefing on the menu, the wine list, and the uproarious bout of sex that followed. But there were new developments.

'Now Lucinda's gone ballistic.'

'I bet she has.'

'Ordered Serena out of the flat. She won't go, of course.'

'Of course not.'

'So Lucinda's put locks on the bathroom and kitchen to drive her out.'

'That would do it.'

Tamara waved to the waitress and ordered a risotto. Simon said he would have the same, and a second bottle.

'So Lucinda phoned me at home at midnight last night, hysterical. She kept sobbing and asking if I thought she was crap in the sack.'

'Is she? I mean, do you?'

'Of course not. That's what Serena told her I'd said.'

He ran his hands through his thinning hair and his bottom lip jutted like a petulant child's. Not for the first time, Tamara marvelled at his success with women. He was overweight, middle-aged and balding. As a young man he must have been chinless, and maturity, compensating for nature's earlier oversight, had given him a concertina pleat of flesh at his throat.

'Blimey.'

'So there I was, trying to placate a hysterical Lucinda down the phone with Jan lying in bed beside me.'

Simon's wife of long standing, posh, plain and pleasant Jan, had apparently never suspected a thing while her husband steadily worked his way through London's Lucindas and Mirandas, Serenas and Marinas, like a bulimic at an all-you-can-eat buffet.

'Tricky.'

'And now, just before we came out, Serena phoned the office in tears. She's furious.'

'Oh no,' Tamara said, pouring another glass.

Their food arrived. Simon didn't even glance at his plate.

'She said I said she had tits like empty bed socks.'

'What?' Tamara put down her fork and tried to summon the image. '*Bed* socks? Has she? Did you?'

'*No*. That's what Lucinda told her I said.'

'Oh. Right.'

'No word from Lucinda now, either,' he said, checking his pager.

Tamara, beginning to tire of his story and keen to embark on her own, ate her lunch in silence. He clipped his pager back on his belt.

'So how's the escape plan?' he asked.

Tamara was baffled, and then she realised he was enquiring about the subject she had been hoping to introduce into the conversation since they arrived.

'She was an obnoxious old witch,' Tamara said. 'Wouldn't tell me a thing about her life, but when she got onto the subject of her brilliant career, about the boring stories she'd broken, about the boring politicians and soldiers she'd known, she wouldn't stop talking. I thought I was never going to get out of there and—'

Simon's mobile phone rang. Tamara looked away to conceal her envy: she really wanted one of those machines. The only people she knew who could afford them were senior editors, who got them on expenses, and drug dealers.

It was Jan, calling about their son's eighteenth birthday party.

'Okay, sweetie . . .' Simon said. 'Go with the marquee . . . Whatever you think . . . Yes . . . Whatever Dexter wants . . . No. Business lunch . . . Can't talk now . . . Bye . . . Love you too.'

He turned off the phone and Tamara continued.

'I've been trying to reach the publishers to arrange another interview and they won't return my calls.'

Simon was drumming his fingers on the table.

'And you know how much this means, this commission,' Tamara added. 'I mean, writing for *S*nday* is a real breakthrough for me.'

He looked up, signalled to the waiter and ordered two more glasses of wine along with the bill. He had not touched his risotto.

'Get a grip, Tamara,' he said, taking out his credit card. 'You've just got to move on.'

'What do you mean?'

'Look, if you really want to pursue this story, you have to show some initiative.'

This was unfair.

'I'm doing my best. I'm not even sure what angle Lyra wants on this piece and she won't answer my messages.'

'You don't need any hand-holding from Lyra,' Simon said.

'I just feel I've reached a dead end. All I've got is a lousy interview, with maybe one halfway decent quote, and some cuttings. I'll never wring four thousand words out of that.'

He took out his pager.

'Come on, Tamara. You can do better than that. Honor Tait's a public figure. She's out there. Watch her at work. Something will turn up.'

The pager was bleeping like a heart monitor. He paid the bill, tucking the receipt into his pocket. He was very good at dispensing brisk professional advice, Tamara thought resentfully, but the only work he would be doing this afternoon would entail locating a paperclip, fastening this receipt to an expenses form and writing: 'Lunch. Contacts. Features Ideas. £36.'

*

The interview had served one useful purpose, kick-starting a process that was long overdue. The disturbing phone call was a further spur. How had she, Honor Tait, the arch anti-materialist, the scoffer at sentimentality, taken so long to get round to this? She had the urge, but not the energy, to strip it all, or, better still, to walk out of the door and chuck a Molotov cocktail behind her. But the freeholders of Holmbrook Mansions would not thank her for it, and her neighbours might object.

This time, without hesitation, she wrenched Tad's hideous seascape from the wall. It was not as heavy as she had feared. Clumsy watercolours of seas and hills, woods and waterfalls gave him a pleasure the landscapes themselves never could. 'Yep,' he would say, coming up behind her as she stood by the window in Glenbuidhe. 'The mountains are still there. And the loch. That's still there too. Let me know when they move 'em.' But he had to be restrained from buying the abysmal paintings of local views offered for sale in folksy tea rooms, alongside souvenir tea towels and handcrafted fudge.

Sunsets, too, left him cold. At the end of each day in Glenbuidhe, when she liked to walk down to the lochside and watch the blazing sky, he had always insisted on accompanying her. But he would stand there in the cooling evening air, stamping his feet impatiently. He didn't get it. Yet he spent a ridiculous sum on a lurid oil, in which broad sweeps of mauve, rose and orange conjured a grotesque pastiche of nature. That was one picture she had happily dumped straight after his death – his god-daughter had expressed a liking for it and was bundled off with it in a taxi after an uneasy tea. Honor hadn't seen her since.

She scooped up armfuls of books and took them with

the painting to the cupboard in the hall – how much time was there left for reading, let alone *re*reading? – and placed them in there with the relics from her recent clearout. She began to gather up the photographs. Who was she doing this for? Would she accede to Ruth's badgering and invite the foolish Tamara back? Or was she expecting another visitor, who might sneer, with some justification, at the display of her vanished splendours? Pompey in happier times, as the caption cliché goes.

She took down the photograph of her younger self with Franco. Much had been made of the fact that she had conducted the interview while costumed like a chorus girl. In fact, she had been holidaying in Tenerife with Thierry and it was Franco – unknown, recently demoted, restless in exile and, it turned out, only weeks away from the uprising that would provoke the Civil War – who had sought *her* out for the interview. Hearing that the young reporter, whose smile had already illuminated several RKO newsreels and who wrote for the American news magazines, was on the island, he had tracked her down and surprised her at a harbourside café. She had concealed her irritation at being disturbed by this officious little man, borrowed a notebook from an amused waiter and politely conducted an interview, only half listening to the answers, about the administrative problems of this cluster of extinct volcanoes moored just north of Africa. Her interview, a few workaday paragraphs in *Collier's*, did not survive. The picture did. A local photographer had caught the moment and must have made more money from that single picture – so often reproduced that, sixty years on, it was a visual cliché – than he did in a lifetime's career spent snapping wedding parties, over-dressed infants and first communions.

The sitting room was beginning to look satisfyingly austere. Who could have guessed that such pleasure was to be had from this systematic pillaging of the past? If only memories could be ordered and dispensed with so easily. She had struggled to make progess with her coda. She worried that, as she got older, she had lost her sure touch as a writer, that her ear for good prose could no longer be trusted, and she found it increasingly difficult to assemble her thoughts in the service of a story. The phone call had been a further distraction, scattering her thoughts.

Fighting exhaustion, she gathered up the proofs of *The Unflinching Eye*. If she could not write, she could surely read.

Morocco, 25 October 1956 – The massacre in Meknes began in a fashion that would have been comic, if the outcome had not been so tragically grisly. A demonstration against French rule in Algiers was proceeding relatively peacefully, until a Moroccan police officer, using the butt of his rifle as a club against more enthusiastic elements of the crowd, accidentally shot himself in the foot. The rumour spread that supporters of the French had opened fire. The mob turned on any Europeans who had the misfortune to be in the area. A husband and

wife were hacked to death with axes in the presence of
their children, a hospital assistant was bludgeoned to
death with paving stones as he knelt to aid a wounded
man in the street and three men were burned alive in
their car as they tried to flee. A total of thirty men and
women, mostly French, were brutally murdered.

She could not go on. She was going through the motions
of work, the pantomime of purposefulness. Why was she
bothering? The world was a mess then. It continued to
be a mess. And rereading her younger self, breathless with
excitement in a place of horror, was disquieting. All that
had changed was her attitude; her youthful solipsism had
persuaded her that she could combat injustice and transform the world. Today she knew better. There was consolation in this, as well as reproach.

Six

It was stubborn pride, and anger with Simon, rather than journalistic zeal, that took Tamara two nights later to the drab parish hall of the Strict and Particular Baptist Church off the Archway Road. As she stood shivering in the queue outside to buy her ticket (the cost equivalent to a night at the pictures, fares included, or a couple of decent bottles of wine), Tamara regretted her choice of wardrobe for the evening. Jill Dando was tonight's role model, but the *Crimewatch* presenter's sensible girl-next-door charm, achieved with some hair gel, pearl earrings and a black trouser suit, marked Tamara out from the crowd as an interloper. Most of the women were dressed in fleeces and waterproofs as if for a trek in the Hindu Kush, while a few in tiered skirts and festooned scarves suggested a delegation from a gypsy camp fire.

The men were mostly crushed academics in quiet corduroy; wraith-like elderly hippies, their surviving wisps of hair, long and grey as carpet underlay, tied back in frail tribute to a pony tail; and a handful of peaky teenagers, shoulders hunched under the weight of book-filled back-packs. In the hall porch, a goateed pensioner in a patch-work waistcoat was sitting at a table selling tickets. Without looking up from his tin cash box he took Tamara's money and handed her a numbered cloakroom ticket. Useless for expenses.

'Could I have a receipt for that?'

'We don't do receipts,' he said, holding his hand out to the teenager behind her. 'Next?'

The rows of red plastic chairs in the hall had already begun to fill. The audience murmured and nodded as they made their way to their seats and the general mood seemed to be one of simmering indignation. Tamara, anticipating a long evening and determined to make a swift exit as soon as she had gathered the information she needed, took an aisle seat in the back row. She planned to follow Honor Tait's advice: 'Through meticulous obser-vation and a ravenous hunger for detail, all will be revealed.'

On the walls, primary coloured posters, pasted up for the benefit of tonight's audience rather than for the Strict and Particulars, celebrated liberation struggles in Latin America, urged the release of political prisoners, called for the boycotting of goods from unfashionable countries, enjoined trade union members to pay their dues and, in a mock-up photograph, showed John Major outside Number Ten Downing Street with a Hitler moustache painted above his simian upper lip and his right arm raised in a Nazi salute. Over the proscenium arch of the small stage, a portrait of the Queen in her comely youth had been partly obliterated for the evening by a plastic plaque depicting Che Guevara, eyes upturned in ascetic rapture like a medieval Christ. Faded velvet drapes framed the stage, which was bare, apart from four bentwood chairs.

Tamara looked around and marvelled that the hall was almost full; so many people for whom a few hours of dreary speeches in a church hall represented a good night out. Most of them, she saw now, were morbidly unattractive, and more conventional evening pleasures would be unavailable to them. As she scanned the audience, she caught sight of only one exception, someone who possibly could have a life if she chose to. Tamara registered the profile, almost saccharine in its delicate perfection and framed by a fall of dark hair that shone like liquid jet, before she recognised its owner: Tania Singh. What was she doing here? Didn't she have a groundbreaking play to go to? Or an opera? Or a web diary to write?

The general murmur faded as a rugged figure with parched sandy hair and combat fatigues, who looked as if he had just choppered in from an Amazonian guerrilla encampment, strode from the wings across the stage towards the microphone. As soon as he spoke, Tamara recognised him as the blunt-jawed correspondent from the TV news programme that preceded *Blind Date*. Paul Tucker, roving reporter, a middle-aged hulk in an Action Man costume, the liberal intelligentsia's equivalent of a celebrity, with a presence on prime-time TV. Though he did not qualify as famous in the proper sense of the word – his private life was not interesting enough to make the tabloids – his name would be worth dropping for *S*nday* readers. The audience applauded tentatively but respectfully, and the sound was of an uncertain scattering of spring rain. Tucker was joined on stage by a tall, angular woman whose disproportionately wide hips, encased in taupe slacks, seemed to have been borrowed from a fat friend. Tucker introduced her as the 'well-known philanthropist and human rights activist, Clemency Twisk'. Well known to whom? To everyone in the audience, apart from Tamara, it seemed. They demonstrated their familiarity with the woman and all her works, in a renewed and amplified round of clapping – a prolonged April shower of noise.

Twisk acknowledged the audience with a modest nod as the next speaker came on to more grudging applause: a local Labour MP, an eager-to-please young barrister and member of the Shadow Cabinet, who had been putting himself about, garnering publicity in advance of the coming election, like an It Girl on the party circuit. Only last week he had been pictured grinning in leathers astride a snorting Harley Davidson on the cover of *Biker's News*, and he had appeared in *Country Life*'s New Year issue in a waxed jacket, squinting dreamily at distant hills. Having covered the Hell's Angels and Barbour constituencies, tonight he was focusing on the traditional Labour voter. He gave the audience a chummy wave as he took his seat and Tucker announced the evening's special guest speaker. The applause increased in volume and intensity – a clamorous monsoon on a vast tin roof – as Honor Tait walked slowly from the wings. She smiled graciously. Some younger members of the audience stood to cheer and whistle and soon everyone was on their feet; a standing ovation before the old woman had even opened her mouth. Tamara remained resolutely seated.

The noise subsided and it was Twisk who walked first to the microphone. Tamara groaned quietly and glanced at her watch. She had hoped Honor Tait would give the opening speech, leaving her free to escape and salvage something of the evening, and as Twisk talked, with high and quavering voice, at length and in detail, of the genesis of the new pressure group, Kids' Crusaders, which had been set up by her foundation, Tamara felt a creeping desolation.

'The purpose of KC,' said Twisk, in a sustained yodel, 'is to fight child exploitation wherever it is to be found, in third-world factories, in the grotesque barbarities of the sex industry, in Eastern European sweatshops, or in the economically privileged but spiritually impoverished environment of the western middle-class home . . .'

Tamara, numb with boredom, gradually drifted into a pleasant daydream involving Tim, his newspaper's irascible proprietor, and some compromising photographs taken in the bedroom of the Georges V Hotel. That the images of Tim, taken at his most sexually playful, when he had used her pink thong as a hairnet, existed solely as an imprint in Tamara's mental photo album did not diminish her enjoyment of the revenge fantasy. She was shaken from it by the crackle and thunder of sudden applause. Honor Tait was on her feet again. Tamara gripped her pencil, steadied her notebook and wrote: *Frail. Small. Dwarfed by microphone.* All eyes in the hall were focused, unblinking, on the speaker. Of Tait's speech, a querulous inventory of cruelty featuring child weavers, underage gold miners (would that be minor miners?) and prostitutes, Tamara took no record; Clemency Twisk's mission statement had exhausted any reserves of social concern. *Rousing. A fury. Reminisces. India. Philippines. Thailand. Lithuania,* were the only notes Tamara made. On it went and, though she tried her best, she could not reclaim her delicious reverie of retribution. She would have to revive it later in bed.

She looked at her watch again and judged by the falling timbre of her voice that Honor Tait was winding up. Quickly glancing behind her to check that her exit route was clear, Tamara saw that it really was standing room only. Leaning against the walls or seated cross-legged on the floor, as if at a yoga class, were several dozen people ranging in age, she guessed, from sixteen to seventy. All of them were gazing enthralled at the tiny figure on the stage.

Tamara's attention was drawn to a tall latecomer who was pushing open the door. His hair was a tangle of Romany curls and, despite the wintry evening, his shirt-sleeves were rolled to the elbows of his muscular arms. He looked incongruously heroic in this hall full of pallid whiners. Lady Chatterley's lover, fresh from some butch business in the potting shed. He was the only attractive man in the room, and he appeared to be alone. Surely *he* could have found something better to do on a cold evening in January?

They were all applauding again. Honor Tait must have finished. Five minutes ago, Tamara would have taken this as the signal for immediate departure, but the prepossessing stranger had added a new element of interest. She willed him to look in her direction. Paul Tucker was speaking now, grasping the microphone in his freckled fist like Henry VIII at a hambone. It was time for questions from the audience and a bustling figure of indeterminate gender in a purple anorak was waving a microphone in the aisle. Only Tamara's curiosity about the brooding figure by the door kept her from bolting for the exit.

'Could Honor Tait tell us something more of her experiences in South East Asia?' asked a blowsy hiker with owlish glasses.

Of course she could. The real question was whether Honor Tait could *stop* telling us more about her South East Asian experiences. Tamara tried taking notes again – *Manila, Chiang Mai, Cambodia, Laos* – but gave up. She could not listen to this stuff, let alone write it down. And who would want to read it? She looked over at the latecomer by the door. His arms were crossed against his broad chest and he was leaning back, one foot braced against the wall, in a pose that suggested defiant boredom, or perhaps rapt surrender to the potency of Honor Tait's oratory. Tamara preferred the first explanation; it was heartening to think of him as a kindred spirit, a fellow contrarian at this prigs' convocation. But she was here in the line of duty. What was his excuse?

She returned to her notes: *She is the diva of dissent, a* bien pensant *superstar, and they are listening in admiring silence to her account of horrors in Hyderabad, calamities in Cambodia, atrocities in Azerbaijan.*

Was she ever going to stop talking? Was there much more of this? There was. Much more. A continent-hopping grand tour of global misfortune.

Tamara glanced round the audience – even these professional pessimists and catastrophiles must have their limits. But no, another question from the audience. The voice, the light yet assertive peal of a summoning hand-bell, was irritatingly familiar. Tania Singh.

'I wanted to say, first of all, what a privilege it is to hear Honor Tait tonight and I wanted to thank her for her inspiring work.'

There was an outbreak of affirming applause. Wasn't this supposed to be a question, not a masterclass in grov-elling? Tamara, seething, looked back towards the door and was gratified to see that, like her, the good-looking loner was not clapping.

Tania continued.

'I wondered, what advice you would give a young woman journalist starting out today?'

Honor Tait hesitated for a moment, plainly displeased.

'Any advice I have would apply just as much to young male journalists as to their female counterparts.'

At the back of the hall, Tamara gloated. It was good to see the old woman turn her blowtorch on Tania Singh. But Tania was implacable. She bounced back with another question.

'What would you say are the most important qualities a journalist requires?'

Tait shrugged, and for a piquant moment Tamara thought she was going to put Tania in her place. But the old woman seemed to relent.

'An ability to really *see*,' she said finally. 'Through patient observation, the accumulation of detail and a hunger for truth, the bigger picture will emerge. The reporter's duty is to champion the weak and to shine a searchlight in the darkest corners of human experience.'

Visibly tiring, Tait was reduced to quoting herself. Tamara had had enough. But more hands were raised as the audience jostled to take the microphone and put questions to which they already seemed to know the answers. Honor Tait's voice wavered as she spoke of child brothels in Asia and sex traffickers in the former Soviet Union but her words were, despite the promising subject, free of enlivening anecdotes and full of generalisations and statistics. She even seemed to be boring herself. Her voice gradually trailed away and she went to sit down, with a final mumbled admission that 'it isn't really my area. Perhaps Clemency would like to add something.'

Clemency most certainly would, and did. Her contribution was heartfelt, vague and self-loving as she vibrated with transcendent righteousness before the microphone.

Tamara's spirits only lifted when the ticket collector with the harlequin waistcoat appeared at the back of the hall swinging a plastic collection bucket. The meeting was drawing to a close. Tamara pushed past him as she made her way to the door, in time to see that she was not the first fugitive. The attractive latecomer was sprinting just ahead of her, wrenching open the door of a white van and nimbly slipping inside. It was raining hard and, as Tamara looked vainly for a cab amid the thunderous convoy of traffic on the Archway Road, he drove off into what remained of the evening, spattering a jet of muddy water over her trouser suit.

*

How had Clemency talked her into it? A new charity? As if there were not sufficient *old* charities crying out for funds. And that banal, ahistorical name? Kids' Crusaders. Self-righteous nonsense. Honor knew the real object of her ire was not Clemency, but herself. She should never have agreed to it. She had become too dependent on Clemency's support, the financial lifeline, the late-night phone calls, all the practical help a wealthy heiress, without family commitments or demanding job, could command at the wave of a chequebook.

In exchange for the generous benefactions, their unwritten contract decreed, Honor must every so often lend her name, and her intellectual and social weight, her years' experience, to some feeble-minded cause which served no purpose but to bolster the ego of its paymistress. The indignity of the experience, of travelling out on a miserable evening to that godforsaken part of London, of enduring Clemency's tiresome speech, of endorsing it by sitting there in silence, of sharing the stage with a grinning booby from the Labour Party, or the New Labour Party as it styled itself these days, who was there simply to harvest votes for the coming election, was too much to bear.

Paul, too, had been reeled in like Honor to lend substance to the new organisation, but he was more pragmatic than Honor – his Mount Rushmore features were untroubled by self-doubt, or any kind of doubt at all – and the idea that the transaction was distasteful would not have detained him for a second. He helicoptered in and helicoptered out. Even the inane questions from the audience – every one of them directed at Honor – did not perturb him. Clemency finally had the grace, or conscience, to suggest in a whisper that it might be time to wind up the meeting.

And here, back at her flat, readying herself for a night of insomnia, Honor was battling a sense of guilt for a crime she could not remember committing. Was this paranoia? She felt like John Berryman's Henry, stirring from a nightmare of murderous mayhem, going over everyone, reckoning them up, reassuring herself at last: 'Nobody is ever missing.' It was all so long ago. Only the guilt was new. She was surely too old for spiritual stocktaking.

She picked up the proofs of *The Unflinching Eye*.

5 July 1950. Ten days and four retreats into war. Despite the reversals, the loss of life and the gruelling conditions, the mood is confident at Taejon headquarters as Major General William Dean takes command of the 24th Division. With the arrival of more troops and guns, American forces could secure victory within six to eight weeks.

She felt revulsion at the intractable confidence of her younger self. Today's reader knew what she could not know then, what no one could have known, that three years later America limped home – 40,000 men down, twice that number maimed, 15,000 missing in action or captured – to regroup for its next bruising conflict. She had prided herself on the acquisition of facts: precise troop numbers, makes and capabilities of armaments, hours of skirmishes, days of battle. That was the style, strengthening the impression of impartiality.

What did she know, this determined young woman, convinced of her immortality, exulting in the exclusive company of men in extremis? And there was rather too much personal detail masquerading as colour writing in here for her liking. The mud, the lice and fleas, the grimness of rations, the squalor. Under fire at Taejon, surrounded by enemy troops, she had been co-opted by medics to help set up drips and administer plasma to the wounded. Initially, in all the confusion, the noise, the smoke and flares, mutilated boys writhing and groaning at her feet, she had found time to feel affronted – was it because she was a woman, the object of suspicion, even derision, to some officers, that she had been singled out for such duties? Then she saw that some of her male colleagues had been drafted in too. She went on to describe that day in a piece reeking of fraudulent humility, which won plaudits from colleagues back home: *Today, your correspondent abandoned her notebook, rolled up her sleeves and became a nurse.*

The sound of a disturbance from the garden drew her to the window. It was not the gatecrashing youths from the council estate but a group of young friends from the flats opposite. They were drinking champagne, wrapped up against the cold in hats and scarves, talking and laughing at full pitch.

These young people were emphatically making their mark on the neighbourhood. Skips lined the nearby roads, gradually filling with old fridges, barque-sized TV sets, perfectly solid pieces of dark furniture and yards of brocade curtains, double lined, mouldering in the January rain. Out with the old. No doubt some of those young people had their eyes on her flat, and the flats of every occupant over sixty left in the building and would, if they could, fill those skips with the stiffened corpses of all the bent-backed greyheads, the fixed-rent bed blockers taking up space in perfectly good three-bedroom mansion flats with secure twenty-four-hour porterage. They probably scoured the obituary columns daily, these thrusting young people, for the good news that would signal vacant possession and a ninety-five-year lease.

Well, she still had something to say before they had their way and bundled her out of here. There had been no new stories in recent years, but she must return to an old one, focus her mind, ransack her diminishing word-hoard and summon the truth. She opened her notebook and read over the opening lines of her coda. No. It would not do. Taking her pencil, she scored through the words and started again.

Buchenwald, 14 April 1945. Four days after liberation, the strongest of the frail survivors gathered by the charred stump of Goethe's Oak for a parade to celebrate their freedom. From paper and rags, they had fashioned their national flags and they waved them now in a spirit of defiance in the spot where they had been forced to parade daily before their barbaric captors. Evidence of that barbarity was witnessed two days ago by soldiers of the American Third Army, who, with members of the press, came across piles of the rigid, naked corpses of those murdered in haste by retreating German troops.

And now, in this parade of defiant national pride, many of the freed prisoners silently wept for those fallen comrades.

Seven

Morning Conference was a demanding affair: a daily tournament of jousting egos performed before an impassive Austin Wedderburn or, in his absence, the quietly anguished Miles Denbigh. At 10 a.m. in the dowdy fourth-floor boardroom, senior editors, or their deputies, vied to break the most interesting news of the day; to offer the most original perspective on that interesting news; to express that perspective with concision and, when taste permitted, sufficient wit to make the corner of Wedderburn's mouth twitch in a scant smile, or to temporarily banish the frown from Denbigh's corrugated forehead; to dismiss most effectively the work of any rival newspaper, except when the performance of that rival newspaper might contrast favourably with the efforts of a department run by a rival senior editor on their own paper; and, most demanding of all, to laugh loudest and longest at any wan simulacrum of a joke that Wedderburn, in a rare outburst of gaiety, might throw out, like a monarch with his Maundy pennies to a grateful peasantry.

No one anticipated the experience with pleasure, but

each morning those journalists who had attained the status necessary to earn a seat at conference, stampeded into the boardroom like bargain hunters on the first day of the January sales. Only those intent on professional suicide would miss it, since any absent senior editors were regarded as fair game by those present, automatically becoming the butt of unflattering comparisons with their counterparts on other papers. Simon was not a self-harmer when it came to his career, though his love life was another matter. He might skip the weekly Features meeting, affecting a lordly disdain for office politics, but even he would never miss Morning Conference. He never asked anyone to deputise for him at the meeting and, like all senior editors, he only took holidays when he knew Wedderburn would be away. Whatever he'd been up to the night before, he would always manage to make an appearance in the boardroom. Once conference was over, he would slip away from the office to catch up on some sleep before returning in time for lunch.

This morning, however, was different. His hangover, incurred after a euphoric reunion with Serena at a champagne bar, was monumentally incapacitating.

'When I finally woke up,' he groaned over the phone to Tamara, 'it wasn't so much a question of "Where am I?", as "Who am I?" I couldn't possibly sit through conference. I'd never make it on time, anyway. Do you think you could cover for me?'

The chance to attend Morning Conference, to sit as an equal among the paper's grandees, in heady, career-making, genuflecting proximity to its absolutist ruler, did not come along often and Tamara, downcast by last night's church hall meeting, which would add little or nothing to her *S*nday* piece, saw the invitation as a fillip; here was a compelling opportunity to present herself, with all her skills and insights, to full advantage before *The Monitor*'s supreme politburo.

At her basement desk in the office, she glanced at the morning papers, mugging up on the main issues of the day, hoping to offer some insightful new angles and rustle up some jokes. The Opposition's education proposals did not offer much scope on either front. Nor did missing yachtsmen, a princess campaigning against landmines, and an ongoing siege in a Peruvian embassy. January was a notoriously dry news month. Pictures of John Major grinning gormlessly in a turban, like an extra from *Carry On Up the Khyber*, on an official trip to meet his Pakistani counterpart would be bound to raise a laugh – these days, anything he did provoked derisive titters, even from Tories – but it was more of a visual gag. Would there be any mileage in the government's plans for a new £60m royal yacht, a bid to gladden the nation's loyal hearts and win votes in the coming elections? Could this be the boat that finally scuppers the Tories? Or could it successfully steer an unpopular government out of choppy waters? Might there be something witty to be said about the Shadow Chancellor's rumoured wedding plans to an attractive public relations executive? Something on planned mergers? Or the married person's tax allowance? Some sparky comparison might be drawn with the planned nuptials of surly popstar Liam Gallagher and Patsy Kensit, the pouting blonde love interest from *Lethal Weapon 2*.

The lift was not working and by the time Tamara had climbed the stairs to the fourth floor at 9.55 a.m. she was panting like a first-time marathon runner. The senior editors, or their deputies, were already there, clustered round the closed door of the boardroom, waiting for the signal to charge. Vida was representing Features, standing in for Johnny, who was on a conflict resolution course in Buckinghamshire. The Home editor, bearded and cardiganed like a Seventies folk singer, was whispering to the Foreign editor, a valkyrie in crush-proof pinstripes, while the new Sports editor, Ricky Clegg, wearing a festive red and white tracksuit, scanned the pages of *Sporting Life* with deceptive nonchalance. It was galling to see Tania Singh – since when was she a senior editor? Or even a deputy senior editor? – standing there, pretending to read the *New York Review of Books*. Lyra Moore, dressed in clinging black and white and precipitous heels as if for a smart cocktail party, was fiddling with the buttons of a mobile phone.

Spotting her chance, Tamara advanced towards her, mentally framing her opening gambit: 'Hi! Just wanted to check in with you about . . .' 'Hi! Lyra! I was wondering if we could have a word . . .' 'Honor Tait, eh? What a character! . . .' Lyra looked up, startled, as she approached but before Tamara could utter a word, they were interrupted by a sudden clamour; the boardroom door was flung open, revealing the burly form of Hazel, a shot-putter in pearls and chintz polyester, who stepped back with surprising agility to avoid being flattened in the scrum. As the senior editors and the deputy senior editors scrambled for seats, and Hazel fled for the safety of the fifth floor, Tamara saw that Austin Wedderburn was presiding today, further raising the stakes for any contribution she would be making to conference. This was, in *Monitor* terms, the ultimate networking forum and here was her chance to shine.

After a few unsuccessful feints at the chairs closest to the Editor, Tamara finally found herself seated next to the tea trolley by the door, out of the direct eyeline of Wedderburn. If this was a theatre, her seat would have been classified as 'restricted view' and sold at half price. She was going to have to work to get his attention. Lyra, an incarnation of sleekness and efficiency, marred only by the top button of her blouse, which seemed to have come undone in the mêlée, was seated on the Editor's left. The Home editor, whose face reflected the gravity of so many of the stories he had to impart, was sitting on Wedderburn's right, by the Foreign editor. Next to the Foreign editor, a couple of seats up from Tamara, was Tania, smiling with feline contentment, her elbows on the table, hands cupping her infuriatingly sweet face, like a spoiled child anticipating a treat only the truly heartless could refuse.

Though an expectant silence had already fallen in the room, Wedderburn rapped his pen like a gavel on the table.

'Before we begin the regular business, I'd like to introduce a guest at this morning's conference,' he said, nodding benignly towards Tamara.

She felt a narcotic pulse of excitement; her heart revved and moved thrillingly up a gear. Wedderburn had seen her after all. And not just this morning. She jerked upright in her seat, and clasped her hands on the table in a pose of alert engagement.

'Many of you will have spotted her around the building,' continued Wedderburn, 'some of you will already be familiar with her work, aware of the mark she has made at *The Monitor*, and I'm pleased to tell you she is going to play an increasing role in the life of the paper.'

Could you go into shock over *good* news? A wave of heat stung Tamara's face like a gust from a suddenly opened oven. She was blushing, she knew it. She hoped she was not sweating. She forced her lips, which seemed oddly mutinous, into a tight, modest smile. Lyra must have spoken to the Editor about her and told him of the Honor Tait commission. It had happened. Tamara had always known, even in her deepest midwinter moods, that it would. Her talents had marked her out, set her apart, lifted her above the commonality, gilded her. She had a sudden memory of a Sunday school picture: a saint (Lucy? Agnes?), her eyes modestly downcast (Who? Me?) as a halo twinkled above her head like a golden frisbee. At last. Tamara was one of The Elect.

Wedderburn had realised that *The Monitor* needed to reach out to younger readers and the appointment of a few under-thirty-year-olds to senior editorial positions would be the first step in a circulation-building campaign. It was unorthodox, certainly, to announce a promotion in such a public way, but Tamara was not going to quibble.

'And, once we've despatched the main business of the conference, I hope she might tell us something about her vision for *The Monitor*,' went on Wedderburn.

Tamara's excitement turned to terror and her temperature plummeted. Vision? The nearest she had got to a vision was when Ross had slipped her a slice of magic mushroom omelette at Glastonbury. She could recite the list of *Psst!*'s stories for the week, she had boned up on the main news of the day, and she had worked up a couple of jokes on the subject of wedding bells, rather than division bells, for Gordon Brown. But vision? Who did he think she was? St Bernadette? She sat in horrified silence, wondering how she was going to get out of this, hoping for the sudden arrival of a secretary bearing a fax carrying news of, say, the death of a leading member of the royal family, something, anything, that might be of sufficient import to demand the immediate dissolution of conference, when another voice – young, female, toweringly confident, the sound of a public school head girl on Founder's Day – rang out in the void.

'Thank you, Austin.'

It was Tania.

'I promise I won't take too much of your time,' Tania continued, turning to address the entire conference. 'But, following several meetings I had with Austin on recent breakthroughs in information technology, he kindly invited me to address you this morning about the World Wide Web and its implications for the paper.'

Tamara leaned forward and looked along the table, incredulous, from Wedderburn to Tania and back again, her feelings alternating between relief and disappointment as the truth revealed itself and her bright halo shrivelled to a limp jester's cap. This was humiliation on a grand scale. Tamara looked across at her colleagues. No one was meeting her eye, no one was smiling or openly relishing her embarrassment. All heads were turned to Tania.

Wedderburn rapped his pen on the table again and the conference swept on. As the morning's papers – *The Monitor* and its rivals – were ritually disinterred, Tamara recovered her composure and waited for her moment to speak. She had not been singled out, the emperor had not smiled on her, he had not even seen her, but she would still get her chance to impress.

Vida was implying, in the nicest possible way, that the News desk's handling of the education policy story left something to be desired, while the News editor suggested, in the most cordial manner, that Features had missed a trick on the lost yachtsman story, which had been addressed so humorously by this morning's *Courier*. Vida struggled to suppress her fury as she pointed out that *Me2*'s deadpan coverage of the story had actually been commissioned by Johnny; the News editor countered with a joke from *The Courier*'s 'Captain Calamity' piece, which elicited a brief facial tremor, possibly a smile, from

Wedderburn. A chorus of light laughter rippled round the table.

Toby Gadge hesitantly suggested that the News desk might have made more of the Tory government's response to allegations that one of its MPs had engaged in an illegal homosexual affair, while the News editor retorted that Politics might have made more of the government's latest crisis, when it slipped into a minority following the sudden death of one of its MPs after an alcoholic binge.

The Money editor, shifty as an accountant on the take, was concerned that his reports of a building society's plans to float on the Stock Exchange were not getting proper play on the front page. Wedderburn yawned openly and, round the table, several of his senior editors felt emboldened to shift in their seats, rub their eyes and stretch their arms. The Arts editor, a shock-haired troll, made his weekly plea for more space for classical music reviews. He received the weekly response, a pained silence, as Tamara mentally refined her lines on the Shadow Chancellor's romance rumours. Before she knew it, the conference had moved on from yesterday's news to today's.

This involved the sombre reading of lists – in which senior editors on the daily paper, or their deputies, outlined the stories being assembled by their respective teams for inclusion in tomorrow's paper. As far as Tamara could tell, the chief task of senior editors was to read the same lists to many of the same people at different meetings, several times during the course of a working day. The trick was in the delivery; variety was all, ensuring that on each hearing, the same list sounded blisteringly new, brought piping hot to the meeting – the scrap metal of rumour forged in the furnace of journalistic enquiry into the glowing ingot of fact. A staccato urgency might be appropriate when addressing a predominantly News-based meeting, languid irony was more effective when addressing Johnny's Features meeting, a 'gather round, children' narrative jauntiness helped to galvanise Circulation and Marketing, while swift robotic detachment, even contempt, worked best at budgetary meetings. List-reading at Morning Conference, however, defined the pace and tone of the working day.

The Home News editor, one laugh up and already ahead of the game, read his with brisk effectiveness, then gave a more expansive description of tomorrow's spoiler, calculated to torpedo *The Courier*'s latest 'exclusive' book serialisation scheduled for Saturday. The book, for which *The Courier* had paid the equivalent of four times Tamara's annual income for four extracts, comprised a rogue MI5 agent's sensational claims of an elaborate assassination plot aimed at destabilising oil-rich countries. *The Monitor*'s News desk had managed to get an advance proof of the book (a cash-strapped security guard at the publisher's warehouse had accepted a three-figure sum) and had rehashed the story, adding outraged quotes from Venezuela and Saudi Arabia, sceptical quotes from ex-colleagues, and a diagnosis, by an obliging media psychiatrist, that the agent was suffering from Histrionic Personality Disorder. *The Monitor*'s story would also be tagged 'exclusive', a cheeky, low-cost trumping of *The Courier*, which had also paid for a stingingly expensive TV advertising campaign to publicise the serialisation. Wedderburn gave a throat-clearing chuckle of satisfaction at the heist, setting off a wave of similar respiratory episodes round the table, then nodded to the Foreign editor.

After the virtuoso performance of Home, Foreign wisely played it straight and read her list – Hebron, Hutus and Tutsis, Aung San Suu Kyi in Burma and President Milosevic in the former Yugoslavia – in a tone that could have gone down equally well at a budgetary meeting. On to Features, and Vida, taking advantage of Johnny's absence, was shelving the more frivolous elements he had planned for *Me2* tomorrow and replacing them with a substantial meditation on domestic violence by the feminist writer Isadora Talbot, a report on dwindling sperm counts, and an upbeat story about an ingenious new anti-rape device. News and Foreign exchanged discreet smirks.

Then it was the turn of Ricky Clegg, who rocked back in his chair like a restless teenager and recited his litany in nasal plainchant. His wisecracking reference to the romantic misfortunes of a Premier League footballer raised a mild laugh from Wedderburn, and a heartier one from everyone else. Sport's small victory was followed by the brisk, telegraphic announcements of stock market falls, retail price rises and exchange rate fluctuations from Money, and Arts' passionate advocacy, before an indifferent audience, of a season of Brechtian theatre. Through it all, Tamara, now sure of her lines and waiting her turn, ground her teeth as she watched Tania taking careful notes.

The main business of tomorrow's paper was despatched and it was now the turn of the weekend senior editors. The S*nday menu was, as usual, not so much a list of stories as a Literary Who's Who – Saul Bellow, Iris Murdoch, Ted Hughes on, respectively, Robert F. Kennedy, writers' block and the mythic resonance of the stickleback – and Lyra read it with the cold poise of a TV anchorwoman. Wedderburn nodded solemnly, his equivalent of the imperial thumbs-up. Then the Books editor, Caspar Dyson, a nervy boffin in wire-rimmed glasses who seemed permanently affronted by the company he was obliged to keep in order to make a living, stammered through his list of reviews – something about colonialism, something else about poetry, something about history, something about politics, and a novel that he described with breathless urgency as 'postmodern meta-narratory poioumenon', none of which ignited the interest of Wedderburn.

There was more enthusiasm for the Travel editor's contribution, an enviable catalogue of freebees – all-expenses-paid jaunts to the Maldives, Caribbean romps, Thai beach idylls and dirty weekends in European boutique hotels – bestowed on favoured members of staff, including Simon (a week in a luxury spa resort in the Seychelles) and Wedderburn (a fortnight's golfing in Mauritius), in exchange for 600-word, land-of-contrasts, ancient-meets-modern, verdant-valleys, mist-shrouded-mountains, East-meets-West, picture-perfect-paradise-island puffs.

Tamara's moment was approaching. She reconsidered her strategy and decided to give special emphasis to her A-List, Top Ten TV Bad Hair Days: Shock Locks and Criminal Cuts of the Telly Stars. Would Paul Tucker qualify as a last-minute addition? His parched thatch looked like an implement for removing limescale from toilets. But did a campaigning news reporter qualify as a TV personality?

Vida was speaking again. She had been granted a second moment in the spotlight to announce plans for a special weekend supplement which she and Johnny had been working on, in conditions of Masonic secrecy, for the past three months. *The Monitor Elite List*, a glossy eighty-page directory naming the Top 100 Figures of Influence in Politics, Arts, Media, Sport and Business, would appear with the Saturday paper in three weeks' time as part of the Spring Circulation Push, backed by a budget-busting prime-time TV advertising campaign. Tamara felt a stab of fury. Lists. Her speciality. No one had consulted her. Well, she would have her moment. Once she had delivered her Honor Tait piece she would not have to spend her time grubbing around the second floor, hoping someone on Features would throw a list her way.

Meanwhile the head of Circulation and Marketing, Erik Havergal, smooth and tanned as a shopfront manne-quin, was delivering a report on the satisfactory sales boost received by the Christmas seed packet giveaway, and the less satisfactory spike in sales generated by the New Year free aspirin offer, which had been undermined by *The Courier*'s spoiler Alka Seltzer promotion.

'On a more positive note,' Havergal said, 'I can reveal our exclusive giveaways planned for the *Elite List* issue: a His 'n' Hers package of faux-gold cufflinks and a faux-gold bracelet, both stamped with the letter E. For elite, of course.'

Wedderburn's jowls trembled, the overture to a smile of deep satisfaction, and one by one, throughout the room, in a domino effect of delight, faces lit up with similar expressions of pure pleasure.

The Fashion editor was next to speak. Today, Xanthippe Sparks' hair was plaited and coiled round her ears, giving the impression that she was wearing stereo headphones, and she was dressed in a dirndl skirt, puff-sleeved blouse and laced bodice, in apparent homage to Heidi. She tripped lightly through her inventory: 'The New Informality . . . Rhapsody in Shoes . . . Daywear for Night Owls . . .', as the Home News editor re-examined his schedule, Austin Wedderburn looked at his watch and Tamara, calculating that it was her turn next, scanned her own list, silently rehearsing its delivery, mentally enunciating any tongue-twisters that might trip her up. Articulacy was essential. And she must not miss her cue.

'. . . and in Menswear, we're looking at the Retro Pimp: white loafers, gold chains, black hearts . . .'

The Home editor gathered his heap of A4 printouts into a neat pile and gave it a card-sharp's tap on the table

while Austin Wedderburn seemed to have found something interesting lodged in the nib of his pen. Xanthippe
finished on a rising note, a little bubble of self-delight
unpricked by the silent derision of her colleagues, and
Tamara steadied herself for her moment. She would be
succinct and witty and resolutely down to earth. The
Fashion editor would be an easy act to follow.

'Thank you, everyone,' said Wedderburn, drumming
the table decisively with his fingers. 'We'll have to cut it
short today. We've got a paper to bring out, after all.'

He grinned, provoking an outbreak of sympathetic
smirking round the table.

'But first,' he went on, 'Tania Singh will talk to us on
the subject of web-readiness.'

Tania stood to deliver her speech, a shining evangelist
from the Information Superhighway bringing the good
news about urls and domain names, portals and page
impressions, dotcoms and digital divides, and the senior
editors watched her with varying degrees of quiet scepticism and idle lust. Tamara, consumed by loathing, could
not take her eyes off her and was startled by a tap on her
shoulder. It was Hazel, who had slipped back into the
room with a kettle. She handed Tamara a bowl of sugar
and a jug of milk and indicated with a nod that she had
been chosen to help distribute the tea. This was probably
on account of her proximity to the trolley, but Tamara
could not help wondering, after this morning's humiliation, whether she was giving off some kind of low-status
mammalian scent.

She did, though, eventually have her moment at conference: a direct encounter with Austin Wedderburn. Miles Denbigh was describing progress on discussions for the new multi-faith prayer room – his own office was to be fitted with an altar and prayer mat in a compromise deal to head off the irate smokers – when the Editor glanced up at Tamara and held a thumb and two fingers aloft. Tamara efficiently stirred three spoonfuls of sugar into his tea and passed him a plate of digestive biscuits. He did not say thank you, but she was sure he looked up again and registered her. He would know who she was, next time.

But over lunch with Simon in the Bubbles later, Tamara was overcome by gloom. He was in a generous mood – things had gone well with Serena and his hangover was finally clearing.

'Come on, Tamara. It's not so bad. You did well last night on the Honor Tait story. You showed some real resourcefulness, going all the way to Archway.'

'Great! You should have been there. There wasn't a sentence worth quoting from the entire evening.'

'Oh, come on! There must have been something you can play with. A bit of colour. A few facts.'

'Facts? They gave us plenty of facts. Facts were *all* they gave us. And what good are they? Four thousand brain-numbing words on an old lady's charity work? Even Lyra won't buy it.'

'You can do better than that,' he said, pouring her another glass.

'I know what I need,' Tamara replied. 'The famous lovers, the celebrity friends, the heartbreak. I just can't get a word out of her on any of it.'

'It's not meant to be easy, is it?' he chided. 'If it was easy, any mug could do it. You have to work at it.'

'What do you think I'm doing?'

Now his pager was bleeping.

'What about the Monday Club?' he asked, absently checking his messages. 'Her gigolos and fancy boys? There's the story. Go along and check them out.'

'She's not likely to invite me to one of her swanky salon evenings, is she?'

Simon raised his eyes from his pager and gave her a withering look.

'Who said anything about an invitation?'

Eight

The Monday *soirées* had evolved, at the Boys' insistence, from *ad hoc* drinks parties to monthly suppers which had become the only fixed points in Honor's calendar. Her only regular meals, in fact. She had always been a defiantly inept cook and, while the maid kept the kitchen cupboard and fridge supplied with essentials – bread, milk, tea, vodka, oatcakes, a little cheese, a few tins – Honor's culinary ambitions since Tad died had never extended beyond toast and its variants. The Monday suppers were, said Bobby, her 'meals on wheels' service. They provided the food and wine, she supplied the venue and the vodka.

To them, she was a *monstre sacrée*, quixotic, witty, sometimes vicious. It was the glamour of her past, the association with greatness, that earned their fealty; they were flattered to spend time in her company, liked to drop her name, could tolerate any amount of abuse from her, and the sense that an ill-judged remark could cast them into permanent outer darkness added a thrilling edge of danger to her company.

Bobby was her stalwart. The Editor of *Zeitgeist*, *The Courier*'s broadsheet weekly culture section, he brought her gossip from Grub Street, wine from the Languedoc, and a stream of handsome neophytes, usually actors newly hatched from drama school, tender Beauties to his swarthy Beast. He was, even by his own estimation, a failed academic. The author of two poorly reviewed biographies of forgotten modernist writers, he had been an acerbic critic for a number of minor Arts Council periodicals, which paid nothing for his pieces. His appointment as Editor of *Zeitgeist* – Neville Titmuss, *The Courier*'s Editor, had been impressed by Bobby's excoriating review of a journalistic memoir by one of Titmuss's old rivals – had surprised no one more than himself.

Bobby seemed to fail upwards, whereas poor Aidan Delaney, a rather good poet, well reviewed and award-winning but with the sales figures that went with his calling, continued to succeed downwards. Honor admired Aidan's steadfastness and found his misanthropy curiously comforting. Inigo Wint, a public school pretty-boy gone to seed, made her laugh in a way that no one else could. He was an artist with a slight, imitative skill and his fashionable work was unstintingly championed in *Zeitgeist*. Though he was industriously heterosexual, Honor sometimes wondered whether he and Bobby had ever been lovers. A louche but loyal friend, Inigo was also, apparently, accomplished in bed. There was something of the changeling about him and his girlfriends found him maddeningly elusive. A succession of young women, not all of them conventionally pretty – his tastes, he liked to say, were as catholic as Cardinal Hume – trailed after him with pitiful solicitousness. He indulged them for a couple of months before abruptly abandoning them for another languid geisha. 'A free upgrade,' he called it.

Paul Tucker, the most uncompromisingly masculine representative of the Monday Club, was silent on the subject of the bedchamber, claimed to have no interest in art or the workings of the imagination and said he had never knowingly read a work of fiction – 'apart from the front page of the *Sunday Times*'.

'Sod the life of the mind,' he would say. 'Give me life!'

He was ill-suited to reflection, television news was his medium. He was out there – angry, unshaven, in his bullet-proof vest, filing to camera against a *son et lumière* of missiles, or shouting over the whirring of helicopter blades, a true inheritor of Honor's tradition of intrepid truth-seeking, a defender of the weak and scourge of the powerful. How ironic that it should be television, a medium she had always despised, that had preserved at least some of the journalistic values jettisoned by newspapers.

Honor had always found men better company than women. Homo or hetero, they were wittier, lighter about matters of the heart, and more engaged with the real world. They were also more trustworthy, free from the atavistic rivalry, the sidelong scrutiny and secret *schadenfreude* that women engage in. Even so, she counted two women among her Monday Boys. Ruth, round and smug as a matryoshka doll, was the efficient one, the fixer, and the paymaster. It was Ruth's capable, gym-mistress approach to life's admin – dismal dealings with plumbers and lawyers, accountants and taxmen, restaurateurs and travel agents – rather than her publishing expertise, that earned her a seat at the monthly suppers. Her editorial skills were, as far as Honor could tell, non-existent, or at least invisible. Which made her the best kind of editor. There had been no wrangling over points of language or structure, no sly tweaking, no 'helpful suggestions'. Ruth had been the respectful handmaiden, ushering *Truth . . .*, out of print for decades, into the public realm with a tasteful new cover, and now she was about to perform the same service for *Dispatches*.

In addition to Ruth, there was Clemency. Tall, homely and bowed with guilt at her enormous inherited wealth, Clemency was a professional philanthropist. She was on the board of several arts organisations and was a rich source of invitations to first nights and gala events. She was also generous with time and money, always available for late-night phone calls, a patient, admiring and re-assuring listener. When Honor was at her lowest, Clemency had insisted on flying her to Lake Garda, where she was pampered at the Twisk Foundation's villa for two months. But Clemency was drawn to the specious, her new charity being a case in point, and could be insufferably sanctimonious. She was a reformed alcoholic and had once made the mistake of expressing pious concern about Honor's occasional indulgence.

Clemency had had to work very hard to gain readmission to the Monday Club.

Tonight, Inigo was the first to arrive. His lopsided smile was a good gauge of Honor's mood. If her spirits were low, she would find it irksomely insincere. If she was buoyant, the half-hitched grin and easy charm would cheer her further.

Still drained and somehow diminished by the recent *Monitor* interview, a feeling compounded by that late-night phone call and her debasing brush with Clemency's latest vanity project, Honor felt only relief at the sight of her most chivalrous and supercilious courtier. He was carrying a prettily packaged box of patisseries. He kissed her cheek – a moist brush against her papery skin.

'Am I the first?'

'Of course.'

'Good. I've got you all to myself then,' he said, his eyebrows twitching, a satirical silent screen seducer.

'You can fix the drinks, darling,' she said.

As he went towards the cabinet the doorbell rang again. Honor sat down while Inigo, with the camp groan of an interrupted suitor, walked back along the hallway to admit the next guest.

It was Aidan, pink and glowing from the gym – surely he was getting a little old for all that weight training? – and mercifully alone. His difficult boyfriend, Jorge, an architect, was working late on an important project.

'A Midlands leisure centre,' Aidan said, with an exaggerated shudder. 'Mutually exclusive concepts, I'd have thought.'

He had brought a carton of fat green olives and a pretty hardback edition of Palgrave's *Golden Treasury*.

He kissed Honor, holding her a little tighter and longer than she felt was sincere or necessary, and embraced Inigo in the way that men seemed to do these days, whatever their sexual preference.

Ruth arrived next, out of breath and flustered, carrying a large tray of Lebanese mezze. She looked a mess as usual: unkempt hair, frock like a beige marquee that had come loose from its guy ropes, orthopaedic shoes, all defiantly declaring her rejection of patriarchal sexual tyranny. She bent to kiss Honor with a grunt of exertion, trying not to drop the tray, then swayed into the kitchen to sort out the plates and cutlery.

'A tithe for the Empress of Maida Vale,' Inigo said, handing Honor a vodka martini.

They heard the lock turn. Bobby had let himself in with the key Honor had given him last year during a bad patch. His contribution to the evening was twofold: a case of Bordeaux, purchased on *Courier* expenses, and his guest, Jason Kelly, a laconic young actor of mesmerising beauty.

'So this is your *amuse-gueule*, Bobby?' Aidan said, taking a step back to appraise the new arrival.

The blond, almond-eyed Kelly, whose fecund love life was the subject of intense tabloid interest, bridled. Inigo handed him a distracting cocktail before steering him over to Honor. Kelly was currently giving his Hamlet at the Old Vic and his visceral reading of the part had attracted garrulous praise from the critics. Honor, who went to the first night with Aidan (Clemency had provided the tickets), had been equally impressed.

'Not quite "fat and scant of breath",' was her only criticism.

Professionally, Kelly was better known, and considerably better paid, for his leading role in the recent blockbuster film version of Enid Blyton's *Magic Faraway Tree*. Honor, though entranced by the young actor's Hamlet, had declined Aidan's invitation to see the film – Hollywood hogwash, obviously – in a multi-screen cinema in a shopping mall.

'I would,' she had said, 'rather spend an evening doing housework, or reading Isadora Talbot.'

But the bedroom scene with Gertrude had been extraordinarily powerful. Honor patted the needlepoint stool by her feet and invited the newcomer to sit.

'Ah. The Seat of Honor,' Inigo said, as he said at every Monday supper.

The doorbell sounded again – two short rings, one long. No one stirred.

'Ruth?' Honor called out to the kitchen. 'Be a darling and let Clemency in.'

'Bringing up the rear as usual,' muttered Inigo, making his regular unkind reference to Clemency's horsewoman's seat.

The Twisk heiress walked in, shoulders slumped apologetically, carrying a large wheel of pungent cheese wrapped in brown paper.

'Mmm,' Inigo said, sniffing the air. 'What's that scent you're wearing, Clemmy? *Eau d'Egout?*'

'By Cloaca?' Aidan threw in.

Clemency ignored Inigo and looked accusingly at Aidan's glass of wine.

'Can I do anything?' she called to Ruth in the kitchen.

The question was rhetorical. Clemency sat down with heavy finality before Ruth had time to answer.

'Are we quorate?' Bobby asked.

'Yes,' Aidan said. 'The Inner Cabinet's here. But Paul's in town so he's going to join us, too.'

'He's on his way from the studio,' Honor said. 'Back from a weekend in Afghanistan.'

'Of course!' Inigo said, refilling the glasses. 'Where else would he be?'

Honor took a long pull at her drink. Inigo had always resented Paul's showy integrity. She liked to see them bickering, her Boys, fighting to catch her eye.

Aidan turned to Jason.

'Congratulations on the reviews.'

'Cheers,' the actor said, raising his glass.

'The glass of fashion and the eye of form,' Aidan went on. 'But never mind Gertrude, the strumpet. Or that daft bint Ophelia. Isn't the real, unexpressed passion for Horatio?'

Jason's pretty mouth crimped with displeasure and Bobby stepped in gallantly, shielding his trophy.

'*You* might think that, Aidan. You might even wish for it. But Horatio's function is to be the audience's proxy: a witness. The more interesting relationship, I think, is with Laertes.'

'Piffle, and you know it,' Inigo said.

'What kind of critical language is that?' Clemency asked.

'Tom Eliot used to say that Hamlet was literature's Mona Lisa,' Honor said wistfully, reaching for the young actor's free hand and giving it a squeeze.

With the subtlety that had earned him plaudits at the Old Vic, Jason Kelly recoiled imperceptibly.

'That's no enigmatic smile,' Aidan said, raising a provocative eyebrow at the actor. 'That's the proud man's contumely.'

The look that darkened Kelly's fair features was more menacing than the stare he summoned nightly for Claudius. Aidan was saved by the doorbell.

'Hercules Tucker!' he said, springing to his feet to open the door. 'Back with the golden apples.'

But it was not Paul. It was the very opposite of Paul. A young woman with the abundant décolletage of a Restoration wench stood in the doorway. She was clearly a gatecrasher and the proof of her outsider status was in her hands – a large bunch of hideous candy-pink blooms.

'I'm sorry to bother you,' Tamara said. 'I'm here to see Honor Tait. I'm a journalist, a friend of hers. I've been trying to get in touch with her about an article I'm writing.'

Aidan, smiling like a malevolent pixie, did not believe a word of it but showed her in; another *amuse-bouche* for the party.

'Welcome to Olympia,' he said.

'Really?' Tamara said, startled. She was sure she was in Maida Vale.

A gleam of spiteful pleasure played across Aidan's eyes.

By now, Honor was feeling woozy, one hand stroking the warm, inert paw of the young actor, the other outstretched as Inigo topped up her drink. She was watching the exchanges around her like a newcomer in the hospitality seats at Wimbledon, unfamiliar with the rules but enjoying the spectacle.

Her first response to the sight of the new arrival was disappointment; it was not her Paul. Who was going to invigorate the evening with dispatches from the Real World? Then her disappointment hardened into irritation; it was the half-witted Tara from *The Monitor*. The girl's face was stamped with a silly rictus of a smile and she was holding another bunch of garage forecourt flowers.

'I'm so sorry,' Tamara said breathlessly, before Honor had time to speak. 'I tried to contact you. I called your publishers but they wouldn't give me your number.'

'You bet I wouldn't,' Ruth said, walking into the sitting room and drying her hands on her voluminous skirt. 'Tamara Sim? You're becoming a nuisance caller.'

Ruth looked towards Honor for endorsement but found that the old woman's attention had shifted towards the hall, down which Paul, flak-jacketed and fuming, was striding.

'Door was open, Honor. Hope you don't mind.'

He knew he did not need to apologise. Honor got to her feet and, dropping Hamlet's unresponsive hand, accepted Paul Tucker's ursine embrace. She shooed the relieved actor away and directed Paul to the needlepoint footstool where he sat, monumental and masculine as Rodin's Thinker.

'So, darling, what's the latest from Kabul? Tell all,' Honor said.

Ruth gave a testy gasp and retreated to the kitchen while Tamara, temporarily forgotten, shrank into a corner. Paul Tucker she recognised straight away. He did not seem to have changed his clothes since the Archway meeting last week and he talked unstoppably, with a level stare, as if permanently addressing a camera. But who were the others?

She recognised Clemency Twisk from the charity event. The little ruddy-faced Scotsman who had answered the door was raising his glass at Tamara and winking in a manner that was not entirely friendly, while another middle-aged man, squat as a frog, with bulging eyes, was waving a cigarette. Her reportorial antennae began to twitch at the sight of a young man who seemed to be backing away from the pop-eyed smoker. He had the blond good looks of a Scandinavian superhero and there was something tantalisingly familiar about him. Tucker's monologue gathered speed, his voice rumbling like an approaching landslide, and Tamara ducked into the kitchen. The publisher was muttering to herself as she unpacked small pastries and arranged them on plates, like counters in a board game.

'Anything I can do to help?' Tamara asked, propping the flowers by the sink. Ruth sighed and poured herself another slug of wine.

'You've got a nerve. You really have. You mess up an interview, completely alienate one of my writers, then you waltz in uninvited – gatecrash her party! – and expect to get a warm welcome.'

'It wasn't like that. Honest,' Tamara pleaded. 'She was difficult. Impossible. I tried my best. They really want this piece in *S*nday* magazine and I'm running out of options.'

'We made it quite plain when we set up the interview. Honor Tait is a very private person.'

'It's not too much to ask, is it? A few details? Family? Her glamorous life? This isn't a hatchet job we're planning. *S*nday* doesn't do hatchet jobs. You know that.'

Ruth unpacked more pastries onto a plate.

'Look, I warned you. She despises all this personal prying. And besides, Honor Tait's writing speaks for itself. Look up her biography if you want. It'll be in the cuttings. But don't expect any quotes from her.'

'Come on. You're her publisher,' Tamara said, her arms outstretched in an appeal for sympathy. 'You're a commercial outfit, not a charity. Don't you want to spread the word about your product? Make some money?'

Ruth licked her fingers.

'We're not a charity, no. But commercial? Chance would be a fine thing.' She passed a plate of pastries to Tamara. 'I suppose you can make yourself useful now you're here. No one else has offered to help. Take these and pass them round.'

Tamara moved deferentially through the sitting room distributing the food, then picked up a couple of bottles

189

and went round refilling glasses. Tucker was still holding court and the only permitted interruptions were from Honor.

'So it's been sealed off?' she asked.

'Yes. Thousands have fled. The place is a ghost town. Only the sick and old, those who can't move, remain, living like rats in basements. You're crunching over spent cartridges in the ruins, past heaps of rubble that were once apartment blocks . . .'

'More wine?' Tamara whispered. He glanced up, his eyes locking briefly onto her chest. Then he held out his glass and continued.

'The infrastructure's been totally trashed . . .'

Tamara retreated to the kitchen where Ruth was noisily washing plates.

'Here,' said the publisher, passing a corkscrew covered in soap suds. 'Open another bottle.'

Tamara refilled Ruth's glass then poured one for herself. They could still hear the TV newsman's voice from the sitting room, as insistent and uninflected as a Black and Decker.

'He's quite something, Paul Tucker,' Tamara said.

'Yes, isn't he just?'

'How well does he know Honor . . . Miss Tait?' Tamara asked, casually picking up a tea towel and wiping a plate.

'If you're trying to ingratiate yourself here,' Ruth said, 'you're doing a pretty good job.'

'I just need another hour with her, to get some quotes on her famous friends.'

Ruth's eyebrows arched in warning.

'You're wasting your time.'

She immersed an enamel saucepan in the suds, holding it down forcefully as if drowning a puppy.

'We need to bring this interview to life,' Tamara said. 'I've got to get an idea about what she's really like, off-duty as it were.'

'I'm not sure I can persuade her to spend another minute with you.'

'It would be really useful to know who's here, for a start. You know, build a picture of her from her circle of friends. Who's the little Scotsman who answered the door, for instance?'

'Aidan Delaney. The poet,' Ruth said. 'Won the Margrave Prize for his last collection, *Strychnine Kisses*?'

'Of course. And the skinny one with the laugh?'

'Inigo Wint. The artist. There was a double-page spread on him in *Zeitgeist* last week.'

'Oh yes, I thought I recognised him,' Tamara lied. Was she meant to be familiar with German newspapers, too?

'You must know Clemency. She's always in the culture pages.'

'Yes. I've seen her around. Human rights meetings, that sort of thing.'

'Everyone knows *Clemency*,' continued Ruth, with an emphasis that suggested buried resentments. She balanced a glass decanter upside down on the draining board. 'She's a "power in the land". You can't go to a first night, a gallery opening or a serious book launch without bumping into Clemency.'

Not so buried then. Tamara reached for the decanter.

'And the chunky man with the . . . large eyes?' she said. 'The smoker . . . ?'

As Tamara gestured with her right hand to indicate a cigarette, the decanter slipped through her fingers and smashed on the floor like a glass grenade. There was a shocked silence in the kitchen but outside, in the sitting room, Paul Tucker did not miss a beat.

'And then the gunfire started again and, for a moment, I thought I was a goner,' they heard him say.

Ruth tutted, reached into a cupboard for a dustpan and brush and thrust them into Tamara's hands.

'That's it. I knew I should have thrown you out.'

Tamara knelt contritely by the shards.

'I really am terribly sorry. I'm only trying to do my job, write my story, do justice to your author.'

'There are proper channels for this sort of thing, you know,' Ruth said. 'Oh, just get up, for heaven's sake.'

Tamara struggled to her feet.

'Shall I take out some more food?' she asked.

Ruth shook her head at the girl's effrontery but there were no other volunteers. She thrust a plate at Tamara and nodded towards the door.

Tamara approached the blond Viking first, bending low over him with the canapés. He declined with a shake of the head.

Paul Tucker was holding Honor Tait's hand with a new intensity and seemed to have paused for breath. The

Scots poet was sounding off on the subject of Telstar, now. Or perhaps it was Tolstoy.

'The extraordinary thing was his transparent admiration for Murat,' he said.

Tamara hovered, hoping to make herself inconspicuous and to keep track of the conversation. The tubby smoker intervened, waving his cigarette like a fairy wand to make some point about St Petersburg and the Caucasus, confirming that they were not, after all, talking about the hit single by the Tornadoes, pioneers of electronic pop, but about the author of the blockbuster *War and Peace*.

'Stuffed vine leaf?' Tamara asked, leaning into Tucker's weather-beaten face.

The room fell silent. He gazed at her cleavage, as if it was that intriguingly contoured arrangement of flesh, rather than the mouth located some way above it, that had addressed him.

Honor Tait appeared to wake from a pleasurable dream and took in Tamara properly for the first time since her arrival.

'Are you still here?'

'Yes. I just—'

'I don't remember inviting you.'

Honor sipped her drink meditatively, as if the glass itself was the repository of her memory. Seated next to the bulk of Paul Tucker, she seemed absurdly tiny and wizened, like an ancient relict of Tamara's childhood doll's house.

'I thought we might have the chance of another chat? For my feature?'

Tamara heard a polyphonic gasp.

'This really is an unpardonable intrusion,' Honor said.

Ruth appeared in the kitchen doorway, holding a roasting fork.

'I just thought . . .' Tamara continued.

'You just *thought*,' Honor said.

Was she mocking Tamara, elongating the vowel in a bad impersonation of her London accent?

'I doubt,' the old woman continued, 'whether you've ever had an original thought in your life.'

'I think you'd better leave,' Ruth said, escorting Tamara down the hallway. 'You've completely ballsed it up now,' she added in a whisper.

Tamara glanced around her, frantic for one more chance, something to hang on to, one thing that would save this evening, this story, her contract. On the hall table was a stack of mail and a small pile of invitations.

'Just one thing. Could you tell me? Please?' pleaded Tamara, backing towards the table as Ruth opened the front door. 'The boy in the corner? The good-looking blond one who didn't say anything. Was that Moonface from the *Faraway Tree*?'

Ruth threw up her hands in exasperation before grabbing Tamara's left arm, firmly leading her into the corridor, closing the door on her beseeching face and securing the bolt behind her.

Nine

She returned to her flat, threw down her bag and walked to her desk with the heavy tread of a condemned woman approaching the gallows. Only 3,800 words stood between her and a contract with the most distinguished magazine in British journalism, between success and failure, recognition and loveless obscurity. But the terrible truth was that she had nothing to say. It was not just the job she needed; it was the life. And not just *her* life; her brother's, too. With a little money, she might be able to reintroduce Ross to other possibilities: to happiness without chemical assistance; to the fulfilment of work and the satisfactions of independence; to the attractions of a pleasing, ordered home; to personal hygiene. Ross could start again. It was not too late.

Tamara had dreamed of putting a deposit on a rented cottage for him, somewhere safe and remote, beyond the reach of his low-life friends. Maybe Cornwall. Ross liked Cornwall. They had gone on holiday there with their parents before the divorce and Ross had talked about going back – 'reconnecting'.

He would probably never hold down a job again, in the conventional sense. He had dropped out of school and worked in a record shop for a while, but his shop-lifting convictions (he was not acquisitive, just feeding his habit) ended any prospect of a career in retail. The routine, the requirement to get up in the morning and be in a certain place at a certain time, would be too much for him now, though when it came to scoring and making assignations with dealers, he hared about London with a determined speed-walker's gait. Maybe he could take up something creative, a job where you could choose your own hours, work through the night and sleep through the day if you wanted. Candle-making, perhaps. There was a lot of candle-making in Cornwall. There were a lot of dealers there, too, she supposed, but if the cottage was sufficiently isolated, it might take Ross a while to track them down, long enough for him to get clean, wake up and realise what he had been missing all these years.

Upstairs, the solicitors had turned on their music. The whole house shuddered to the sound – Tod Maloney, a suburban boy in mascara, yowling about 'Life on the Dark Side'. Tamara reached for her earplugs. She loved her flat, and worked hard to pay for it. She would not be driven out. The rent was a struggle, but most nights, after hurrying along the tapering corridor of her street, stealthily feeling her way down the unlit external stairs and turning her key with fumbling haste, she felt a rush of pleasure once she closed the door and stepped inside. This was her sanctuary, her place of safety. The neighbours were an occasional nuisance, certainly, but nothing bad could ever happen here, within the confines of her flat. Except, perhaps, failure and a silent phone.

She leaned across her desk to check her answering machine. The display was flashing a mocking red zero, but she wanted to be sure. She pressed the replay button.

'You have no new messages.'

Was there an element of malice in the digitalised female voice, a hint of jubilation in the emphatically lilted *'no'*?

'And if you think anyone – a single person in the whole world – cares about you,' was the subtext, 'think again, sweetheart.'

Resisting misery, she looked around at the sitting room, which also served as an office, and was comforted. With its blue walls, green sofa and aquamarine rug (the colour scheme copied from *The Monitor*'s monthly *Dé-COR!* supplement), and the strings of conch shell fairy lights over the mirror, it looked like a mermaid's *pied-à-mer*, 20,000 leagues under the sea. Here were her treasures: souvenirs of family holidays (the tube of coloured sand, in layered stripes, from the Isle of Wight and the chipped plaster cat won at a Dorset funfair on the mantelpiece, the panting-puppy pyjama case, bought in a St Ives gift shop, at the foot of her bed next door); every letter and birthday card she had ever received; every Christmas card since she had left home at eighteen; and family photographs, in labelled, colour-coded box files stacked in a corner, as carefully catalogued as anything in the British Library.

Gemma, her old flatmate from Brighton Poly, had said

that Tamara's mementoes of her mother, laid out on a small bamboo table in her bedroom, were 'a bit creepy'. But Gemma had never been bereaved. There was an irreparably broken coral necklace that Tamara's mother had worn as a teenager, a Waterford crystal vase she had kept on her bedside till the end, some of the little glass animals she had collected – two horses, a poodle and a fragile-necked giraffe – which seemed to have been chipped from ice by tiny elves, a larky red feather boa, a silk scarf edged with sequins that she had used to cover her thinning hair during chemotherapy, and a photograph of her in her twenties, sitting on a beach, her pin-up's curves straining against her modest swimsuit, her head thrown back in laughter, arms enfolding two wriggling children who stared at the camera with frank hostility.

The religious would have called Tamara's collection a reliquary, but it was precisely because she was unsure about the existence of life after death that these souvenirs were precious. They had been chosen by her mother, cherished and touched by her. When Tamara traced a finger along the rim of the vase or held the scarf to her face, sniffing the sweet, mossy smell which no bottled fragrance could capture, she was holding her mother. Tamara had been comforted by that scent, which lingered like an afterglow for months after her mother's death. And then one day, when she picked up the scarf the reassuring smell had vanished and she realised she could no longer accurately recall it. She had wept helplessly. These keepsakes, meaningless to everyone else, must still bear traces of her mother's DNA. And that was all that was left of her.

Tamara went to her kitchenette, an alcove just off the sitting room, and opened the fridge. It was empty apart from a tub of low-fat yoghurt, two weeks past its sell-by date, a pint of skimmed milk and a bottle of wine, half empty, vacuum-sealed with a rubber stopper. She opened the wine, filled a glass and watched the liquid shivering to the vibrations of the upstairs din before she raised it to her lips. Didn't they have law books thick as London telephone directories to memorise?

If she really could have everything she wanted, she would dig a trench round her flat and prise it out from under this ugly villa, slide it onto a gurney and wheel it from hard-pressed Hornsey to a better, grander part of town, say Holland Park. She would slot it beneath a big white Regency house garlanded with wisteria. She could take to life in a peaceful haven of gardens, lush with lilac and roses, among wide avenues and interesting little boutiques, a place of silence and contentment where a single woman could turn her key in her lock at night without glancing over her shoulder and gripping her rape alarm.

She went back to the sitting room, clamped the padded headphones from her stereo over her already plugged ears, picked up her bag and returned to her desk. There was always the possibility that with *S*nday*'s reputation, once her piece had been published she could break into the American market: *Vanity Fair*, *Time*, *Esquire*. Then there were the women's glossies: *Sassy*, perhaps *Vogue*. And she could always write features for *Entertainment Weekly*. They liked lists. It was, as Tania Singh demonstrated, all about spreading yourself as widely as possible.

Tamara opened her bag and took out her swag. This was tonight's sole haul: a handful of letters, the product of what Simon would call 'a little light larceny', a legitimate tactic in pursuit of a story, especially when the subject of the story was so obstructive. She had not taken too many; she did not want to arouse suspicion.

So what had her lucky dip yielded? An electricity bill. This could only be of use if it revealed that Honor Tait was mired in debt. *Tragic end of top journalist, friend-of-the-famous, ex-beauty, debt-ridden and alone, shivering by candlelight*? But no, Tait seemed to have paid her unexceptional bills, which was more than Tamara herself had done lately. She wrote reminder on a Post-it note and stuck it on the phone. There was a bank statement, by the look of the envelope, and a doctor's bill for a 'consultation', which could mean anything, from ingrown toenail treatment to a post-face-lift follow-up. The face-lift option would obviously make a better story. There were also three letters, hand-addressed, as well as a circular for stair lifts. Promisingly, one of the letters had already been opened. It contained a postcard. A dated saucy seaside cartoon depicting a pair of leering spivs in striped bathing trunks eyeing up two women in swimsuits who were holding large ice-cream cones. One woman was bent, toothless and decrepit, a withered granny in a floral rubber cap. The other was a pouting blonde doll with enormous upthrust breasts. Both men, the double speech bubble indicated, were speaking at the same time. And both said the same thing: 'I don't fancy yours.' Tamara turned the card over. The handwriting, in purple ink, was spiky and affected, with open, forked 'e's and fat-bellied printers' 'a's, and the message brief and cryptic: *Surprise! Need to see you soonest. No cheques this time. Cash will do. Your Darling Boy.* That was it. No 'Dear Honor', or 'all the best'. No signature. It must be a private joke. One of her posturing groupies. Tamara puzzled over the picture again. It was amazing what used to pass for humour.

The bank statement, though oblique on details, was more interesting – Tait seemed to be nudging the outer edge of her £4,000 overdraft limit. She was broke and she needed her book to be a success. She needed the publicity, which made her sabotage of the interview more perverse. But for all Tamara could tell from the cryptic lists of numbers, the standing orders and cheques could be made out to massage parlours, casinos or cat rescue charities. She turned to the two remaining letters. They turned out to be annoyingly impersonal: an invitation to an art exhibition in Soho and a brochure advertising a string quartet series at a London concert hall. She threw them theatrically into the wastepaper basket.

She was angry with herself for being so cautious and wished she had been more professional. She should have scooped up a bigger handful of Tait's post. The risk would have been the same but the outcome would have been more rewarding. She went over to the wastepaper basket and fished out the invitation; its bright lettering, printed over cartoons of old-fashioned schoolboys in caps and crumpled shorts waving catapults, announced a party next week to mark the launch of the exhibition. Of course. The painter, Inigo Wint, with the falsetto laugh, had been at Tait's flat tonight. Tamara sifted through the cuttings again; there he was, cited in *Vogue* as a 'flamboyant draughtsman using seminal images of British popular culture to interrogate conventional mores' and a 'prominent member of Honor Tait's Salon', along with Bobby Ward-Moore, 'waspish literary journalist and flaneur' (the frog-featured smoker), and Aidan Delaney, 'writer of verse as satisfyingly mordant as fifteen-year-old malt' (the Glaswegian leprechaun). In addition, there was a thumbnail picture of one of Wint's pictures, which the caption described as 'a witty postmodern take on the stories of Richmal Crompton'. Whoever he might be.

In the absence of anything else, the exhibition might provide some sort of lead. As Tamara turned to her keyboard, she felt a slowly percolating optimism.

I step into the dimly lit corridor and enter not so much a flat as a hermetic casket of memories; the walls lined with pictures, photographs and paintings, exquisite landscapes of her beloved Scottish countryside, old master portraits, the shelves stacked with an eclectic collection of books and souvenirs of a long and exotic life at the heart of a century's action.

She indicates a chair in the crepuscular drawing room
and goes into the kitchen to fetch a vase for my lilies,
which she lovingly places alongside the photograph of her
late husband, Tad Challis, director of classic Ealing
comedy films. Finally, she sits down and I can study her
features more closely.

Tamara wrote another Post-it note and stuck it on the
phone: *chk Challis films.* Her memory of Ealing comedies
– glimpsed on Sunday-afternoon TV when she was too
hungover to reach for the remote – was that they were
black and white and distinguished by an absence of humour
and a lack of stars: the leading men were unappetising
baldies and the actresses were either busy old trouts like
Bernice Bullingdon or frigid English roses. She should
take another look, get a few videos, maybe buy a boxed set
on expenses. But she must not be distracted. The goal was
clear. Nothing must stand in her way. Not 4,000 words.
Not anything. She picked up Tait's first book and turned
again to the Pulitzer Prize-winning essay. She could at
least filch a few chunks from it to pad out her article.

One hundred and ten years later, in July 1937, Goethe's
transcendental picnic spot was chosen as the site of the
concentration camp the Nazis called Buchenwald. The
prisoners forced to clear the area and prepare the ground
to build the camp were ordered by their guards to leave
one tree standing as the citadel of misery was erected
around it; that tree was Goethe's Oak, seen by Hitler's

troops as 'Verkörperung des deutschen Geiste' – the embodiment of the German Spirit.

This week, I stood in that camp, newly liberated by the US Third Army, and saw grim evidence of the barbarity of the Nazi regime and the sickening debasement of that spirit.

For Honor Tait, rich girl with a charmed life, the shock must have been great. At the time she was writing, the liberation of the camps, the enormity of Nazi crimes, must have seemed like the ultimate scoop. But from this end of history, the hard fact was that it was stale news, almost cliché. Accounts of Viking raids or the activities of Attila the Hun would have made riveting reading in the Middle Ages, but their impact these days was minimal. Besides, coverage of atrocities was best left to television.

Tamara had never seen a corpse in person – she couldn't, in the end, face seeing her mother's lifeless body in the funeral parlour – but she had attended several harrowing inquests for the *Sydenham Advertiser* and imagined that for her, from a background far less sheltered and privileged than Honor Tait's, the professional reflexes would soon kick in. And she was certain that when she came to write up such a story, she would not have wasted space on the insipid musings of a long-dead nob in a frock coat.

Damn. The phone. Its red light was flashing, jolting her, irritated, back to the present.

And then she remembered that she had been willing

it to ring all week. It must be Tim. He wanted to see her again after all. This was just the sort of interruption she needed. With a smile of triumph she took out her earplugs and picked up the handset. But instead of Tim's teasing plea for forgiveness, she heard urgent mechanical pips followed by the rattle and clunk of a coin. A phonebox. She knew, before a word was spoken, that it was her brother.

'Ross?'

Silence. Tamara's heart faltered. She had to calm herself, take a deep breath. She needed to be in control.

'Ross?' she tried again.

Had she got it wrong? Was it a crank caller? She felt the familiar churn of self-loathing; would she *rather* it was a crank caller instead of her brother?

'Sis!'

It was Ross and he was excited. High. But not on heroin. Too alert for heroin. Maybe too alert altogether. Was he back on amphetamines?

'You okay?' Tamara asked.

'Course I'm okay.'

Part of her tried to imagine her brother at the end of the line; another part of her, the self-hating, selfish coward, did not want to know, wanted to shut him out, erase the nightmare images of him – haggard, filthy, his skinny body deformed by fear and craving – that were lining up in a grotesque beauty pageant, each contestant more hideous than the next.

'Only it's late.'

'Well, I'll piss off then if I'm bothering you.'

'No. No. Don't go, Ross. I was just worried you were in trouble.'

'Don't you worry about me, Tam. I'm doing great.'

His voice was pitched half an octave higher than usual, borne up by a helium exhilaration. Or perhaps agitation.

'Have you eaten lately?' Tamara asked.

'Yeah, yeah. I'm good. Taking care of myself.'

Tamara knew her questions were futile. Ross's dishonesty was automatic. He lied by default, especially to himself. Other people might let themselves go a little, have a few off-days now and again, but Ross's self-abandonment was total, heroic.

'Is the flat okay?' Tamara asked.

'Yeah. Been tricky, though. Those bastards, the Brummies in the flat above, had it in for me. They tried to bug me. Microphones. I sussed them out, though. Found a camera in the ceiling, too.'

'Oh, Ross.'

It had started again.

'No problem, Tam.' His laugh, a hacking variation on his bronchitic cough and calculated to convey carefree merriment, suggested its opposite. 'I'm too clever for them. Rumbled their game. Crystal helped me sort it.'

Crystal – the hopeless junkie ex-girlfriend he had met in a psychiatric unit. She was eleven years older than him: a raddled hippy with an extra decade of substance abuse under her beaded Navajo belt.

'Crystal's been around,' he had said with unsavoury

relish five years ago when he first described his new girlfriend to Tamara. 'She's a gypsy spirit – studied with gurus in India, lived in a cave in Ios, hung out with Maoris in New Zealand, worked as a snake charmer in Morocco . . .'

Her Romany caravan had finally rolled into King's Cross, where she and Ross had got together in detox and cemented their relationship in successive sprees of retox.

'Is that Crystal as in methamphetamine, or as in semi-precious stones with healing powers?' Tamara had asked.

'Actually,' he'd replied with injured insouciance, 'she has highly developed psychic abilities.'

When Ross first met her, her younger sister had just died of an overdose, which clairvoyant Crystal had failed to foresee. It was a family business, this kind of screw-up. Crystal was bad news. But then Ross was bad news, too.

Tamara felt a cold spike of anxiety, as if she had just injected some rough speed herself. She remembered how she had found her brother in his flat after his last split from Crystal – was that three times now? – cowering in his own dirt among a pack of feral cats. There was no furniture, apart from a suppurating mattress on the floor, partly covered by one of the bedspreads their mother had crocheted, irreparably soiled and torn. (Tamara's, clean and nursery bright, was on her bed even now.) The flat was in darkness. Newspapers had been taped over the windows and the light fittings and electrical sockets had been dismantled in his meticulous search for the cameras he knew were there, filming him and beaming his plight to TV sets all over Britain.

'Have you been taking your medication?' Tamara asked now, knowing that if Ross were ever to make the mistake of telling the truth, it would not be on this subject. Any pharmaceuticals he was taking would be unprescribed.

'Yeah, yeah. Don't worry about me.'

Tamara felt a helpless swoon of affection; she wished she could make everything all right for him. Ross was her big brother but most of the time he seemed like her child. Her damaged child.

'Do you need anything? Are you warm enough?'

She had tried to find ways of helping him directly – sending parcels, tokens, paying his electricity bills, phoning credit card food orders to his local supermarket. Cash, Tamara learned early, ended up in his dealer's pocket.

'No, I'm fine. Sorted. The cooker's packed up, though. But I'm going to apply for a loan from the social. Get meself straight.'

'You don't have a cooker? How are you feeding yourself?'

Tamara knew she sounded like their mother. She also knew that there was some hypocrisy here; her own dietary habits – her erratic reliance on canteen fry-ups and party canapés – were not exemplary.

'I'm okay. Like I said. Crystal's cooking for me.'

Tamara imagined Crystal in the kitchen. The only dish she would be cooking would be crack cocaine.

'Oh, Ross. You've got to take care of yourself.'

'Don't nag. I can stand on my own two feet. I'm doing fine.'

His tone had changed, as it often did, from chipper defiance to aggression. If she wasn't careful, he would turn on her, accuse her of belittling him and slam down the phone.

'I'm not nagging. I want to help.'

'You're always helping, Tam.' Now he was wheedling, flattering her. 'It's not fair on you. I'll be all right.'

'But you weren't all right in the past.'

'That's right. Rub it in. Don't you worry about me. You've got your own life to lead.'

He was pulling away, rejecting her.

'Ross, you know it makes me happy to help you out. You're my *brother*.'

She was aware of the language, the therapy-speak. She knew she should not be drawn in, or rather she should not throw herself in. But what was the alternative to co-dependency? The cold shoulder? Let them sink as low as they could, turn your back and walk away, until they could fall no further. Only then, was the conventional wisdom, could they start to help themselves. But what if they disappeared altogether? She could not do it.

'I'm okay.' That sulky voice again. 'Crystal's helping me out.'

That was exactly what Tamara feared.

'Look, let me send you some money.'

'Only if you're sure you can spare it.'

The ready capitulation. Was this the purpose of his

call? A little ice stiletto entered Tamara's heart, then melted. What difference did it make? Her brother needed help; that was certain. Who would choose to live the way he did? She thought again of that hellhole flat, the chaos and grime, the *smell*. Tamara reassured him; yes, honestly, she could spare it. But Ross had no bank account and the complexities of a postal order, requiring a visit to a post office and the need to produce identification, were beyond him. Tamara would draw out £80 in cash from her building society savings tomorrow, put it in an envelope and send it by registered mail to his address.

'Thanks, Tam. You're the best. I'll pay you back as soon as I get straight.'

The idea that Ross would pay her back was almost as ludicrous as the notion that he would ever get straight.

'Don't worry about it. Just—'

She never finished her sentence. The phonebox pips broke in. The line clicked, then lapsed into its sinister purr. He had gone. Misery tugged at her, like a horror-movie hand reaching up from a drain to grab at her ankles. She poured another glass of wine. The smoking abyss was always present, but she did not have to stare into it. There was always work. It was a necessity, and it could also be an escape.

She opened Tait's book again.

Outside one of the huts that had been the scene of such sustained brutality, stood the jagged stump of a once mighty tree. This was all that remained of Goethe's Oak after an

allied air strike only days before, aimed at a nearby muni-
tions factory, had sent incendiary bombs raining on the
camp. There were many casualties among the inmates.
Goethe's symbolic tree was another victim of the raid.

A tree? Did Tait think she was writing for the Gardening
pages? Tamara could not bear much more of this.

She tidied the distracting heap of gossip glossies and
TV magazines into a neat pile and stuffed them under her
futon, logged on to her Amiga, fed it a floppy disk and
opened her latest draft. The bright screen of her computer
blazed, a chilly hearth, in the darkness of her flat.

Those eyes, once wide and Wedgwood blue, set in a face
of palest porcelain, which had mesmerised some of the
leading figures of the last half century, are now potholes
in an Ordnance Survey contour map, and are focused
flirtatiously on our photographer as he snaps away.

As I express my admiration for her work and encourage
her to reminisce about past glories, her carapace begins
to crack and I can at last see the vestiges of beauty in
the ancient ruin of her face.

'Yes,' she says, smiling almost girlishly, recalling her
love affair with Bing Crosby, immortal crooner, 'they
were marvellous times, marvellous. He had the most
wonderful feet, you know. Whenever he held me in his
arms, I felt like a gossip columnist.'

*

It must have been around 2 a.m. when they finally left, Paul still trying to engage Bobby and his phlegmatic actor friend on the subject of the Sarobi field hospital, the laughter of Aidan and Inigo fading away down the corridor, Clemency and Ruth en route to the bottle bank with sacks of empties clanking like distant church bells. Honor had also persuaded Ruth to take away the hideous flowers that the pushy young reporter had brought.

She poured a drink and settled back in her chair. Thanks to Ruth, the ashtrays had been emptied and the flat was now cleaner than it had been before they had arrived. Cleaner, and sadder too. Their departure had sucked all sound and life from the place.

She switched on the wireless. The World Service. How debased it had become. A man with the deliberate speech and oscillating tone of a children's entertainer was patronising a group of African women about a clean water project. Once, Honor had been a regular contributor to the Service, broadcasting news and features from what were then – before the influx of airborne charabanc parties and credit-card-carrying backpackers – some of the most remote regions of the world. She could be accused of many things, she was sure, but she had never patronised listeners, or readers. Nor could she be indicted for cheeriness.

Tad was the one for bonhomie. Though he had his dark moments, too. But only Honor was party to those. As a director, Tad was known for the convivial atmosphere he encouraged on set, if not for the intellectual rigour of his filmmaking.

'He was a lovely man,' one broken-nosed gaffer had said to her after the funeral.

'A real gent,' said another.

She had thanked them sombrely, but tonight, remembering, alone in her icy flat, she laughed aloud, and was startled by the eeriness of the sound, an echoing cackle. She struggled to her feet to fetch her shawl from her bedroom. The busy hum of the evening had not entirely done the trick. Bobby's wine and the pleasingly disputatious conversation had temporarily warmed her core as effectively as Glenbuidhe's Rayburn, but now she was shivering and her fingers were stiff with cold. She had found herself, despite the evening's distractions, like an infatuated schoolgirl, constantly returning to that recent phone call, mentally replaying it, word for word. A ghost of times past. She was a rationalist by conviction but superstitious by nature – the legacy of an Anglo-Scots background, she supposed – and felt that it was only her fervent wishing, and its more judicious counterpoint of dread, that had generated this visitation. Here she was again, racing towards the ravine.

In bleaker moments, her entire life – even her work – had seemed a sequence of Lilliputian diversions, futile displacement activities. The flights and fights, the sleepless fevers of writing, the manoeuvres and machinations, the dogged progress across the planet, like Robert the Bruce's spider, millimetre by millimetre – and for what? The pleasures of success and catastrophes of failure, sexually as well as professionally, all the incessant busyness, to weave this cobweb in a dusty corner. She was shivering again. If she were to succumb to remorse now, she would have a seventy-year backlog to get through.

As for kinship, real or assumed, it had always been poisoned by betrayal and estrangement. And motherhood, the saintly state – who would ever admit the desolate truth about that? Not poor Lois, whose unconditional love for Daniel and her bitter loss had sent her tumbling over the edge. Even the pleasures of music and landscape seemed tainted to Honor now. The hills were scarred by tarmac and infestations of tax-break pine plantations, the lochs disfigured by fish farms, and music, once consolation and delight, had largely become an irritant, an audible manifestation of anxiety.

She poured another drink and set it down on the table by Tad's picture. Their marriage, if not quite 'open', as they used to say in the Sixties – Tad had been too babyishly jealous for that civilised arrangement – had been far from closed. There had been an unspoken understanding, or at any rate an assumption on Honor's part, that the occasional fling was permissible as long as it did not interfere with their marriage. The passion of their affair – he had been a vigorous and attentive lover – had, five years after the wedding, subsided into a comfortable, if spiky, sibling affection that neither of them wished to relinquish. But a receipt from a French lingerie shop, carelessly dropped by Tad on the bedroom floor, had been the first indication of a seismic shift in their domestic arrangements.

Honor assumed he must have a regular mistress and

she rebuked herself for caring so much, and for being so surprised. She herself had been his mistress, drawn to him after their first meeting at a screenwriters' cocktail party, by his kindness, his uncomplicated optimism and his canine devotion. She had tired of complexity, and Tad's Labrador temperament seemed marvellously exotic after a succession of affairs with tormented egomaniacs and miserabilists. His work reflected his nature – light-hearted and warm, with a blitheness that tipped over into silliness. Honor had, against her inclinations, liked his silliness.

In his company, in the early years, the horrors of the day and terrors of the night receded. He was not entirely indifferent to suffering, and shook his head at her stories of famine from the Horn of Africa, or child poverty on the Indian subcontinent, but he never seemed to truly feel it. Mortality did not perturb him, not because he was wisely resigned to it, or saw it with a philosopher's equanimity as part of life, but because it never occurred to him that it had any relevance to him. Death, like unhappiness and poverty, was something that happened to others. He was devoid of misanthropy and his frivolity was a sparkling foil to her brooding *sturm und drang*. At bottom, he had been a far better human being than she could ever be. He did not have to work at it. There was no hinterland, no undercurrent of resentment or regret. Only his jealousy, irrational and all-consuming, had given her any sort of moral advantage.

She felt shame, now, to admit that at first she had found his jealousy flattering. She did not even have the excuse of youth or innocence; she had been an urbane fifty-year-old when they first met. But he had been so handsome, with a broad, safari-suited virility (a look that Paul could only aspire to) that made her feel – and she would confess this to no one – protected. It was a novelty. The straightforward affair, without a trace of existential anguish. It was then, in their first year of stolen meetings, that he had bought her pastel silk and lace underthings, flimsy clichés of male fantasy wrapped in pink tissue, from the same bespoke Paris atelier.

But six years into their easy marriage, looking more closely at the discarded receipt, she saw that the bustier he had bought, in vulgar '*rouge et noir*', was built to accommodate a *belle poitrine* of 117cm, a 46DD. Was Tad in the grip of a helpless passion for a giantess? Was obesity now 'his bag'? As a man with a certain status in the film industry, he had always enjoyed the attentions of pretty young actresses. But had his tastes, jaded by the predictable amusements of slender-hipped ingénues, grown more arcane?

After much interrogation and many tears (she asked the questions, he wept) it finally emerged. Tad had a secret hobby. The lurid corset, with its integral garter belt, was for him. Tad Challis, the bluff and affable American gent of Pinewood Studios, liked to wear women's clothing. Red-eyed and begging forgiveness, he brought out a tin trunk, concealed in a cupboard in the spare room of the flat. He unlocked it and a tangle of brightly coloured silks, satins, brocades and floral cottons spilled out, like the contents of a monstrous child's dressing-up box.

Even in her rage – Honor could not bear it that he had concealed all this from her – it would have seemed cruel to point out that at 6 foot 3, weighing 200 pounds, with the physique of a dissipated rugby player and an out-thrust jaw stippled with grey bristle, he would make the most implausible woman. He was nothing like a dame, unless the dame was appearing in a pantomime.

Under the pretext of trips to discuss film projects that never materialised, while Honor was pursuing her own work, or assignations, he would check into a corporate hotel at an airport and, in the harsh lighting of his hotel room, proceed to transform himself, with an immense padded bra, floral frock, wig and copious make-up, into what he saw as Gina Lollobrigida in her prime. Widow Twankey would have been nearer the mark. Thus attired, he would – by his account, and Honor chose not to press him further – go down to the bar, drink a couple of cocktails, eat a solitary meal in the restaurant and retire inviolate and alone to bed in peach chiffon nightwear.

For all that, it had been a happy marriage. Tad's confession had left her freer to pursue her own interests. They asked fewer questions of each other and Tad curbed his jealousy, or at least was a little more abashed when he expressed it, and when they were together it was an agreeable reunion of old friends.

She picked up the photo again and looked at it closely, as if her stare could charge the image with life. She took in the familiar expression of delight, the little twist of pleasure in the corners of his mouth. He was one of the privileged few, and he gloried in it. His status had nothing to do with economic advantage; Tad had the gift of happiness. But there was something withheld, too, a cast of secretiveness about the eyes that she came to recognise later. No matter. Vanished. She traced the outline of his lips with her finger, set the picture back on the table and fetched another drink. The flats opposite were in darkness and she was seized by a sense, thrilling and irrational, that she was the only person awake in a city of sleepers.

When was Inigo's opening? Ruth had put a three-line whip on it. Honor knew she had to get out, overcome this reclusiveness – a dry run for the grave – and see people. In the same spirit, she had accepted Bobby's invitation to the Press Awards dinner next week. She should find Inigo's invitation and transfer the date to her diary. She must not forget. Lately, she was becoming more absent-minded, she was sure of it. Losing things. Missing appointments. That was how it had started with Lois.

Honor sifted through the mail in the hall on the small tiered table that Tad had insisted on calling an *étagère*. She was sure Inigo's invitation had been here – she clearly remembered the moment she had opened the envelope – but there was no sign of it. Had she imagined it? Had she also imagined the taunting postcard, in an envelope bearing a London postmark? And the phone call, which had robbed her of the few hours' sleep that was her nightly allocation these days?

*

It was getting light now. The strip of sky visible above the flats opposite was saturated with a fleshy glow. Dawn. The loveliest, loneliest, hour. She summoned her most recent memory of Lois, dozing in a wheelchair, her tooth-less mouth open. Lois's course, so hard to discern at the beginning, had been as clear and true as a Roman road. First she lost things, keys, spectacles, occasional words, and then she began to lose herself. There was a brief period of religiosity, painful to watch in such a rationalist, before she succumbed to full-blown visual and aural hallu-cinations. Daniel was there, restored, and then he would be gone again, a cause of consuming anxiety. The dead returned to her, the living ceased to exist. Was that, Honor wondered, the way ahead for her, too? And her dead? Were they waiting for her?

She picked up her notebook.

Buchenwald, 14 April 1945. Liberation Day Four. In that defiant parade, surviving prisoners waved the makeshift flags of their nations – Russia, France, Romania, Yugoslavia, Greece, Italy, Hungary, Great Britain and Germany – the flag of the Weimar Republic . . .

She could not work. Nor could she sleep. Insomnia was another curse of age. How cruel that you needed less sleep as you got older, leaving more waking hours to contemplate encroaching oblivion.

Ten

Tamara murmured a polite greeting to Courtney and walked towards her desk. She could not believe it. Tania was sitting there again and had arranged another pile of books on top of Tamara's back copies of *OK!* and *Hello!*.

'Oh, sorry!' Tania said, with a vixen's smile. 'Computer's down again.'

'Shouldn't you be doing something about it? Isn't that *your* department, computers?'

'Well, no actually. We're not technicians. We're journalists. If you'd like to spend a morning on the website to see what we really do, I'd happily show you around.'

'No thanks,' Tamara said airily, reaching for a copy of *OK!* and upsetting Tania's stack of books. 'I gave up Space Invaders years ago. Strictly for spotty teenagers.'

'But that's where you're wrong,' said Tania, whose blemish-free complexion was a radiant rebuttal. 'It's the future. For all of us.'

'That's what they used to say about unisex silver jumpsuits and time travel.'

Tania laughed, a tinselly chime, and gathered up her books. Tamara looked at the spines: one by Martha Gellhorn – Tamara squirmed at the memory of her recent gaffe with Honor Tait. One by John Pilger, the Australian yachtsman, and a history of World War Two. Didn't she ever relax?

Seated at her reclaimed desk, Tamara drew out her notebook from her bag. There were captions to be written – Tod Maloney and Pernilla Perssen, the Swedish super-model turned lingerie designer, had been pictured squint-eyed outside a West End nightclub – and she still had to finish this week's A-List: Skinny Minnies and Manorexics.

First, though, she needed to write up her notes from Honor Tait's salon. Then she would put in another call to Uncumber Press. Discretion was essential. Courtney and Jim were conspiring in a corner again.

Paul Tucker, macho newsman, a cut-price Robert Redford, has returned with news from some far-flung battlefront. Honor Tait sits in the centre of the room like Queen Guinevere, surrounded by her knights of the realm. Jason Kelly, fresh from his blockbuster screen triumph in Faraway Tree, *adorns the evening with his smouldering presence. Ruth Lavenham, publisher and bustling Mrs Tiggywinkle, knocks up some canapés in the kitchen. A small German with hyperthyroidic eyes (fill in name later) . . .*

Across the top of her screen, a message flashed. It was from Simon: *Lunch?*

She typed: *Great! Just finishing the A-List.*

He called over to her, 'Fantastic. Half an hour?'

Ignoring Courtney's scornful stare, she got down to work.

If looks could kill, there would have been a massacre in Maida Vale on Monday when Jason Kelly attended one of Honor Tait's famous salons. As she clasps the young heartthrob to her bony chest, a small, grinning Scot, the well-known versifier Aidan Delaney, sits around quoting Tolstoy; a sniggering dandy, the artist Inigo Wint, and an overweight German exchange brilliant aperçus on the meaning of Shakespeare and swap witticisms while knocking back fine wines.

Meanwhile, Honor Tait sits inscrutably in the centre of the room like a spider in the heart of her web. All around her, lesser insects hang, transfixed.

They took their table in the centre booth at the Bubbles. Simon needed to unburden himself.

'So Lucinda's thrown Serena out of the flat.'

'Well, it was bound to happen,' Tamara said. 'I mean, once Lucinda found out you were sleeping with her flatmate, what else could she do?'

'And now Serena's homeless, she's threatening to come round and confront Jan.'

'What's *she* meant to do about it?'

'Quite.'

'I mean, it's not as if your wife's going to say, "You're welcome to move into the spare room", is she?'

'No. Plus which, she's got her hands full with Dexter's eighteenth coming up.'

His mobile phone rang.

'Yes, darling . . . Of course . . . No one . . .' he said.

Tamara bit viciously into a breadstick. Perhaps she could insist on a mobile phone as part of her *S*nday* contract.

'Look, Serry . . .' Simon continued, 'I know how awful this is for you . . . I'm doing my best to sort it out . . . I'm getting the deposit together this afternoon . . . What doesn't kill us makes us stronger . . . It's going to be fine, darling . . .'

At a nearby table, Tania, a rare visitor to the Bubbles, was in animated conversation with Vida over a shared bottle of sparkling water.

'Byee . . . Love you . . . Byee,' Simon cooed into the phone.

Tamara pounced before he turned off the phone.

'So, I went to the salon.'

He looked at her blankly for a moment then sat back, smiling.

'Of course. I meant to say. Nice. Really suits you.'

'No,' she said. 'Not the hairdresser's. Honor Tait's salon. The Monday Club.'

'Oh, right.'

His phone rang again.

'Thank God . . .' he whispered into the receiver, turning his face towards the wall. 'I've been so worried about you, darling . . . No . . . No one . . . I'm on my own . . . Of course not . . . You know it was all a terrible mistake . . .

It's you that I love . . . No really, Luce . . . I need to see you. We can work through this . . . What doesn't kill us makes us stronger . . . Okay, sweetheart . . . Call me later . . . Please . . . Love you . . .'

He switched the phone off and pensively poured himself another glass, reached for a breadstick and then looked across at Tamara with a start, as if surprised to find her there.

'Lucinda,' he said, nodding towards the phone.

Tamara's face was tense and unsmiling.

'Where were we?' he said. 'Ah yes, Honor Tait's harem. Did you get the goods on her gigolos?'

'Not exactly. I got in, but there didn't seem to be much going on, apart from a lot of drinking and high-flown talk.'

'Who was there?'

'A few queeny nonentities. And Paul Tucker . . . Jason Kelly.'

Simon whistled softly.

'Kelly. Now he's hot. That would make a tasty front-page splash. Especially if he'd do a kiss-and-tell.'

'I didn't see any kissing.'

'No problem. It's all in the telling.'

'He didn't say much either.'

'It's not talking he's famous for. Tucker might make a para or two, depending on quotes. No one wants to hear him on famines and genocide any more – not even the readers of S*nday. But Kelly . . .'

'Well, it was all very sedate. Nothing of interest to report.'

224

'Don't tell me they remained fully clothed all evening.'

'I couldn't say. They threw me out.'

Simon laughed.

'Well, I'd take that as an admission of guilt – and a declaration of war.'

His phone rang again.

'Hello, darling . . . Yes. Fine . . . No. On my own . . . Sounds good . . . Did you get the quote from the other caterers? . . . Of course. Up to you, sweetie . . . Yes . . . See you later . . . Bye, Jan . . . Love you.'

Tamara folded her arms huffily. If he answered his phone again, she would snatch it from him and hurl it across the room. If it hit Tania Singh, so much the better.

'The thing is,' she continued, 'I don't know how to take this piece further. I drew a blank at her little party last night and she's unlikely to let me cross her threshold again. What's my next step?'

'It's obvious, isn't it?'

'No.'

Simon groaned. 'Look, if she won't give you another interview, if you can't get what you need legitimately, then you've got no choice but to raise your game. Follow her. Dog her footsteps. Get your colour that way,' he said, looking up at the passing waitress, his finger miming a signature in the air. 'You've done that often enough before. Watch her in her unguarded moments, gather details of her daily life, find out more about her young men. Stake her out.'

He tucked the receipt into his pocket. Lunch. Contacts. Features ideas.

They pushed their way out through the bar, nodding to colleagues who were suffused with a second-bottle glow. Tania and Vida had already left.

As they walked back to the office, Tamara asked him the question she had been reframing all morning.

'Do you think you could have a word with Lyra?'

He stopped in his tracks and looked at her sharply.

'What sort of word?'

'I just wanted a firmer briefing from her on this article. I've been trying to talk to her, phoning, sending messages, but she's impossible to get hold of. I thought you might mention it casually when you saw her at Morning Conference or a Features meeting.'

'What exactly do you expect me to say?'

'You know: "About that commission you've given my writer, Tamara Sim. She'd really like to know what angle you're looking for, exactly. Are you thinking more Hollywood? Love life? Or fancy arty friends? Or is it the war stuff you're after?"'

'I really don't think that would be very helpful.'

'Well, what do you suggest?'

He shook his head.

'Haven't the faintest.'

'I thought you knew her pretty well.'

'We've crossed paths, yes. Swords even.'

Had he made a pass at Lyra?

'Well, maybe you can advise me on the best way of approaching her.'

'Approaching her?'

Now she thought about it, Simon had been curiously unsupportive when Tamara had first told him about the *S*nday* commission. She knew that his time at *S*nday* had ended swiftly and badly with the Aurora Witherspoon debacle. Was he concerned that Lyra was trying to poach Tamara from *Psst!*? Surely he didn't see *S*nday* as a threat. Jealousy would be out of character. He had reservations about Tamara writing for *Me2*, concerned that Johnny would use her inside knowledge to plunder *Psst!* stories for his daily pages, but Simon had been generous to her. It was he who had first introduced her to Tim, brokering her Lucy Hartson exclusive and suggesting that she might do some shifts for the *Sunday Sphere*.

'I just need more clarification about what exactly Lyra wants on Honor Tait,' Tamara said.

'How much more clarification do you need? It's an interview, isn't it? Publicising a book? And if you can get the goods on the toyboys, you're looking at an exclusive everyone, not just *S*nday*'s toffs, will want a piece of. It's pretty elementary – hardly stem cell research.'

That was unfair. Tamara had spent most of the last year listening to the plot summary of his love life, an X-rated TV sitcom set in countless London flats and hotel rooms. Five minutes of his time was all she asked. Occasional advice on her career, in exchange for unflagging, non-judgemental attentiveness on the subject of his sexual adventures, that was the deal. That, and her solitary evenings spent forging receipts for his expenses claims.

'I just want to know what angle they'd like me to go on.'

They reached the pedestrian crossing opposite *The Monitor*. Simon seemed irritated as they waited for the lights to change.

'Just write it all up and leave out the boring bits.'

Tamara turned to him.

'Simon, please. You know this *S*nday* job means a lot to me.'

'I know. I know. Look, don't take Lyra's silence personally. You know she doesn't answer her messages – unless you're Austin Wedderburn or you've shaken hands with the King of Sweden.'

The lights changed and they started to cross.

'What if I just went up to the fifth floor, hung around her office until she was free and had a word with her in person?'

Simon's step faltered. He laid his hand on Tamara's arm. Was he restraining or reassuring her? Perhaps he was simply trying to steady himself after all that wine.

'No. I wouldn't do that, Tam, if I were you. Take it from me, any approach to the fifth floor could be counterproductive right now. Just get on with the piece. Go and see Lyra when it's done and dusted. Present it as an irresistible fait accompli.'

His pager bleeped as they walked into the building.

'Sorry. Just got to make a call.'

Eleven

The walls were decorated with bright frescoes, painted in a more deferential and stoical era, showing pink-cheeked maidens in virginal white ministering to the picturesque sick. Glimpsed through mullioned windows, a bucolic Olde England – towering elms, thatched cottages, cheerful labourers, sturdy children dancing round maypoles – beckoned the lovingly tended infirm back to health.

As Honor walked along the hospital corridors, late-twentieth-century reality played out in drab vignettes all around her. A woman in soiled overalls was ineffectually mopping the rusty smears – blood? viscera? excrement? – on the floors as nurses, not so young, some of them male, all tired and unkempt, few if any virginal, hurried by in what looked like pastel-hued nylon housecoats and slacks. They could have been chicken pluckers or fish gutters. And the sick? Like the old and the poor, they were never picturesque. Even ethereal consumptives, dying for love and too beautiful for this world, as the Romantics had it, coughed up gouts of blood and were reduced to double incontinence. Ill health was a great leveller. No one looked dignified in a dressing gown wired up to a drip, surrounded by the squalid clutter of convalescence and life support, the engorged bags of blood and saline solution, the bedpans and the sick bowls.

And Lois, beautiful clever Lois, was down among them now, her body racing to catch up with her disintegrating mind. Cancer. Of course. They said she was at her best in the morning, so here was Honor at 8 a.m. on Saturday, standing over her friend's hospital bed wondering what Lois's 'worst' would be like. Her eyes were open and remarkably clear. Open and unseeing. They scanned the ward, Honor's face, the nurse adjusting her drip, with what could have been mute amazement, like a newborn taking in the shifting shapes and shadows around its cot. Or it could have been simple animal restlessness, a meaningless flexing of the orbital muscle. Behind the inky blue depths, there was no sense of any intelligence.

From some corners of the ward there were occasional outbursts of muted merriment and – how Lois would have loathed this – the debilitating drone of a television set. Other visitors, husbands, dutiful adult children, families with unruly toddlers, came and went to neighbouring beds, bearing fruit and chocolates and flowers, wholesome emissaries from a promised land of peak health and cast-iron constitutions. Honor suspected that there was an element of display, triumphalism even, about this parade of robust family life, and the cheery greetings cards around the ward. Get Well Soon! Was there a greetings card to cover the other eventuality? Die Swiftly! Honor had come empty-handed and on her friend's bedside table there was only a stainless-steel kidney dish containing a used syringe. It occurred to Honor that, for form's sake, she should have brought the garish bunch of flowers – another one – that arrived this morning from the foolish reporter. Honor had thrown them straight down the chute. But Lois, if she still had her senses, would have loathed them too.

A nurse, a boy with pitted skin and an earring, came to check the drain that led from Lois's wound into a bottle below the bed.

'All right, Louise?' he said, and then he turned to Honor and winked. 'Doesn't understand a word we say, poor soul, but every so often she gives a little mumble.' He leaned over the bed again and Honor thought she saw her friend's eyes widen in terror as he added: 'Don't you, Lou darling?'

*

Tamara stowed her thesaurus, tape recorder, cuttings, notes and printouts of her early drafts of the *S*nday* article, along with Tait's two books, in a small backpack, and caught a tube to Maida Vale on Saturday morning. The jumbo bouquet of pink lilies, enough to fill a hearse, sent with an apologetic note to Holmbrook Mansions, had gone unacknowledged and Ruth Lavenham had not returned her calls. What else could Tamara do?

She had handled subterfuge at a far higher level, most successfully when she had snared the drug-taking son of the police chief. She had staked out the media-shy too, camping on the pavement for three days outside Caleb Hawkins' flat in Ladbroke Grove after the footballer had been secretly photographed holding hands with a transsexual at a gay nightclub. She had also been with the paparazzi when they had snapped Pernilla Perssen checking into a Hampshire rehab clinic. But Tamara's new assignment would not be straightforward door-stepping. There would be no foot stamping in the cold outside Honor Tait's mansion block, waiting to ambush her with a few questions. There would be no point in bringing a photographer along. There would be nothing to see. Not yet, anyway.

She paced the area that was to be her patch for the next three days, sizing up the small parade of shops and the pub, the Gut and Bucket, next door to the café where she had waited for Bucknell before the interview. The café would be her base. One of its vinyl tables, set at a wide window, gave a clear view directly across the road to the entrance of Holmbrook Mansions. But first, she needed to talk to a few locals. She crossed the road to the small supermarket and picked up a can of cola from the fridge. Sitting behind the till, the shopkeeper, so luminously pale and obese that he appeared to be crafted from melted candle wax, was breathing heavily and leafing through a tabloid.

'Been here long?' Tamara asked brightly.

'Since seven this morning.'

He yawned, illustrating the point.

'No. I mean the shop. How long has it been here?'

'Dunno. I only work here.'

'You must have lots of regulars. Customers, I mean.'

He looked up from the pages of his newspaper then stared at the drink in her hand.

'You paying for that, or what?'

She handed over the coins. There was no point in pushing it. She would build the rapport later. She walked back to the café. It was run by two middle-aged Eastern Europeans, brothers, she would have guessed: one genial, one sullenly preoccupied, both broad and moustached. Their business was not sufficiently brisk to require a high turnover of tables. Tamara smiled at them and they seemed happy to let her sit in a window seat, sipping at an infrequently replenished cup of weak coffee.

She opened her notebook and, occasionally turning her head to check on the main entrance of the mansion block, continued with her revisions.

Honor Tait doesn't like to talk about her background. This champion of the poor was born and raised in a big country house in Scotland. She is discreet about her past, preferring to talk about her work, but with her crisp English accent she's a House of Windsor sound-alike.

It was easy to get swept away with the prose. She accepted another grey coffee from the glum brother and gazed across the road at Holmbrook Mansions. There was not a lot going on. She could just make out the figure of the doorman, who seemed to be slumbering behind his desk in the foyer, his peaked cap tipped over his eyes.

Honor Tait, former Press Corps Golden Girl, was born
and raised in aristocratic splendour in Scotland. She is
discreet about her background, 'it's the work that matters',
but with her crisp upper-class English tones she could
plausibly read the Queen's Christmas Message if Her
Majesty ever threw a sickie.

Half an hour later, the doorman stirred. A woman, fiftyish,
brittly thin, wearing a silk headscarf knotted under her
chin, pushed through the revolving doors and picked her
way carefully down the wide stone steps into the street.
She hesitated, looking left and right, as if unsure of her
next move, then hurried away in the direction of the tube.

Honor Tait, friend of the stars, once the Marlene Dietrich
of the newsroom, would never be a GI's pin-up these
days, but, for all her years, she is still what Humphrey
Bogart would call a fine-looking woman. Under her
corrugated skin, the cheekbones, once no doubt rendered
in paint by artist lovers, are still visible, the hair, a
formerly lustrous strawberry blonde, now a handful of
white feathers scattered over the rosy dome of her scalp.

Outside the mansion block an elderly man, plump and
florid, in houndstooth check, walked up the steps into
the foyer.

Her voice testifies to a life of comfort, propriety and innu-
merable servants bustling about a grand stately home.

If the old bat refused to come across with the biographical details, she could not blame Tamara for taking a few poetic liberties, drawn from her familiarity with BBC costume dramas.

In this crepuscular world of governesses, hunt balls and muslin frocks, little Honor's ambitions must have seemed deeply transgressive.

Now the miserable brother was standing over her with a glass jug of vile coffee. She held out her cup and smiled. Perhaps she should order a sandwich to appease them.

At Honor Tait's hermetic mansion block, residents and visitors are clearly top drawer and strangely ageless. There, in her crepuscular fourth-floor apartment, the doyenne of journalists exerts a chthonic hold over her followers.

The smiling brother brought over her sandwich, a fibrous flap of chicken breast, garnished with a yellow pickle, which oozed like industrial effluent through the spongy casing of bread.

Residents and visitors alike have a timeless, unmistakeably patrician air at Holmbrook Mansions. She presides there, a secular guru, a gnostic of news, whose hermeneutic mission has been to carry the flickering candle of truth into the world's darkest corners.

She bit into her sandwich, then regretted it. Ah – the first sighting of someone under fifty. A small boy in a maroon cap and grey school uniform, like an extra from a made-for-TV heritage film. He was carrying a violin case and skipping down the steps accompanied by a sturdy teenager in a denim skirt, presumably his nanny. Neither, Tamara guessed, would be on nodding terms with Honor Tait. Somehow she could not imagine the old woman with children – they would be too chaotic, too noisy, too demanding. Tamara had some sympathy with this view. Gemma's pair of squabbling toddlers were always poking their grubby fingers into orifices – noses, mouths, bottoms, electrical sockets – while their mother looked on with an indulgent smile. Tamara had invited them round to her flat only once and it was like being besieged by a horde of unhygienic dwarves. It had taken weeks to clean the finger marks from the walls.

The good-natured brother was signalling to her.

'Delicious thanks,' she said, taking an enthusiastic bite of her sandwich and dabbing with a napkin at the yellow slime trickling down her chin.

Honor Tait maintains a tight-lipped silence on the subject of her background. Perhaps understandably, because this firebrand champion of the underprivileged was born and raised in a Scottish castle. With her crisp English accent she's the aural Doppelgänger of Her Majesty the Queen.

Reluctantly, and with a sense of grim duty, Tamara put aside her notes, opened Tait's first book and returned to the Pulitzer Prize-winning essay.

According to survivors I spoke to, once the air raid was over, guards and prisoners joined in a frantic scramble for surviving splinters, looking for souvenirs of that shattered tree. For the Nazis, those charred fragments represented the ancestral dream of German supremacy; to the prisoners, too, Goethe's Oak had assumed a sacred status. The shady bower where the poet, scientist, playwright, musician and novelist Johann Wolfgang von Goethe had sat and contemplated 'the kingdoms of the world, and their glories' had come to represent for the captives, even in their despair, the enlightened humanism of pre-Nazi Germany. And there it stands today, mutilated, in the midst of horror.

Exasperated, Tamara closed the book and turned back to her own work.

On the subject of her illustrious forebears, whose portraits glowered from the panelled wall of her ancestral castle in Scotland, Honor Tait maintains an omerta. But this silence itself is, perhaps, hermeneutic . . .

It was getting dark outside now and the smiling brother was lifting the chairs onto the tables while his moody brother swept the floors.

*She sits in the centre of the room like an empress,
surrounded by her courtiers. The brooding Jason Kelly,
fresh from his blockbuster screen triumph in* Faraway
Tree, *kneels adoringly at her feet. Ruth Lavenham,
publisher and earth mother, whips ups some exotic deli-
cacies in the kitchen. A loquacious Scot* . . .

If Tamara had not been so absorbed in her work at that
moment, she might have seen the bent figure of an old
woman walking slowly up the steps and through the doors
of Holmbrook Mansion.

In the café, the shutters were lowered and the miserable
brother rang up the till and counted out the cash. Tamara
paid her bill, adding a generous tip, and they handed her
two blank receipts. She would be back.

*

It was dark when Honor got home. She switched on the
wireless. Bach. Like Inigo's smile, Bach's music was a
sound barometer of Honor's emotional weather. In spells
of good cheer, she thought the partitas and fugues, even
the inventions, offered rational mortals the most persua-
sive glimpse of paradise they were ever likely to be granted.
On darker days, the keyboard pieces could sound as trite
and mechanical as a child's music box: a hellish hurdy-
gurdy. She turned off the radio. Silence was preferable.
But she felt an urge to talk, to describe today's hospital
visit, to describe the Lois she had known and in describing

her, to bring her back to life. Honor poured a glass and reached for her address book. So many names crossed out, some excised by the attrition of feuds and fallings-out, so many arbitrarily annulled by death. One day soon the book would be as obsolete as its owner.

And her Boys? Ideally, Honor liked to see them singly, to eke them out. That way she could maximise her pleasures – have each one all to herself – and minimise any treacherous sub-alliances. They fought each other for the scraps of her approval, knowing that there would never be enough to go around, and she encouraged their competitiveness. The idea that they might talk about her in her absence, pity her, laugh about her, have fun without her, was loathesome to her. Though she had no concept of an afterlife, she sometimes imagined that death would be like this: lying mute and immobile, listening to the muffled sounds of a merry party next door.

There would be tears, at first. Ruth might wail the loudest. She had the physique and dress sense of a professional mourner, the beefy Greek chorus sort, born to hurl herself, shrieking, over the passing coffins of strangers. Bobby would sob more fastidiously and lean on his latest young friend for support, and Inigo would weep into a large silk handkerchief and drink too much – 'If you can't binge at a dear friend's funeral,' she could hear him saying, 'when can you?' Aidan would be silent and inconsolable, shrugging away his frightful boyfriend, while Clemency would probably set up a trust fund in her name: The Tait Award For Young Journalists. Honor shuddered. And

Paul? Well, Paul was like her. She could see him facing news of her death with virile gravity. But tears? She doubted if he had ever shed them in his life.

There would be the respectfully inaccurate obituaries and a memorial service, in which weeping false friends, distant associates and old rivals – who would claim victory at last by simply outliving her – would utter humbug from the pulpit about her exemplary integrity and professionalism. She had no illusions, least of all on the question of mortality. Soon, even to her regular intimates, her Boys, the Monday Club, she would be reduced to an amusing anecdote, a murmur of regret and, with time, would become the butt of black humour. Inigo, she suspected, would crack the first post-mortem joke and the others would laugh with gratitude and relief. Then the party would go on, without her. It might even be jollier in her absence.

Only now it occurred to her that the person she really wanted to talk to about today's hospital visit was Lois herself. She closed her address book and picked up her pen. Despair could be as good a provocation to work as any. While she still had her wits, she must write her coda.

Buchenwald, 14 April 1945. Liberation Day Four. Still in the striped uniforms of the concentration camp, the survivors lined up by the shattered stump of Goethe's Oak to celebrate their freedom, each holding a makeshift national flag. They had came to celebrate, but also to grieve for their fellow prisoners who did not survive the brutal regime. Many wept silently, and some of their liberators, the soldiers of the American Third Army, who had seen the evidence of Nazi barbarity with their own eyes, wept with them.

*

In the acrid warmth of the pub, where the staff and patrons were gaping glitter-eyed at a football game on a vast TV set, Tamara ordered a large gin and tonic and took it outside. This vantage point was going to be a lot less comfortable but she could put another tape in her recorder and use it to dictate her copy.

I ask about her childhood and the octogenarian Honor Tait, once known as 'the high IQ in a low-cut gown', fixes me with a basilisk stare. She maintains a chilly omerta on the subject of her childhood, spent in a rambling Scottish castle. This champion of the world's down-trodden spent her early years waited on hand and foot by servants and, with her crisp English accent, she's Her Majesty the Queen's sound-alike twin . . .

At 11 p.m., as the pub closed, it started to rain. She had not brought an umbrella and her tape recorder was getting wet. She stowed it in her backpack and moved across the road to stand sentinel outside Holmbrook Mansions. The foyer seemed ghostly in the bluish light. The doorman was sleeping again.

Twelve

Honor finally rose from her bed at 7.30 a.m. on Monday, drew back the curtains and, if she was not quite ready to embrace the day, felt more prepared to face it than she had been when she closed the curtains on Saturday, after visiting Lois. She had not stirred from the flat for the rest of the weekend, turned off the phone, cleared out more junk, ate half a packet of oatcakes and drank one and a half bottles of vodka. Clemency would tut over the empties.

Now she bathed to the sound of Radio 3 – some playful harpsichord music by Rameau – and dressed in her silk-lined grey skirt and mulberry cashmere cardigan; their softness against her skin was pleasing, a kind of intimacy. The radio news came on. What had she missed? Not much. Labour pledging a national trust for culture in the event of their election victory; a former soldier charged with the murder of his missing stepdaughter; accusations of 'ageism' at the BBC made by middle-aged male presenters. She reconnected the telephone and checked her diary in the hall. Yes, her Wimpole Street appointment was at 9 a.m. No breakfast was the stipulation. This suited her. And then there was the lunch. She must steel herself.

*

Tamara was in the window seat on her third cup of coffee. Today was her last chance – she could not afford to take more unpaid leave from *Psst!* – and, after spending Sunday in the same café without a single sighting of Honor Tait, she had dragged herself to Maida Vale at an absurdly early hour on Monday anticipating a third day of fruitless observation. Even the good-humoured brother had muttered ungraciously when she walked through the café door at 8 a.m. She would have to order another sandwich, and the prospect depressed her further as she stared blankly out of the window.

When it finally happened, she thought for a moment that it was a mirage, conjured by hope. She wiped the misted window and looked again. Honor Tait! There she was, emerging from Holmbrook Mansions at 8.30 on Monday morning. Tamara leapt up, scattered some change on the table, turned up the collar of her coat and ran into the street. She need not have hurried. The old lady was still standing on the pavement, timorously scanning the road, looking as tiny and vulnerable as a child who had slipped her mother's hand. Tamara slowed her pace, keeping to the opposite pavement, and stopped outside the estate agent's on the corner. There she pretended to examine photographs of expensive flats while keeping an eye on her target, reflected in the shop window. Suddenly, the old woman raised her arm. A black taxi came into view and stopped. As the old woman stepped into it, Tamara scanned the road for one of her own. She was in luck. It swerved obligingly into the kerb and she got in, indicated Honor Tait's cab, idling at traffic lights 100 yards down the road and, shrinking from the cliché – but what else could she say? – commanded: 'Follow that taxi!'

The driver shot her a quizzical look in the rear-view mirror. The traffic lights were in their favour, delaying Honor Tait long enough for Tamara to catch up.

'What's your game?' he asked.

'Game?'

She craned her neck to keep sight of the other cab, which had shot ahead.

'Tax inspector? Disability fraud investigator?'

'No. No. I'm a journalist.'

'A story! Used to be in the print myself. Old Fleet Street. Happy days.'

Soon they were in the Marylebone Road.

'Ever drink in the Stab in the Back?' he asked.

'No.'

'You missed yourself there, love,' he said, shaking his head at memories of better times, as he nipped between a couple of idling Routemasters.

'We're losing them!' she said.

He cut up a post office van and the other taxi was back in view.

'Keep your hair on, Sherlock.'

At the next set of lights they drew alongside Honor Tait's taxi and Tamara shrank into her seat. Her cabbie wound down his window and gestured to the other driver.

'All right, John?'

'Yeah. Not so bad.'

Honor Tait's strained little face was clearly visible, staring ahead at the broad neck of her cabbie. Tamara, pressing herself against the far door, slid further down the seat.

'Haven't seen you down the clubhouse in months.'

'Rotator cuff tendonitis been playing up.'

'Tough one. You want to watch that. Can lead to excessive anterior translation of your humerus head.'

'Got an ultrasound Monday. Checking for calcification.'

'Nasty. Could play havoc with your follow-through.'

The lights changed and both taxis turned companionably in parallel into Harley Street and then into Wimpole Street. There, Tamara's driver finally had the wit to hold back, waving on his colleague with a genial, 'Be Lucky!' Tait's taxi pulled in thirty yards ahead, outside a grand house with wide stone steps and two prim topiary trees flanking double doors.

'Here's fine,' Tamara said, watching the old woman mount the steps and ring the bell.

As soon as Tait disappeared inside, Tamara paid her driver, giving him a generous tip.

'You're in luck, Sherlock,' he said, handing her a book of blank receipts. 'I usually charge extra for undercover work.'

The double door was black and glossy, framed by strips of bevelled glass whose facets sparkled in the winter sunlight. The polished brass door knob was as big as a cantaloupe. Tamara squinted through the glass into the entrance hall. It was tiled in black and white like a chessboard, and she could make out the curved wooden banisters of a stone staircase. Outside, to the right of the door, was an entryphone with a brass name-plate, engraved with the perplexing consonant clusters that declared this was a warren of private doctors' consulting rooms.

She made a note of the names and initials: Professor Hereward Browning MBChB FRCS(Plast); Miss Isabella Kerr MBBS FRCS(Glas); Rose A. McCotter MBBS FRCS(OFMS); Dr Didier Mooney MBChB FRCP; Mr F. Bose Dch DGM FRCOG; Mr Eliot J. Tregunter BDS FDSRCS.

Now, all Tamara had to do was wait. As she turned from the door an elderly woman in a fur coat, her snowy hair as stiffly peaked as meringue, brushed past her with a lofty tilt of the head and pressed the buzzer for Professor Browning. Another candidate for cosmetic surgery, innately hostile to the young and attractive.

There was something especially repugnant about these ancient women who allowed white-coated mercenaries to dismantle and rearrange their faces, like tailors altering an ill-fitting suit. All the pain, the blood, the bruising, the money. And for what? No one would actually fancy them, no matter how much surplus skin had been sheared off or fat had been sucked out. They were beyond desire. Their own, or other people's. They should take up lace making, cultivate their grandchildren, or their gardens. They had had their go; it was someone else's turn. My turn, thought Tamara.

It was not entirely rational, but she could not help thinking that the visible effects of extreme old age – the withered skin, the drooping jowls and shrivelled lips – were the result of simple carelessness. The crones had not paid attention. They had let themselves go. Though discipline was not her strongest suit, Tamara was scrupulous about her beauty regime. She cleansed, toned and moisturised regularly, and never left the flat without applying factor 15 sunblock. Honor Tait was reaping the consequences of a lifetime's negligence – Tamara guessed the old woman had never used sunscreen and had probably washed her face with soap and water all her life.

Across the road, a smaller, shabbier and vaguely municipal building, a visa office for a former Eastern bloc country, would serve as an observation post. They were not exactly queuing up here. Tamara leaned against the wrought-iron railings bordering the steps and got out her notebook.

Honor Tait's face is a palimpsest of experience. Beneath the folds and wrinkles conferred by her extended existence that no amount of cosmetic surgery can ever quite eliminate, there are the remnants of the glamour girl, the high IQ in a low-cut gown who charmed her way to some of the greatest scoops of the last century.

*

As she lay on the bed and closed her eyes, Honor considered the pain to come. There had been many worse pains, psychic and physical. And in the scale of things – say, compared to the sufferings of an average citizen of sub-Saharan Africa – her travails were nothing. Less than a pinprick. To make the comparison was an indulgence. No, she did not feel calm in the face of this little laceration. She was anticipating it with pleasure. At least her neural pathways were in working order, unlike those of poor Lois. Prick me and I will bleed, and I will also wince with pain. She welcomed the insults to her body as a reminder that she was alive and of this world. Pain was also an apt punishment for the cowardly impulse that had brought her here, rather than to the workhouse democracy of an NHS clinic. The cost was preposterous. For the same sum, she could have supplied clean water to an African village for a year, financed 300 eye operations for the third-world blind, funded a small field hospital in Kurdish Iraq. Perhaps she should have foregone the anaesthetic altogether. She deserved to suffer. But it was too late.

Mr Bose, in mask and gloves, leaned in on her, his implements glinting in the overhead surgery lights. His eyes, their lashes fluttering above the starched yashmak, looked startlingly girlish.

'Are you ready for this, Miss Tait?'

She nodded.

Pain. This is how it begins, the brutal clamour of life. And how it ends.

Thirteen

Lulled by boredom after three and a half hours, Tamara did not immediately recognise the small figure pausing in the doorway of the surgery. She was wearing unseasonal dark glasses and her scarf cocooned her face in the style of an incognito Fifties starlet. She was unsteady, too, grasping the railings as she descended the steps to the street. She regained her poise – whatever procedure she had undergone, it must have been comparatively minor – and walked, slowly but purposefully, towards Wigmore Street, passing Tamara on the opposite pavement without turning her head.

Tamara had to slow her pace, in a careful game of grandmother's footsteps, to avoid overtaking Tait and was led, fifteen minutes later, down a narrow side street to the exterior of a small Italian restaurant. As Tait went inside, Tamara hovered by the window, pretending to examine the framed menu while watching the stooped figure, still wearing sunglasses, talking by the door to a waiter. The restaurant was cramped and obligingly overlit. The waiter led the old woman to a table in the corner.

If she moved closer to the window, Tamara would have a clear view of it. Someone was waiting for Honor Tait. He was in his early thirties, shabbily bohemian – faded denims, fashionably unkempt hair, creased linen jacket – and there was something familiar about him. Was he one of the Monday Club? One of her writers? Tamara shaded her eyes and pressed herself against the window. No. Too good-looking to be an intellectual, too dark and curly-headed to be Jason Kelly. Another actor? He rose to greet the old woman, who took off her scarf and sunglasses and accepted his embrace stiffly. As they sat down he reached for a bottle of red wine and poured her a glass. It was then, with a cardiac jolt, that Tamara recognised him: the handsome hero of the Strict and Particular hall.

Was it for this encounter, and others like it, that Honor Tait had endured scalpel and stitches? Today's visit to the cosmetic surgeon must have been one of many similar visits, an express repair – a quick stitch – or perhaps a preliminary consultation before a major refit. They were leaning towards each other, talking intently, when the waiter reappeared with his pad. The frail octogenarian – looking, from Tamara's vantage point, no more youthful than she had done at their interview – glanced at the menu, a glossy card the size of a tabloid, and raised her glass to her lips. The old woman's chief interest was not the cuisine. Her companion was still deliberating, massaging his forehead, lips pursed, as the waiter impatiently jiggled his pen. Finally, they gave their orders and, alone again, began to talk, huddled together, their profiles almost touching, the sculpted angles and planes of his face an unkind contrast to the collapsed asymmetry of hers.

Their exchange was quick-fire and fervent, then the old woman pulled away from him and leaned back in her seat, silent, as he continued to talk. There was something of the eco-warrior about him; a cleaned-up, Armani version of those tunnelling protestors who'd just been evicted from the Devon road protest. His brow was furrowed and his animated features suggested anger or complaint. It was hard to read Honor Tait's expression as she suddenly reached down for her handbag. Now he was silent, watching her, pushing back his hair with his fingers, as she produced a brown envelope, which she slid across the table. He opened it and rifled through a thick sheaf of banknotes. Then he closed the envelope, put it in his jacket pocket and took a quick swig from his glass.

Tamara's eyes widened. 'Yes!' she whispered. This was better than she could have hoped for. The old woman's body language, intimate and defensive, and the intensity of the conversation, did not suggest that she was here to pay her builder on the quiet, VAT-free, for a new bath-room suite. What other services could a freakishly good-looking young man plausibly provide to a lonely old woman that would merit a discreet lunch and cash-stuffed envelopes?

The waiter returned to the table with a plate of pasta for Tait's companion. She had settled for a bowl of soup.

Fluids only for the post-operative plastic surgery patient, Tamara wrote.

He was talking again. Honor Tait listened, immobile, her lips parted, as if breathing in his words, then she reached across the table and stroked his fingers. He looked from her face to her hand. He must be feeling disgust, Tamara thought, but he let her crabbed claw rest there. A corner of the envelope was just visible in his jacket pocket. It could not be plainer. He leaned towards the old woman and gave her a complicit smile.

'Make your mind up, love.'

Tamara started. It was the waiter, standing in the doorway with a gingham cloth over his arm.

'Do you want lunch?' he asked. 'Or are you going to move away and let someone else take a look at the menu?'

She stammered an apology and walked down the street to the doorway of a piano showroom. From here she still had a view of the restaurant entrance. The waiter stood scrutinising her for a moment longer then shook his head and went inside.

After fifty fretful minutes, Tamara was rewarded. The pair emerged into the silvery winter light, and there it was: proof. He bent his face to Honor Tait's and Tamara thrilled to see her story confirmed. He had pocketed the money and now this striking young man was kissing his eighty-year-old benefactress full on the lips.

The truth was revealed – 'through patient observation, the meticulous accumulation of detail and a ravening hunger for truth' – just as Honor Tait said it would be.

They stood, the oddest of couples, talking intently and then, as if suddenly aware of being watched, they parted. The old woman walked towards Oxford Circus while he turned and headed in the opposite direction.

Tamara felt a leap of dismay. She had to let one of them go. But which one? Of course. She should go after him. She needed to know who he was, where he lived. How he made a living, she had a pretty good idea. She had to talk to him. Without him there would be no story. Honor Tait could wait. By the time Tamara had caught up with him in Marylebone High Street, he was stepping into a taxi. And this time, there was no other cab in sight. She cursed herself as he was driven off, who knows where. She had let the key player in the story slip away. Perhaps Honor Tait's lunchtime envelope had been a final settlement, severance pay, and neither of them would ever see him again.

*

Honor let herself into her flat. The moment of relief at arriving home was fleeting. Her flat was dark and cold, more sepulchre than sanctuary. She hung her coat behind the door and went straight to the kitchen to fetch a drink. Now the pain was kicking in – the physical pain, which had been temporarily diverted by the other sort. And sleep would be impossible. She had generated an overdraft of sleep over the weekend. Chastened and scarified, she had emerged from Mr Bose's suite, after a light doze induced by local anaesthesia, longing for nothing more than to lie down in a darkened room. But the lunch had to be got through.

To yearn for something and yet to fear it. Love – in its fiercest and most destructive form – could be like that. Childbirth too, she supposed. For the foreign correspondent in an overlooked region, the local skirmish that becomes an international war brings guilty exultation. The higher the body count, the bigger the story, the greater the glory. And the personal engagement with death? You could want that, too, seek it out, the infinite peace, while fearing the moments of terror you know will precede it.

The restaurant had been brash and uncomfortable. But if it had been the *Galerie des Glaces* at Versailles, the effect would have been the same. It had all faded away; the setting, the other diners, the clatter and murmurs. He was all she had seen and heard. His beautiful face, though webbed by a faint tracery of lines, was still beautiful. He still had his curls, though there was now an early frost of grey at the temples. She had suppressed the urge to touch him, to gently push his hair from his face. He was not in bad shape either. A little leaner, maybe, more weathered. More manly. But not drawn and devastated, as she had feared. He was fit and handsome, heading towards louche middle age. And where did that leave her? Where, precisely, was she heading?

'Let's get business out of the way first.'

His first words to her. Had his voice, still sweetly

resonant, acquired a demotic tinge, an elision of consonants, which she had not picked up on the phone? He could never quite conceal the unfashionable patrician accent conferred by a costly education. He must have really worked at it, but he could never shake off the mantle of privilege, the public schoolboy's permanent ermine.

She had ordered soup – it was pleasant to use her Italian again, even for this simple transaction – to keep him company as he forked his way through a plate of pasta. And, as he talked, that familiar threnody of complaint, she found herself, irrationally, longing to be sitting with him under a hot blue Italian sky, at a harbourside restaurant in some chic little port.

The darkness of the flat was not helping her mood. She went to the window and looked down on the scrubby disc of garden, where one of her neighbours, a senior civil servant, was averting his face, arm outstretched, as his terrier strained at its lead and squatted to defecate in the hellebores. There was a sudden incongruously blithe clamour of birdsong. The leafless trees usually harboured only wheezing pigeons – shabby vagrants who would, if they could, badger passers-by with requests for spare change – but these were songbirds. What had lured them here, of all places, when they could be nesting in the oaks of the Tarn, or the chestnut woods of Monte Falterona, or even among the spectral beeches of Ettersberg? Spring was a long way off. Were they – blackbirds? thrushes? – serenading lovers or warning off rivals?

How strange it was that it should be here, in glum

London, that she had ended up. 'End' was the word. It could have been Rome. Or Paris. Or New York. It was in postwar Berlin, improbably, where she had been happiest, living in unexpectedly festive comfort after the privations of war, in a requisitioned lakeside villa with a cellar of good wine and a German cook. She had shared the villa with two Americans, who introduced her to the witty young interpreter Lois Meyer, and the rivalries and intrigues of the press corps had been innocent variations of the greater game of deadly realpolitik playing out around them.

She switched on the light and the portrait of Tad sprang into relief on the rosewood table. 'For all its bleakness,' he had said once, 'London is more accommodating to its old, particularly its female old, than New York or Paris.'

There was some truth in that, though at the time she had disliked his assumption that she would ever belong to that particular interest group. Since then, she had seen wealthy women of her own age in Paris and New York, living alone (except perhaps for an odious small dog), wearing couture designed for girls a third of their age, hair curled or wigged, glossy as a vinyl doll's, and under it their faces, after years of intervention, as taut as Munch's *Scream*, the embodiment of affluent urban fear: death's heads in designer wear. Perhaps there were simply better cosmetic surgeons in London. What did it matter? If he had been shocked by her deterioration today, he was not letting on. So much to talk about, so little to say.

Enough. Old age was a discrete dystopia; there was nothing communal about it, no shared experience. It was your own personalised, monogrammed hell. In London or Limavaddy, Paris or Poughkeepsie, your sixties and seventies were bad enough, but beyond that you were trapped like a wasp in a bottle, alone and raging, with the world outside a swirl of colour and distant noise.

Buchenwald, 14 April 1945. Liberation Day Four. I watched the camp survivors, still in their prison uniforms, line up by the shattered stump of Goethe's Oak to celebrate their freedom and mourn their fellow prisoners who did not survive the brutal regime. Many wept silently, and some of their liberators, the soldiers of the American Third Army, who had seen the evidence of Nazi barbarity with their own eyes, wept with them.

I left the camp to gather my thoughts, and walked alone in the woods outside the perimeter fence . . .

Fourteen

Celebrity Cellulite was the theme. Tamara spent an undemanding morning looking through the picture library's shiny haul: photographs of off-duty models, actresses and singers, including two Spice Girls, Lucy Hartson, Liselotte Selsby and Pernilla Perssen, wearing short skirts or swimwear which revealed, in close-up, an unsightly dimpling of thighs and buttocks. The pictures of Liselotte had to be spiked because of her connection with *The Monitor* but, even so, there were enough pictures of flaccid female flesh to fill a double-page feature. As Tamara showed the results of her morning's work to Simon, Tania walked by and looked over their shoulders at the vibrant paste-up centre spread, with its bold headline set at a cheeky angle: ROCK BOTTOM! STARS AND THE CURSE OF CELLULITE! Tania groaned and walked on.

'Just a bit of fun, Tania!' Simon called out to her retreating back. 'Prig,' he muttered, when she was out of hearing.

'Actually, it's more than fun,' Tamara said. 'It has an important social purpose, too.'

'Oh yeah? How's that then?'

'I'm serious,' she said. 'By demonstrating that even the most glamorous stars, without the airbrush, are flawed, it makes ordinary women feel better about themselves. It's kind of levelling, like communism.'

'Hmm. Sounds like you've been spending too much time in the company of Honor Tait's pals. How's all that going anyway?'

'Not bad. Not bad at all.'

'Want to tell me all about it over lunch?'

Half an hour later, in their booth at the Bubbles, Tamara gave a swift summary of last week's Kids' Crusaders meeting, and described the enigmatic figure at the back of the hall.

Simon was puzzled.

'Didn't you tell me about this meeting already?'

'Yes, but I missed out the bit about this fantastically handsome latecomer.'

'Okay,' Simon said, reaching for his pager. 'So you fancied him? And then he disappears? Shame for you, on a bad night out, I can see that. But I'm not getting much of a picture of Honor Tait here.'

'Wait . . .'

Tamara, too excited to eat, gripped the edge of the table and described what she had seen in the restaurant. Simon did not interrupt, even when his pager went off. Keeping his eyes fixed on hers, he silenced the machine, put down his panini and reached for his glass.

'The old hypocrite!' he said finally. 'She's toast. A cradle-snatching, toyboy-humping, gigolo's pay mistress. What a story! Deep smut and high culture – an unbeatable combination.'

In the warm glow of the bar's simulated candlelight, Tamara felt anointed, illuminated by success, as Simon signalled for another bottle to celebrate and, when he diverted the conversation to Serena (on again) and accepted a call from Jan (a question of table decorations), she smiled benignly. It was the most convivial few hours she'd had in weeks.

Their walk back to the office was high-spirited and unsteady and her attempt to generate an A-List stock-pile, a stash that she could call on when time was pressing, was unproductive. She sketched out a few themes – Fashion Faux Pas, Ugly Babies, Tiffs 'n' Rifts – and ransacked the picture library to illustrate them but, though the research was diverting, when she actually tried to compile the lists she found them strangely taxing.

As the afternoon wore on, however, the effects of the wine receded and the office sprang into focus. There were seditious stirrings in her gut and her right temple was throbbing. She longed to lie down. Simon was suddenly at her shoulder.

'One other thing, Tam. Valentine's Day on Friday week.'

This was cruel, particularly from Simon, who would regard a night in with his wife as a night spent alone and would have to draw lots to determine his Valentine's Day date. She bristled, before she realised he was talking about work.

'Think we'd better slip something on the love theme in the issue this Saturday,' he said.

'Of course. Celebrity Snogs do the trick?'

She shuffled a stack of photos of kissing couples. It was remarkable, the infinite variations of that simple human gesture, and what an unhygienic exchange of bodily fluids it looked to the non-participant. She yawned and glanced down at the patch of carpet tiles on the floor under her desk. Would anyone notice if she slipped under there and stretched out for half an hour? She could use a couple of padded postal bags as pillows. Fifteen minutes would do it. But Courtney was giving her a look of bottomless loathing and Tania was prowling their corner of the office, on the lookout for transgressions of taste.

Courtney's departure at 6 p.m. would normally be the signal for Tamara to put on her jacket and head out, perhaps with a brief diversion to the Bubbles before going home. Tonight, all she wanted was a lie-down with a cold compress on her forehead and a bucket by her bed. Instead, she faced another demanding night's work. Truth was a hard taskmistress, and the possibility of another sighting of Honor Tait's plaything was an irresistible incentive.

The party was well underway when she arrived at the Rodel Gallery, tucked at the end of a quiet cul-de-sac off Old Compton Street. The press of bodies spilled into the gallery's shopfront window, and from the street you could be mistaken for thinking that the revellers, rather than the paintings, were for sale. And what would you bid for this lot? A large woman in bright ethnic prints, her earrings swinging like chandeliers against her jowls, loomed over a small man with dark ringed eyes who was cowering like a cornered marmoset. Wedged in behind a framed cartoon, which depicted two dishevelled, bare-bottomed schoolboys joyfully administering canes to each other, a faded roué in a velvet suit and a beret – an artist, clearly – was thoughtfully rolling the stem of his wineglass between his fingers. He nodded gravely as an ancient buccaneer in an eye patch gesticulated with ink-stained hands. Another artist. Or maybe a critic. The place must be full of them.

As she pushed open the door and made her way through the noisy crowd, Tamara felt giddy at the thought of so much pretentiousness crammed into such a confined space. Intuition, and sickening thirst, led her through the crush to a small table at the back of the gallery where a harassed boy in shirtsleeves was pouring wine. She took a glass of white, gulped it down, held it out for a refill and then forced her way into the throng.

Though little old ladies appeared to be out in force tonight, along with lecherous old men – she was sure she felt a hand lingering on, if not actively caressing, her rump – she could not see Honor Tait. Tamara recognised the artist, Inigo Wint, flushed, animated and mobbed by admirers, in the centre of the room. The Scottish poet was there, too, buttonholing a man wearing glasses with such thick frames that he looked like a welder on emergency call-out. A group of young girls in skimpy party frocks, publicity girls presumably, huddled in another corner, giggling like a crowd of sixth-formers at a school dance. No sign of the brooding gigolo. Tamara's disappointment was not simply professional.

Slowly, keeping to the walls, she circumnavigated the room. There was more space there; in fact, there seemed to be a *cordon sanitaire* around the exhibits. Everyone was avoiding them, as if to do otherwise would be bad manners. Tamara studied the pictures closely: more schoolboys doing unspeakable things – oral sex, dope smoking, bondage – in primary colours. Might there be a story in this? In her weekly paper days, she had wrung a front-page lead out of the local students' rag week magazine, the usual compendium of puerile cartoons and obscene jokes, sold in aid of charity and paid for by adverts from local shops and businesses. In a slow news week, she had taken the trouble to ring round all the advertisers. She had a hunch that none of them – all civic-minded members of the local Chamber of Commerce – had actually read the magazine.

'So, Mr Higgins, could you tell us your views, as a "long-established high street family butcher", on the subject of bestiality? . . . Sexual congress between humans and animals? . . . You're against it? . . . Strongly? . . . I just wondered about your decision to place an advert on page sixteen, just opposite the joke about the lonely sheep farmer and his obliging flock.'

The advertisers withdrew their money, the rag week

was cancelled, the student editors were suspended from college and Tamara's front-page bylined story attracted brief national interest and a jokey aside from Chris Evans on *The Big Breakfast*.

Similarly, she could, if she had the time, track down the Rodel Gallery's sponsors, past and present (there was always corporate money behind commercial arts organisations, even if it was only the local off-licence providing free booze), and ask them whether they endorsed cannabis, bondage and underage sex. The *Mail* would snap it up. The prospect of mischief enlivened her further and she waved at the boy with the wine.

Raised voices and a flurry of action by the door alerted Tamara to the arrival of Ruth Lavenham and, behind her, Honor Tait on the arm of Paul Tucker. The crowd parted deferentially before them. Using her elbows like oars to make her way through the reconfiguring mob, Tamara advanced towards Tait's group. Inigo Wint was kissing and fussing over the *grande dame*, as if she were the artist and this was her party. They were joined by the poet and the glum Twisk heiress. As Tamara squeezed her way into the inner circle, she was startled by the sight of Tania Singh gliding towards them through the crowd, a killer shark in a silk sheath. What did she want? Was this part of her networking strategy? She ignored Tamara and headed straight for Inigo Wint, congratulating him loudly on his 'groundbreaking exhibition'. Next, in an expert move worthy of a chess grandmaster, Tania homed in on Honor Tait, blocking Tamara's route to the old woman. Tamara was going to have to wait her turn.

A teenage girl in braids and braces was forcing her way through the party with a tray of canapés. The guests surveyed the food – grey paste and sliced green olives on diamonds of toast, mashed egg and parsley in pallid pastry cups, asparagus spears peeking obscenely from pink cylinders of compressed meat – as they might a questionably attributed work of art, and continued their conversations without a pause.

Tania's moment with Honor Tait was over and she was now expressing her admiration for the poet. But Tait's little upturned face was still receiving kisses, and her right hand was still bestowing benedictions. Tamara took her place in the queue and absently grabbed a canapé from the tray. She raised the savoury lozenge to her lips and, as she took an exploratory bite, the scent of fish paste reached her nostrils. She felt a sudden swell of nausea and spat the mouthful, as discreetly as possible, into her hand along with the uneaten remains of the gobbet. But it was too late. The swell, just above her solar plexus, became a wave, alarmingly crested with flecks of foam, and was in danger of becoming a geyser. She had two thoughts: the first, how to get rid of the horrible mush in her hand; the second, more urgent, could she get out of there before disgracing herself?

Some Samaritan had anticipated her problem and was offering a perfect receptacle: an outstretched hand. Tamara dropped the unpleasant mush into the kindly cupped palm before rushing for the door.

As she retched, exhausted, in the street outside, she became aware of a figure loitering in the shadows by the entrance to the gallery. She looked up to see Honor Tait's lunchtime companion staring into the window. If only Tamara had not been feeling so ill, this would have been her moment. She would have leaped on him and guided him to a wine bar round the corner for a long chat, beneficial to them both, and a couple of bottles of champagne (expenses would cover it). He turned away from the window and was walking towards her. Here was her chance. But her stomach had not done with her yet. She doubled over once more and heaved loudly as he walked past her towards the night-time crowds of Old Compton Street.

It was then that she heard the approaching click of stilettos on cobblestones. Wiping her mouth on her sleeve, she was startled to see that the sharp-suited silhouette stepping round her and making its way into the gallery belonged to Lyra Moore. Had she recognised Tamara? This would not be the moment to return to the party and press the editor of S*nday to expand on her commissioning requirements. Vomiting in a gutter was not the conventional precursor to a serious conversation with a prospective boss. Tamara wondered whether she could invent a pregnancy as a plausible excuse. But then pregnancy, she remembered, entailed *morning* sickness.

To return to the gallery was out of the question and her quarry, Honor Tait's gigolo, had eluded her. At least the abasement of nausea had passed, but as she turned into Old Compton Street she confronted a new horror.

Of course! The outstretched hand! Her perceptions in the last fifteen minutes had been distorted by physical turmoil. Now, as her stomach settled, the mirage was clearing, but in its place was something far worse. The Samaritan's hand had been wormy with veins, swollen-knuckled and arthritic. The hand of an old woman. It was Honor Tait who had offered her palm to Tamara. Honor Tait, kissed and fussed over to full mutual satisfaction by her groupies, had magnanimously extended her hand in greeting to the next person queuing to pay court. Tamara was meant to shake that hand, not fill it with bread and fish paste.

*

In the end it had been, as Honor had anticipated, another futile evening. The gallery had been too crowded and she had endured much jostling and fawning. Her feelings about finding herself once more, so many years after her prime, an object of popular curiosity and affection, were no longer so ambivalent. Age had conferred on her an unfamiliar aura of sanctity. She was, said Inigo after the *South Bank Show*, and an approach – rebuffed – by the producers of *Desert Island Discs*, in danger of becoming a National Treasure. And she didn't like it one bit. At the gallery, an importunate Asian girl had detained her with overweeningly respectful details of her personal response to *Dispatches*, then Honor had turned from her, relieved, to shake another hand, only to find her palm inexplicably filled with a mound of foul-smelling grey paste. The donor of this disgusting offering, whom Honor recognised only as she turned and left the gallery without a word, was the dim young woman who had interviewed her for *The Monitor* and had later come to supper uninvited. Was it some kind of joke? Was Tara Sim's real mission not to profile her but to insult her?

Honor had insisted on leaving immediately and was then obliged to sit through a dismal meal between Inigo, inflated as a dirigible with first-night grandiosity, and Aidan, spraying caustic asides over Inigo's boasts like a crazed tail gunner. Ruth was unable to persuade Paul to stay beyond the first course: he had a story to file. And how Honor had wished, as he scraped back his chair and rushed self-importantly to the waiting taxi, that it had been she who was fleeing this table – the smeared wine-glasses, the blasted landscape of soiled china and half-eaten food, the ring of tired familiar faces, the din of small talk and mindless conviviality rising from it like noxious fumes – and rushing off to deliver her account of grave matters, of war and strife, hunger and pestilence.

Alone in her flat, she poured a drink. She was not done yet. No one was clamouring for it, but she had one more piece to file.

Buchenwald, 14 April 1945. Liberation Day Four. As I walked alone outside the perimeter fence of the camp, I was alerted by a sound in the undergrowth. I heard him before I saw him.

Fifteen

Pernilla Perssen was back on the bottle. She was photographed in the early hours of the morning, puking outside a nightclub in the West End, hair tumbling over her face, looking up at the camera with a perplexed squint. That settled the question of this week's A-List: Losers and Boozers – Top Ten Rehab Write-Offs. Caleb Hawkins, recently suspended from his Premier League side, and Tod Maloney would also make an appearance. Tamara just had time to put in a quick call to Ruth Lavenham before Simon got back from Morning Conference. There was a chance that no one had recognised Tamara in the mêlée at the gallery, but if they had, she needed to get in her apology before any complaints reached Lyra Moore or Austin Wedderburn.

The publisher's phone switched immediately to the answering machine.

'Got your glad rags for the awards tonight?' Simon called out as he walked into the office.

Courtney scowled.

'You bet,' Tamara said.

They left the office early. Courtney had grudgingly arranged a fleet of cabs to take the basement invitees to the dinner. Tamara found it as soothing as intravenous valium to sit in the taxi in her scarlet halterneck, abandoning anxieties about last night's setback, anticipating an evening of excitements, and vaguely listening in passive silence to Simon's latest plot summary. Lucinda was out of the picture and he was tiring of Serena, who was making unreasonable demands about holidays, flats and divorce. She was a lovely girl, he conceded, but the spark had gone. Davina, however, was another proposition. Had he told Tamara about Davina? The polo-playing blonde in food PR he had met last week at a Thames Valley pork pie launch?

'She's really something, Davina,' he said, shaking his head in pleasurable despair over the impossibility of summoning sufficient superlatives to describe her. 'Ravishing. A free spirit. Great form. And we've got so much in common. She makes me laugh like no one else. Plus which, she's loaded.'

'Sounds great.'

He shook his head again and whistled softly.

'Amazing. I tell you. The real thing.'

Right on cue, his mobile phone rang. His eyes widened and, looking over at Tamara, he pointed at the phone.

'*That's her*,' he mouthed, as if Davina might overhear him before he had even answered the phone.

'Go ahead,' Tamara whispered.

Even more restful than vaguely listening to Simon talking to her about his love life, was the prospect of vaguely listening to Simon talking to someone else. She did not even have to make the effort of nodding and smiling.

*

It had been two decades since Honor attended one of these events. Then she had been presented with a Lifetime Achievement award – a clunky tangle of copper, supposed to represent a pen and notepad, which looked like a distressed sundial by that old fraud Dali. Did it seem indecent, or even ghoulish, to return to the press awards, albeit in a non-speaking role as Bobby's companion for the evening? She must have been the oldest person in the room, and she was unsettled by the glances of apparent recognition and the deferential smiles she received as they made their way into the Belvedere Park Hotel.

The ceremony was held in the ballroom, an impersonal arena framed by smoked-glass mirrors, with brutalist chandeliers cascading from the ceiling like shards of ice. Sixty circular tables radiated from the stage in a mandala of fractured light – silver cutlery, glinting glass, winking bottles – and were gradually filled by journalists and executives, the women rustling self-importantly in taffeta and silk as if at a Glyndebourne first night, the men swaggering in tuxedos like hired thugs.

The Bishop of Limehouse, in a crimson robe almost identical to the floor-length gown worn by the *Sphere's* bosomy agony aunt, stood to say grace, and Honor watched the heads of atheists, blasphemers and habitual sinners bow respectfully in prayer for truth and integrity and give humble thanks for the gifts that were about to be bestowed.

The food was execrable, served by anxious illegal immigrants costumed like footmen and parlour maids, and the wine was poisonous and plentiful. Bobby's table was relatively temperate, but waiters struggled to keep up with the demand for more bottles elsewhere as the evening began its slow unravelling. Honor, pushing aside her smoked salmon parcels, pink as prostheses, wondered whether it was her emeritus presence that was restraining Bobby's colleagues.

Around them, greetings and insults were roared to friends and rivals, faces grew ruddy, bow ties slipped their horizontal axes and stilettos dangled absently from stockinged feet. Impossible to tell the tabloids from the broadsheets. Shouting over the boisterous din, Bobby, sitting by Honor's good ear, gave a commentary. That braying popinjay, an old Harrovian with a first from Cambridge and a doctorate in Gaelic panegyrics, was chief leader writer on the *Daily Mirror*. The hefty skinhead with a diamond stud in his ear was a comprehensive-educated Dagenham boy, said to have worked as a merchant seaman before turning to journalism. A first-rate sub, he edited *The Times's* Court Circular page. The scowling girl in lawyer's monochrome, resentfully cradling a glass of mineral water and looking at her watch, put Honor in mind of the young Margaret Thatcher, with her bright centurion's helmet of lacquered hair. A former head girl of Cheltenham Ladies' College and an Oxford Economics scholar, this formidable young woman was now the disciplinarian Foreign editor of the *Guardian*.

The volume dipped again and there was applause as the compère took the stage. He was a plump little man with a Midlands accent and an emphysemic laugh.

'Jimmy Whipple,' Bobby explained to Honor. 'TV comedian. Got a gong in the New Year's honours.'

He was savagely cheerful and his patter was coarse, derisive and tailored for his audience. He had been well briefed and there was strident appreciation for his insiderish references to a Sports desk coup at *The Monitor*, a News desk punch-up at *The Courier* and the expenses claims of an unnamed Features editor on an unspecified paper for weekly sessions at a Mile End massage parlour.

'No, but seriously,' was his catchphrase, greeted each time he said it with an outburst of inexplicable laughter from the audience. Bobby pointed out *The Monitor* table, where its Editor, Austin Wedderburn, presided warily over his disorderly charges like an elderly virgin at the Feast of Lupercal.

There were whistles and whoops as Whipple was joined on stage by four young vamps in brief, low-cut black frocks and fishnet tights. Honor assumed they were there to hand out the awards, like mutely decorative game show hostesses, until musical instruments were produced. They were members of a string quartet, winners of a recent television talent contest. This was clever programming – Haydn for the broadsheets, played by Page Three Girls for the tabloids. The ballroom fell silent as the musicians sawed with grim competence through a single movement of Opus 33 No. 1. The applause was appreciative. Whipple sighed and said: 'In my next life, I want to come back as a cello.'

The puddings, vivid gelatine squares, like miniature Mondrians on a slick of crimson sauce, were toyed with, the demitasses of coffee poured and the chocolate mints distributed. Some tables were becoming raucously impatient, demanding arcane liqueurs, and Whipple departed from his script and began to taunt the rowdier male elements.

'No, but seriously. You lot. Big noise, small members. Saw it with my own eyes in the john just before I came on. Microtechnology isn't in it.'

Several men, including the *Mirror* leader writer, stamped their feet and whistled. It was time for the prizes.

Honor had anticipated a childish element of inter-table barracking as the winners were announced and they stepped up to the stage to receive awards – for Scoop, News Reporter, Sports Writer, and Feature Writer of the Year. There had been some mild, affable heckling twenty years ago, though a respectful silence had fallen when she had walked on stage to receive her own prize. But she was unprepared for this degree of hostility. Acceptance speeches were shouted ineffectually against a storm of boos and catcalls while more belligerent winners semaphored their success with raised fists, or two fingers thrust defiantly at their rivals.

Bobby, who thought the evening far more diverting than his usual high table dinners or poetry book launches, registered Honor's astonishment.

'Cocaine,' he whispered.

Twenty-two tables away, towards the back of the hall, by the kitchen's swing doors, Tamara Sim sat with her elbow on the table, fondling her wineglass. The evening was not panning out as she had hoped. The food was elaborate and tasteless and they'd just had to endure some pompous classical music played by Goth schoolgirls. She had spotted Tim earlier in the foyer with an anorexic nymphet and she was sure he had dodged into the Gents to avoid her. Now she was straining to give the appearance of rapt interest as Alistair Potter, the weasel-featured picture editor of *Psst!*, described the latest managerial outrage.

'Thing is, you know we're fully stretched already and once Jamal goes . . .'

Tamara frowned sympathetically over her Merlot – at least the wine was not bad, and the supply was limitless – and silently cursed Simon. Why had he sat her next to this earnest creep? On her other side was Tania, whose tawny back, visible through an artful slit in her lime silk dress, was eloquently turned. She was lecturing Simon on the relative merits of various web browsers, about 'the greenhouse effect', and about Kosovan politics. Treacherously, he seemed to be enthralled.

All the interesting and useful people were on *The Monitor*'s main table, 150 feet away. Tamara had located them by taking a circuitous route to the Ladies before pudding. The Head of Circulation and Marketing, Erik Havergal, was confiding in Lyra Moore, aloof and impeccable in pristine navy, while Johnny Malkinson, in fuchsia cummerbund, matching bow tie and grey tails, market testing a Fashion special on The New Formality, was gesturing vigorously at the managing editor, who was staring aghast at his untouched plate. Austin Wedderburn was listening with apparent interest to the paper's majority shareholder, a pock-faced property millionaire from Vilnius who owned a string of Isthmian league football clubs. These were the career-makers, yet here she was, marooned at the back of the room, in career-breaking social exile, listening to the feeble complaints of no-hoper Alistair Potter.

He drank greedily as he spoke.

'Thing is, they can't just take my parking space away . . .'

As he droned on, Tamara clung to the hope that there would be opportunities for networking at the bar later. The decibel levels were rising again. There was a fanfare – a blast of recorded trumpets – and on stage, Jimmy Whipple said, 'No, but seriously, the moment you've all been waiting for . . .'

Relieved, Tamara turned from Alistair to the stage.

All around the ballroom, men – and some women – were heckling now, stamping their feet and whistling at the tiny figures on the distant stage. The scarlet-cheeked northerner, stout as a circus strongman, who was crowned Regional Journalist of the Year had apparently prepared his speech on the train down from Doncaster. Prevented by the din from delivering it, he turned his back on the howling audience, bent over and dropped his trousers. He received another distinction: the loudest cheers of the evening.

*

'The Fall of Rome,' Honor said, nodding vigorously. The strain of the evening had set off her tic.

'The tenth circle of hell,' said Bobby. 'I'm sorry I put you through this.'

The scene on the next table, occupied, according to Bobby, by the tabloid *Sunday Sphere*, could have been painted by Hogarth. One man, bald and violet-cheeked, was drinking straight from the bottle, apparently unaware of the rivulet of red wine running down his shirt front, and another seemed to have fallen asleep on the table, like the Dormouse in *Alice in Wonderland*, while next to him a woman with a sulphurous suntan and wrinkled décolletage was silently weeping. A wan girl in a pink slip sat on the lap of an overweight executive and looped her bony arms round his neck. His extravagant froth of grey hair resembled an eighteenth-century periwig and he seemed to be fellating an oversized cigar.

Honor was tired. She knew Bobby's colleagues would interpret her disapproval as old-maidish prudery. But even in terms of debauchery these people were amateurs. How would they have fared at Henry's Laurel Canyon parties in the 1950s? It was the vulgarity that was so repellent. Once she might have felt dishonoured by association, experiencing a sense of collective disgrace in the company of colleagues capable of such boorishness. Now she felt no connection at all with these people, and her exile from the trade that had once defined her suddenly seemed like liberation.

*

It was easy to lose track of the events on stage from this distance but Tamara echoed the cheers and taunts of her colleagues. The compère was racing though them now; he had reached the bottom of the list, the sediment – Sports Headline of the Year, Layout Sub of the Year, Business Reporter of the Year – and the audience was beginning to lose interest.

Alistair resumed his inventory of grievances.

'And now they're rearranging our shift system so—'

Suddenly the *Psst!* team were on their feet, roaring their approval. Tamara pushed back her chair and whooped. It was Alistair, the parking space soliloquist. Her dull dinner partner was the toast of the ballroom, king of the moment. As he stood up, acknowledging the shouts and cheers of congratulation, Tamara saw that she had been unfair. His modesty was attractive – he was more surprised than anyone else in the room by the announcement – and as he walked towards the stage to pick up his award for Picture Editor of the Year (Supplements), his slight frame and awkward smile seemed endearingly boyish. He really was not so bad looking.

*

The prize-giving was winding down. The shouts and whoops had died away as diners moved between tables, congratulating winners they had mocked from the floor only half an hour ago and embracing old enemies, on their way to more unbuttoned celebrations at the long bar outside the ballroom. The real business of the evening was about to begin. Bobby offered to escort Honor to the hotel entrance and put her in a taxi.

'I'm fine. I really am,' she said. 'Just exhausted.'

As they filed out of the room a photographer, taking group pictures of tonight's prize-winners, called out to Bobby.

'Would the lady mind coming on to the stage for a couple of photos?'

'The "lady" can speak for herself.'

Honor affected weariness as she was helped up the steps.

'Is this really necessary?' she asked.

Her picture was taken in various combinations with the winners and then with the compère, who put his arm around her and mugged to the camera. Though she protested, she submitted, flattered to be remembered.

One of the younger prize-winners, a sweet-faced boy who looked barely old enough to be out of school, asked her for her autograph.

'You're a real heroine,' he said, holding out a pen and the back of the evening's menu. 'That stuff you did in Spain was brilliant. And your Vietnam coverage was amazing.'

She signed the menu and handed it back with a gracious smile.

'Thanks very much, Martha,' he said. 'That means a lot.'

Bobby did not hear the exchange, but Honor's face was expressive.

*

Tamara watched Tania break away from the *Psst!* table and head straight for *The Monitor*'s main table. There, she tried to engage Johnny Malkinson, who was now wearing his fuchsia bow tie round his head like an Alice band. She had more luck with the Latvian shareholder, who beckoned her to sit next to him in the seat vacated by Austin Wedderburn.

Never mind Tania. Linking her arm proprietarily to Alistair's, Tamara made her way to the bar with the victorious *Psst!* team for some celebratory champagne. Was it good timing or bad that Tim should be standing in the corner, rumpled, perspiring and momentarily alone? His schoolgirl companion was giggling in a corner with the *Mirror* leader writer. Alistair extricated himself from Tamara, squeezed her hand to reassure her he would be back, and turned to place his order at the bar.

It happened so quickly, and the wine had already taken such a toll, that it was only the next day, after talking to a number of witnesses, that Tamara was able to piece together the sequence of events. The only moments she remembered with any clarity were the overture – the sensation of a cool finger tracing a line down her spine – and the triumphant finale. At first she had assumed the hand belonged to Alistair and shivered with pleasure, but when she turned round, smiling, she found herself facing Tim, whose face was crumpling in a series of grotesque winks and pouts.

'What the hell . . . ?' she asked.

'Don't be like that, Tamara.'

'You've got a real cheek. Blanking me for weeks – what was it, pressure of work? Family crises? – then spending the evening pawing your underage lingerie model over there.'

He was not going to give up.

'Come on, Tammy. You weren't so unfriendly in Paris, were you?'

He reached out and cupped her right breast in his hand, as if testing ripe fruit on a greengrocer's stall. She brushed him away angrily.

'You can't just—'

She did not finish her sentence because Alistair was there, holding an uncorked bottle of champagne.

'Back off, granddad,' he growled at Tim.

Tamara was beginning to see just how much she had underestimated Alistair.

'What you going to do about it?' Tim slurred. He was swaying now and seemed to be having difficulty focusing. 'This!'

In a single swift and fluid move Alistair passed the bottle to Tamara and jabbed his fist at Tim's leering face. Tamara's ex-lover, about whom she was sobbing only yesterday, toppled slowly backwards, rigid as a felled oak, and crashed to the floor. There were yelps of surprise from the crowd.

The head barman squeezed through the throng and rushed to feel Tim's pulse. Satisfying himself that the victim was still alive, and judging that the loss of consciousness had been caused by alcohol, he tutted loudly and went to fetch the hotel doctor. Tim's jaw slackened and he began to snore loudly. The crowd around him laughed, relieved yet disappointed, and began to disperse. Someone took a playful kick at the recumbent figure while senior editors from the *Sphere* stood around awkwardly, trying to gauge the acceptable response. Should they defend their boss's honour and take out the wide-boys from *Psst!*, or should they laugh it off and order another round? None of them really had any taste for action. The boss would get over it, if he even remembered it. The night had only just started, the bar was still free and there were some likely girls around clearly looking for action.

At the bar, Tamara fussed over the fine spray of blood – Tim's – stippling Alistair's white shirt. Arms linked, they walked towards the hotel reception to book a room for the night, and as they passed Tim, still stretched out on the floor, she upended the bottle she was carrying, sending a stream of champagne splashing over his sleeping head.

It was late but, back at her flat, Honor felt an urge to continue the purification ritual she had started on the morning of that dreadful interview. Was it a fortnight ago? She turned on the radio – a documentary about preparations for the handover of Hong Kong – and turned it off again, then went to the bookshelves and upended a pile of books and magazines: a Christie's catalogue for a photography sale, a critical study of Lucian Freud's work, a couple of *New York Review*s. More candidates for permanent exile. She gathered up a history of the Scottish Enlightenment, the latest *New Statesman*, Ian Crichton Smith – generating a light shower of bills, receipts and, aptly cruel, an old card from Lois, who had bought the book on the Enlightenment when history, her own included, was still accessible to her.

Honor poured herself another drink and sat down by the fire, the scattered books still lying at her feet. She picked up the card. Graphology was obvious tosh but in Lois's large-looped handwriting Honor had always seen the mark of her nature: optimistic, impatient and avid for experience, excitement and answers. Lois had been a great encourager, too, and had followed Honor's career with an attention that it had never occurred to Honor to reciprocate.

Lois would send detailed and critically intelligent letters about each of Honor's articles and had suggested several of her best stories, tipping her off about Mme Chiang Kai-shek's whereabouts, setting up her interviews with MacArthur, Henry Wallace and Dominic Behan, proposing her report on the return trip to Weimar, on the thirtieth anniversary of the founding of Buchenwald, and arranging the visit to the orphanage. She had even brokered that article's publication in *Time*, through an old neighbour from her Brentwood days, when Honor was in the wilderness, personally and professionally. Lois had been her supporter and her sounding board. There was so much to tell her, and ask her, now. The squalor of the evening seemed a reflection of Honor's personal disgrace. It wasn't until Lois became so definitively unavailable, that Honor realised how much she had depended on her. She put down her glass. This was a pain she could choose to indulge, or not. She tore the card in two, poured another drink and picked up the proofs of *The Unflinching Eye*.

More reports on Korean skirmishes. The Kum River . . . Sumgyo . . . Amsong . . . Pusan . . . Advance . . . Retreat . . . Attack . . . Counter-attack . . . She closed her eyes. This faithful accounting of troop movements and battle positions had once mattered so much to her. Now, it seemed as effortful and pointless as one of those dreadful dances she had been forced to endure as a child. Pointless and murderous – a deadly Dashing White Sergeant.

She was exhausted but knew she could not sleep. She was beating her own ignominious retreat. In the time that remained she should get her affairs in order. She reached for her notebook.

Buchenwald, 14 April 1945. Liberation Day Four. They gathered in their prison uniforms for a liberation parade by the stump of that great symbol, Goethe's Oak, and waved their national flags.

It was under this once mighty tree on Ettersberg mountain that the poet was said to have picnicked in the golden light of an autumn day in 1827, gazing out over the city of Weimar below and exulting in the glory of nature and the greatness of man. This tree had become a dual symbol, representing an ancestral dream of fascist supremacy to the Third Reich and, to its prisoners, signifying the enlightened humanism of pre-Nazi Germany.

Walking, alone, outside the camp's perimeter fence, I was alerted by a noise in the undergrowth. It was then that I saw him.

Sixteen

Tamara had no idea how she had managed it but, after last night's triathlon of excess, she had wrested herself from the bed at the Belvedere, leaving Alistair snoring like a sluggish starter motor, dashed back to her flat to change and hauled herself into work. It was some comfort to know that she was not alone in her agony. The office was like an A and E department, with stricken figures sprawled around the building, quietly groaning.

Alistair had called in sick and Simon arrived late, still in his tuxedo, with a wad of surgical gauze taped to his ear – he had tripped on a paving stone, he said. No one in the building who had attended the awards ceremony, with the exception of Tania, spoke above a whisper all day and, as if to compensate for the unusual silence, Courtney's voice seemed amplified to a megaphone blare. Tania, the personification of good health and clean living, walked among her distressed colleagues, a gleaming rebuke to debauchery.

Simon proposed an early lunch. The wine bar was filled with afflicted colleagues, though the virtuous Tania was there – again – in animated conversation with the Books editor, Caspar, who had also escaped the effects of last night's bacchanal, on account of not being invited.

Over two healing bottles and a basket of bread, Simon confessed to Tamara that he had not sustained his injury on an inadequately laid pavement. After leaving the awards dinner he had gone round to Lucinda's flat, using his old key, which he had neglected to return. He had wanted to surprise her.

'The thing is, it hit me suddenly, with the force of divine revelation: it's got to be her. I realised I'd been messing around – Serena, Davina – just killing time. It's so obvious. Lucinda is the one.'

She was also the one for Wayne, her personal fitness trainer, who happened to be sharing her bed when Simon let himself into the flat. Wayne had not appreciated the surprise visit. Simon thought there had been a triumphant light in Lucinda's eyes as she watched, arms folded, looking delectable in the satin baby-doll that Simon himself had bought her, while Wayne attended to the personal fitness of her ex-lover.

'So it hit you, this revelation. Then he hit you,' Tamara said.

Simon tentatively nibbled his baguette and ignored the remark.

'Now I know I've got to get her back. Somehow.'

His mobile phone rang. It was Jan, with more news of plans for Dexter's birthday next weekend. The catering company had gone bankrupt.

'Well, find another one,' Simon said, rolling his eyes

at Tamara. 'No . . . I don't know,' he snapped. 'Try the Yellow Pages.'

He switched off the phone and poured another glass.

'What's the point of keeping a dog and barking yourself?' he said.

'I know,' Tamara mumbled, though she wasn't entirely clear what he meant.

'That was some night last night,' he said, ruefully patting his surgical dressing.

'You're not kidding.'

'Massive punch-up in the bar later, while you were upstairs in the victors' suite discussing the finer points of paparazzi photography with our mutual colleague.'

She flushed. She was beginning to regret last night's impulsiveness.

'What was the fight about?'

'*The Courier* News desk weighed into our boys over some spoiler, Ricky Clegg had a scrap with his old deputy from the *Sphere,* and someone from the *People* took a swing at the compère. It was pure Dodge City.'

'So when did you leave?'

'Can't exactly recall. I remember having a full and frank exchange with *The Courier* Sports desk about their FA Cup supplement – no sense of humour, that lot. And then everything's a blank – until Lucinda's.'

'See any sign of Tim Farrow later?'

Simon suddenly brightened at the memory of someone who had come off worse than him and whose disgrace had been so public.

'Completely banjaxed, wasn't he? Carried off on a palanquin, apparently. Who'd have thought? Little Al, eh.'

'Mmm.'

'So how was your night?' he asked, with a music hall leer.

'Fine,' she said, anxious to change the subject. 'Better than Tim's, anyway.'

'Best not to gloat too openly over the misfortunes of a potential employer,' Simon said with sudden seriousness. 'Tim may be a prat, but he's a useful prat. You never know when a staff job on the *Sphere* might come in handy.'

Tamara snorted.

'The *Sphere*? I'm finished with that dross, remember? I've got S*nday in my sights.'

Simon gestured for the bill then clasped his hands and leaned towards her with avuncular concern, though his authority was undermined by the bandage.

'Tam, look, you should know by now that you can't count on anything in this business.'

'There's no need to be patronising. I'm allowed to aim a little higher than the *Sphere*, aren't I? Lyra thinks so, even if you don't.'

'Don't say I didn't warn you,' he said, getting to his feet.

'Thanks for your concern.'

He patted her shoulder, anxious to restore the light-hearted mood.

'Come on, Tam. Right now we both face the highest

calling of all – a restive public awaits its weekly *Psst!*.
What's this week's A-List?'

'Corkers to Porkers – From Fab to Flab.'

Back at the office, Tamara retrieved the results of this
morning's research and handed him the bundle of photographs.

'Take a look at the recent picture of Pernilla Perssen,'
she said. 'She's piling on the pounds. She'll be modelling
for Weight Watchers soon.'

Simon laughed.

'Not exactly tubby by normal standards, but definite
signs of a beer gut there. Fantastic. And next week?'

'The Pits – Underarm Hair Horror of the Stars.'

'Cracking. *You're* the star, Tamara. You're not going
anywhere. *Psst!* needs you.'

This was exactly what she feared.

She looked through the evening papers to see if Tim's
disgrace had made the diary pages yet, tidied up her
Porkers list, sent it over to Simon, sketched out a draft
of the Pits list and spent much of the afternoon harvesting
background material for the next few weeks' A-Lists: Top
Ten Soap Star Love Rats; Telly Catfights; Best and Worst
Boob Jobs. Johnny sent a message asking her to do a
ring-round for *Me2* on Deadbeat God-dads – one of the
tabloids had run a piece on a septuagenarian soap star
whose middle-aged god-son, an unemployed plumber with
mental health problems, claimed the actor had never sent
him a birthday card or postal order in forty years. Calls

to the usual suspects harvested a workable yield of confessions and complaints.

It was, in the end, a satisfactory day's work and, considering her condition, it was remarkable that she had managed to report for duty at all. She yearned for a quiet night at home, but duty called.

She took the tube to Maida Vale and arrived to find the café still open. But someone was sitting in her seat, his broad shoulders maddeningly obscuring her view of the entrance to Holmbrook Mansions. With a loud sigh, which she hoped would unsettle him, she sat down at the next table. She looked across at the trespasser, and felt a charge of shock. It was Honor Tait's male escort. He was preoccupied, delicately sipping a small cup of black coffee while sorting through some coins. Close up, he was even better looking: a rangy, lightly tanned, soft-eyed metropolitan hippy in a white T-shirt under an artfully creased linen jacket. Around his neck was a loop of brown beads, and a plaited leather cuff was fastened round his wrist.

Tamara willed him to look up but when he did, and shook back his dark tangle of hair, it was to signal one of the brothers for the bill. He did not notice her. His face had the wide-jawed symmetry of a stained-glass saint, a fine, aquiline nose that could have been chiselled by Michelangelo, and lips designed for more than prayer. He pushed back his seat, dropped a handful of coins by his cup and left the café, calling 'Thanks!' over his shoulder to the brothers.

Tamara picked up her bag and moved to claim his chair. The warmth of the seat seemed an intimate gift, something to bask in. As she watched him jaywalking across the road and running up the steps into Holmbrook Mansions, she felt the high of total engagement. After all her work, and several false starts, everything was falling into place. But his work? She gazed up at the fourth-floor windows of the building. What was going on up there? It was unfathomable.

It had never occurred to her that old people could have sexual feelings, but she guessed it might be technically possible. When the elderly, particularly old men, displayed an interest in sex, she had always assumed that other forces were at work. It was a statement of potency, loudly asserted in the season of impotence. Her father, though fifteen years younger than Honor Tait, was a case in point. He couldn't see how foolish he looked, scrawny and hairless, cravated and cologned, arm in arm with the pearl-skinned, lanky Ludmilla, a gargantuan swan to his miniature bald eagle. Athough Tamara had tried, fighting her natural squeamishness, she could not envisage the physical act that brought sturdy Boris, a freakish miracle of hybridisation, into the world. It was an affront to nature, like inter-species copulation, surely only possible under laboratory conditions. And Honor Tait and her escort? It was beyond bestiality.

But for Tait, unlike Tamara's father, the element of display was absent. Women were not so easily fooled into believing that the company of a younger lover, particularly one who had been bought, lent any kind of status or glamour to the senior partner. Honor Tait's escort was not squiring her around town; other young men volunteered that service for free. He was hired by the hour. This was a private transaction, a source of mutual shame as well as mutual convenience. Tamara was sickened by the thought of the old woman's appetites. How unjust it was that a shrivelled pensioner should be enjoying regular sessions with a striking specimen of manhood while she, young, pretty and in her prime, should lie alone and unmolested each night in her king-sized bed. These days, her vast white duvet called to mind an Arctic snowfield – deserted and miserably cold. And under her bed, in an improbable variety of shapes, and in colours that owed little to nature, were the unwieldy fruits of her latest consumer report for *Oestrus* magazine: her hoard of vibrators, her cock stock, still in their boxes, keeping company with her slippers and mocking her loveless nights.

She accepted a mug of watery coffee from the surly brother, ordered a sandwich – anything but chicken – opened her notebook, took out her thesaurus and the clippings, and got down to work.

The conversation at her salons is of world affairs and Russian literature, Hegelian philosophy, aleatoric music, the single European currency and the future of artificial intelligence. Paul Tucker, fresh from the battlefields of Eastern Europe, is a favourite. His macho style and line-of-fire reminiscences set Honor Tait swooning like

a lovesick teenager. Aidan Delaney, the award-winning
poet, provides a seasoning of wit and erudition – and
not a little blarney. But there is one young man whose
company she prefers above all the others. Tall, Hollywood-
handsome [name to come]. And when he pays his discreet
late-night calls, conversation is the very last thing on
Honor Tait's mind.

By the time Honor Tait's visitor finally left Holmbrook
Mansions, the café had closed and Tamara was sipping
a gin and tonic at her chilly berth outside the Gut and
Bucket. Did she imagine the hurried furtiveness in his
manner as he walked away, head bowed, from the building,
as if he was escaping the scene of a crime? If crime it
was, he was the victim rather than the perpetrator. She
left her drink and ran across the road to follow him. Too
late. He got into his van and drove off. Was he returning
to a communal squat in Hampstead, or an austere bach-
elor flat in Ladbroke Grove? Perhaps there was a wife
and kids in Clapham and Honor Tait's tainted money
was putting his children through private school. This
seemed the least plausible scenario. He was too attractive
to be a family man.

As he drove away, an ugly vision took shape in her
mind of the old woman's passion and his cold resignation.
Tamara asked herself once more if she could have got it
wrong. Could he be a member of Honor Tait's salon, after
all? One of her platonic pals, an out-of-work Shakespearian
actor, perhaps, or a hopeless but charming playwright?

None of these explanations could account for the cash, the furtiveness of their meeting or the intimacy of their kiss. And besides, Honor Tait had history in this area.

Behind Tamara, there was an outbreak of rowdy laughter as a young couple left the pub, pushing open the door, arm in arm, and releasing a blast of catcalls on a current of rank air. There was little point in standing here alone in the cold. The real prize had slipped away. He had fulfilled his task. He would not be back tonight and Honor Tait would be lying in the dark, exhausted, her grisly desires sated. Tamara struggled to banish these thoughts. She was working at *Psst!* tomorrow, then she had to spend most of the weekend writing up another overdue travel feature for *Mile High* – on the Krakelingen live fish swallowing festival in Belgium – and the editor of *Oestrus* was pressing hard for the vibrator report. She needed to focus. The *S*nday* article had to be delivered in less than a fortnight and Lyra Moore, elusive on so many matters, was unambiguous in this area at least; she would give no quarter on deadlines.

*

He had come, as he said he would. That was something. That, in the end, had to be everything. This bitterness was becoming habitual. Today's visit was less hurried. He had observed the proprieties, expressed interest in her, asked her what she had been doing, who she had been seeing, how she felt. To an outsider, his embrace could have looked like tenderness. But it was a simple transaction. For him, it was about money. It had always been about money. Why, then, did she feel such anguish at the thought of him walking away? The boy – yes, he was still a boy – was unfinished business. Her feelings for him were dark, primordial; the sediment shifting at the bottom of her stagnant heart. Stir it up at your peril.

There had been many people in her life. In her darkest moments she counted them up, looking for embers in the ash pit. Sometimes it seemed those old loves, those long friendships, had generated barely enough heat to warm her hands. She thought again of Lois. Honor could not shake off this new sense that she had deserted her. Had she started pulling away, quietly appalled, distancing herself, inching out of the picture, as soon as she realised what was happening, and what lay ahead? In Mantua, on what was to be their last trip together, they had spent one morning apart; Lois was touring the churches with the dogged attention only a lifelong atheist could give, while Honor, ironically, given the perilous state of her marriage at that time, was visiting the Camera degli Sposi. When Lois failed to turn up for their lunchtime rendezvous, Honor had gone looking for her. She had been horrified, fifty minutes later, to find her fearless, clever and resourceful friend, lost and weeping in the Piazza Sordello. It had taken a shared bottle of prosecco to calm her down and later that evening they had laughed about it. But no one was laughing now. Least of all Lois.

The night chorus had started in the garden. Honor

did not mind the ululating tots, so much, or the self-righteous parents with their geometric haircuts and fancy baby carriages. It was the teenage boys from the council flats behind the tube station who caused the problems. They had no right to use the garden but they got in somehow, climbing the railings after dark, trampling on the shrubs, baying and hooting into the early hours. Sleep was difficult enough.

It was worse in the summer, with the long hot nights, when the denatured vegetation struggled to re-enact some species-memory of lushness and fragrance, and the boys – where were the girls? – lay around on the grass, bantering and smoking, marijuana no doubt, between bouts of soccer that laid waste to the flowerbeds and lasted until dawn. Forced to close the window against the cacophony, Honor would lie all night, breathless and alert, longing for a downpour. Like Glenbuidhe midges, London teenagers could not take the rain.

She looked up at the clock. It was late. Almost too late. Work was all she had. More unfinished business.

Buchenwald, 14 April 1945. Liberation Day Four. We wept as we watched them, these gaunt survivors – those strong enough to stand – as they gathered in their prison uniforms by Goethe's shattered oak. They shed their own tears, for their compatriots who did not live to see this day of freedom, and there was pride as they waved their national flags – fashioned from coloured paper – in the cold spring air.

More than a century ago, here in the beech forest – the Buchenwald – on Ettersberg mountain, the poet Goethe had rested his broad back against a mighty oak tree as he picnicked in the golden autumn light, gazing out over the city of Weimar below and exulting in the glory of nature and the greatness of man. 'Here he feels great and free – great and free as the scene he has before his eyes, and as he ought properly always to be'.

This tree had become a dual symbol, representing to the Third Reich an ancestral dream of fascist supremacy and, to its prisoners, signifying the enlightened humanism of pre-Nazi Germany.

And standing in what would once have been the shade of its branches, I witnessed – no, participated in – a scene which demonstrated that cruelty was not the sole prerogative of an evil regime, that it could be, given certain conditions, a human universal.

*

The clamour of an alarm pierced Tamara's dream – her mother, smiling in chef's whites, was serving her in *The Monitor* canteen. Fire or theft? It was the telephone. Tamara drowsily reached for the receiver.

'Tam?'

'Ross.'

She stirred into consciousness. Her mouth was parched, filled with a foul toilet-bowl tang, and dried spittle sealed the corners of her lips.

'You okay, Tam?'

Well, here was a rare moment of role reversal.

'I'm okay. Are you okay, more to the point?'

He said he was, but he clearly was not. He sounded shivery and afraid.

'Where are you?' Tamara asked.

'Crystal's.'

Not again.

'Why? What's happened?'

'I've had to leave my place.'

'What happened?'

'Nothing that can't be sorted.'

Tamara sat up, fully awake, and switched on the bedside light.

'Just tell me what's been going on.'

'No big deal, sis.' His laugh was hollow, a dry bark. 'Run up a few debts. Got a few arrears on my rent. If I don't pay up, they evict me.'

'Jesus, Ross, not again. How can you have rent arrears? You're on housing benefit.'

'Been a mix-up down the DHSS. And then the neighbours, some snotty Christian couple, have been making complaints. They want me out.'

'What happened to the money I sent you?'

'What money?'

Was he serious?

'The eighty pounds I sent you, registered mail, last week?'

'Oh. Right . . . Never turned up. The post has got really dodgy round here.'

Was he lying? Or had he blown it on a binge he couldn't remember?

'I can claim it back from the post office. I've got the receipt.'

'You don't want to be bothered with all that, sis.'

He was right.

'How much rent do you owe?'

'I'm not asking you to pay it.'

'Just tell me how much rent you owe.'

'Two hundred quid.'

'How the hell did you manage that?' She instantly regretted her anger. 'No, never mind. Don't tell me.'

'I don't know. I'm not asking you to pay it,' he repeated huffily. 'Anyway, Crystal says I can stay with her as long as I like.'

That was the last thing he needed.

'I'm not sure that's a good idea – you and Crystal.'

'What do you mean? You've always been down on her . . .'

'Come on, Ross. You've not exactly been good for each other.'

'What do you know about it?' His voice cracked with indignation. 'Since when have you been an expert on relationships?'

Tamara had learned early to defend herself from his insults – he was just lashing out because he was in pain himself.

'I'm only trying to say, Crystal's got her own problems,' she answered quietly.

'Yeah. And that's why I'm not going to turn my back on her. She's a woman in grief.'

'Grief?'

'Yeah. Her sister, Dawn—'

'But her sister died *five years ago.*'

'You know, Tam, sometimes, if I didn't know you were my baby sister, I'd mistake you for a heartless bastard.'

Tamara looked at the clock. Three a.m. It was too early – or too late – for this. She had to be in the office in a few hours. Her head was pounding. Could it be a second-wave hangover from the Press Awards?

'I'm only worrying about you. I want you to be okay,' she said.

'I'll be okay. Once my disability allowance comes through in a fortnight.'

'But how will you survive until then? And what about your rent arrears?'

'I'll manage.'

'Are you sure your money hasn't gone on drugs?'

'You think I'm lying, don't you? You're just like Dad. Mum was the only one who ever believed me.'

He began to cry, a low keening that grew into an awful, wounded-dog howl.

'No, of course not, Ross. I believe you.'

Her eyes filled with tears. She could not bear to hear him hurt and hopeless.

'You think I'm lying. You do.' He was angry now. 'I can tell. I'm sick of you people writing me off, judging me.'

You people? Tamara could not risk rising to the bait.

302

Nor could she risk allowing him to fall into Crystal's hands again. There was no way of knowing whether Ross was telling the truth. But if she pressed him, she risked him slamming down the phone and then she would endure months of worrying silence.

She had £220 left in her building society account – she was saving for a new computer – and she would draw it out tomorrow. This had to be the last time. Appeasing her brother, protecting him, was becoming an expensive habit. But what else could she do? Her mother would have paid out. Ross was vulnerable. He could not help it. This must be mental illness; for who, in their right minds, would volunteer to live like that?

'Look, I'll bring it over to you tomorrow night. To Crystal's, if you want. Put the money in your hands. After work. Then you can move back to your own place. You going to be all right till then? Can you get any food? Go to your corner shop. Try to get some on credit. Tell him I'll pay him over the phone with a card. He can call me at *The Monitor*.'

Seventeen

Dishevelled after a fitful sleep, Tamara arrived at the office to discover an impromptu meeting in progress. The *Psst!* team stood clustered around Simon, whispering. Their expressions were grave. Only Courtney remained at her desk, opening the post with a conspicuous smile. Simon was silent and pale.

'What's happened?' Tamara asked Alistair.

They had not spoken since the Press Awards. It had been sheepish distaste on her part – after the awards, the hero's lustre had dissolved and he looked and sounded like the little loser he had always been. Guilt was the cause of *his* awkwardness – his wife had given birth to their first baby the week before their night at the Belvedere. An office crisis was a good moment to restore diplomatic relations.

'We've been downgraded,' said Alistair.

'Downgraded? Who? How?'

'*Psst!*. We've been sidelined.'

Downgraded *and* sidelined. This was serious.

'Simon's been shafted. We're all working for the website now.'

'No! The *website*?'

How could they possibly work for the website? Print was their medium. They knew nothing about computers and cared about them even less.

'I know,' said Alistair. 'It's insane.'

'But who's taking over from Simon?'

'Tania Singh.'

It could not be true. Had Tamara really lost her champion? Was the smug stuck-up Tania really to be her next boss? Impossible. Tamara looked at the faces of her colleagues and at Simon's shocked pallor. The office had been one area of her life where she'd felt secure and in control. Now she'd been cut adrift, Simon had been vanquished and the enemy, a humourless office automaton, was victorious.

'I don't believe it,' Tamara said.

Alistair showed her the proof: a memo from Wedderburn. While it did not actually use the terms downgrading or sidelining, it offered no comfort. 'Integration' was the word. And Simon had not been sacked but 'redeployed'. He was now Content editor, in an arrangement which the memo described as a promotion. But the implications were clear. Tania was to be Editor-in-Chief of *Psst!* and from next month, the magazine was, 'as part of a bold experiment', to be primarily a website, and its paper original, that friendly, tactile, shiny artefact, as familiar and comforting as a box of cheap chocolates, would shrink, becoming a diminutive two-page appetiser, a mere leaflet advertising the colossal online banquet.

The unofficial meeting reconvened in the Beaded Bubbles for an early lunch. No one, except Courtney, had any appetite for food.

'We're goners. Dinosaurs and dodos, trampled beneath the jackboot of progress,' Simon said.

Jim was unusually supportive.

'It won't last, believe me,' he said. 'This internet business is just a fad, bound for obsolescence. It's the hot-air gramophone and the Sinclair C5 all over again. They'll never make any money with it long-term.'

But it was the short-term that was preoccupying the *Psst!* team.

'This isn't what I won my award for,' Alistair said. 'I didn't come into this business to spend my days staring at a screen playing the photographic equivalent of Pacman—'

'Hold on a minute, Al,' Courtney interrupted. 'It's no good coming on like Sebastiao Salgado. We know what you do. It's not pictures of oppressed Bolivian tin miners we're talking about here. It's snatched photos of pissed TV stars. The website seems a perfect outlet for your stuff.'

'Traitor,' Alistair muttered.

'What exactly does Content editor mean, anyway?' Tamara asked.

'Well, it's got nothing to do with contentment,' Simon said. 'They don't want to be sued for constructive dismissal so they invent this nonsense role, supposed to span digital and print, bung me a few more quid and say I've been promoted. But no one's fooled. Tania's the boss now.'

'That's it, then,' Tamara said. 'The golden age is over.'

'The gravy train has been derailed, you mean,' said Courtney, ordering a bottle of champagne. 'No fatalities. Just a few cuts and bruises in the First Class compartment. All change please!'

Back at the office, dejected and mildly drunk, the *Psst!* staff were summoned by Tania for a 'team briefing' in the canteen.

Simon took his jacket from the back of his chair.

'I'm off. You can tell the Warrior Queen I'm out foraging for content,' he said.

Tania sat on one of the canteen tables – still damp from a recent wipe-down, Tamara was pleased to note, though this mild charge of pleasure was short-circuited by the sight of a silver mobile phone glinting in Tania's hand. A company phone, too.

The *Psst!* team slumped in chairs around her like moody teenagers on the first day of term. Arms folded, her suede-booted legs crossed, right foot swinging prettily, their new editor, as enchanted by herself as a girl in a shampoo advert, tossed back her shimmering hair and spoke of opportunities and excitements, web-readiness, interactivity and responsiveness, reader participation and page impressions, breaking news and instant updates.

'Hang on,' Alistair said. 'Breaking news? Instant updates? What exactly does this mean for our weekly deadline?'

Tania smiled beguilingly.

'That's old thinking, Alistair. We've got a new model here. In the future – maybe two years, maybe five, down the line – *The Monitor* will no longer merely be a daily national newspaper with weekly supplements; it will be a twenty-four-hour, seven-day-a-week multi-platform information and comment outlet with a global readership, straddling borders and time zones.'

'What about our four-day week?' Jim Frost asked, pointing the chewed end of his briar pipe towards Tania.

Tania gave him a pitying smile.

'And our days off in lieu?' Alistair added.

It was as if they had not spoken. Their new boss unfolded her arms, uncrossed her legs and gripped the edge of the table. As if about to share a thrilling secret, she leaned towards her audience.

'And the really exciting thing is that I, I mean we, or rather you, have been chosen as the vanguard – you will be trailblazers for this pioneering operation. *Psst!*'s adaptation to the new cyber dispensation will set the template for the rest of *The Monitor*. And, by extension, the future of the entire newspaper industry!'

'When do we start?' Courtney asked.

The meeting broke up in glum silence and Tamara returned to her desk resolved to pursue her own course of web-readiness. She would be ready all right. The prospect of no Simon, no flexible working, and the smiling Tania, a sleek enforcer presiding with merciless enthusiasm over galleys of cyber slaves, was too bleak to contemplate.

She had to get away from Tania's twenty-four-hour,

seven-day-a-week, multi-platform universe, in which every newspaper and magazine would be sucked up by the technological twister, swirling skywards from newsagents and tube stations, from desks and coffee tables, cafés and kitchens, dustbins and gutters, recycling centres and landfill sites, darkening the sky before shrinking to a shower of pixels and falling to earth as magic dust, minute particles of information that would shimmer in plastic boxes in every house in the land.

S*nday – too august to be annexed by Tania's digital dystopia – was no longer an optional escape route but a lifeline. Tamara must nail the Honor Tait story. But first she had another duty to attend to, and a month of fruitless stalking outside Holmbrook Mansions would be preferable to this evening's desolate journey.

*

Purged, exhausted and faintly soiled, Honor Tait submitted herself to the latest indignity. Dwarfed by the machinery, she lay on a paper-covered pallet, cold and shrivelled, naked under the thin cotton gown, while a distant technician, shielded from the harmful rays by glass and lead, fed her by remote control, inch by inch, into the white tunnel.

'Breathe in,' said the radiologist's disembodied voice, broadcast through a small grid at the entrance to the tunnel. 'Hold it . . . keep very still . . . hold it . . .'

Compliantly, full of mute rage, she held her breath. A

simple instruction but so hard to obey. She struggled, with her failing body, with her worn-out respiratory system, and with her natural obstreperousness, to do the voice's bidding. To submit. It had never come easily.

'Now breathe normally.'

She looked around at the tunnel's cold walls. She had never suffered from claustrophobia, but here, now, she could imagine how it might feel. No way out. A dwindling supply of oxygen, a narrowing of options, helplessness, then terror. The human condition. The ageing human condition.

'Breathe in . . . hold it . . . keep very still . . . hold it.'

She had to give it her full attention. That was, above all, what she resented. The machine made an oddly domestic noise as it captured its pictures: a soft swishing and clicking, like the sound of a big-buttoned shirt slowly rotating in a tumble dryer.

'Now breathe normally.'

All the experience, the interests of a lively, long-lived mind, the hard-won achievements, the passions and prejudices, reduced to this, wrapped in the hospital's flower-sprigged shroud, moving powerlessly along the conveyor belt into the scanner, she amounted to nothing more than a series of grainy images – black-and-white splices, cross sections of tissue and bone rendered by technology into pulses of light and pools of darkness – as impersonal as a telescopic view of distant galaxies.

'You're doing very well,' the radiographer said. She could have been talking to an imbecile, or a child. 'Not long now.'

Not long now. There it was, her life, a comet's tail streaking unobserved across the night sky. A falling star. One among countless billions.

'Breathe in . . . hold it . . . keep very still . . . hold it.'

All her life she had enjoyed such exceptional good health that she had come to think of it as a moral quality, perhaps her only real virtue, a corollary of a purposeful life. Apart from certain difficulties in her thirties, after two terminations, she had got off lightly.

'Just one more now. Breathe in . . . hold it . . . keep very still . . . hold it.'

Finally, in doctors' waiting rooms and hospital out-patient departments, she had been conscripted into the tattered army of the sick – old and young, bright and stupid, rich and poor, good and malign. The only thing they had in common was their imperfection; their bodies, the fleshy housing of their essential selves, had become their chief enemy.

'If you could just lie there and wait,' the radiologist said, as jauntily as a hairdresser, 'in case we need to redo any of them, I'll get someone to check through the films.'

Yes, thought Honor. I'll wait. What else is there to do, but wait?

*

Tamara made her way into the grim amphitheatre of the estate, past the carcasses of two abandoned cars, a discarded mattress with a sepia map of stains, trashed TV sets, white plastic garden chairs, arranged primly in a row as if for some interrupted post-apocalypse tea party, a brace of the inevitable supermarket trolleys, upended frames like glistening webs in the sodium blaze of street-lights, and a sinister pushchair, lying on its side, its soiled fabric seat hideously slashed from top to bottom.

The place was deserted, apart from a few kids kicking a football on a sparse patch of grass. Dogs seemed to bark from every flat. She knew these were no eager Labradors or pampered lapdogs but lumps of muscle with chainsaw teeth, programmed to rip through human flesh; creditors or debtors, police or dealers, hostile adults or sleeping babies, they did not discriminate. Even their owners weren't safe.

The open walkway that linked the flats was a foul-scented corridor of graffiti, an extended Jackson Pollock of insult – someone's mother liked it this way, someone did it with their dog, someone was a slag – and pathetic territorial pride: SyncKrew4ever, GBlokRule, KodyisKing. As Tamara penetrated deeper into the estate, human voices joined the barks – the rumbling bass call of complaint and soprano response of protest that presaged a marital spat; a baby's defenceless wail – and above them the choral blare of countless TV sets. Some doors were barred and covered by metal grids; cages with locks on the inside. Outside others were ragged lines of children's shoes, pushchairs, plastic go-karts – the cheerfully chaotic paraphernalia of family life. One fortress, its smashed front window sealed with a sheet of steel, was so tightly boarded and barricaded that it was impossible to imagine anyone lived there but, as she passed, Tamara heard a murmur of voices and a TV football match, with a hectic commentator shouting over the crowd's swelling roars. The neighbouring flat, its door painted proud pillar-box red, had an optimistic welcome mat and a plastic trough of hyacinths. The tenant was probably an old person, a survivor of a prelapsarian age when the enemy was the Luftwaffe overhead, not the crackhead downstairs.

There was no welcome mat outside Crystal's flat, but there was no metal cage either. Her net curtains were cobweb grey, but the windows were not broken, and at least there were curtains. Over the years, as hopes for Ross's life had dwindled, Tamara and her mother had learned to take comfort from such small signs. Standards had plummeted, along with Ross.

After the shock of his first shoplifting conviction, news that he had only received probation had seemed like redemption. Here was the chance of a new beginning for the family. The three of them would be better, stronger people, back on track after this stumble, reinvigorated, clear-eyed. His second offence, or more precisely the second offence for which he was arrested, had earned a four-month prison sentence, rather than the threatened eighteen months, and, after the agony of foreboding before the trial, their mother had embarked on what seemed like a month-long festival of rejoicing, which had, coincidentally, eclipsed any celebration of Tamara's A-level success. It really had seemed as if a stretch in an open prison in Northamptonshire was a shrewder career move than a degree course at Brighton Poly.

Since then, in her bitterest moments, Tamara saw their continuing optimism about the possibility of Ross reclaiming his life – ditching the drugs, regaining his old spark, starting a job, getting a decent flat – as self-delusion on an even grander scale than her brother's. His spell in a psychiatric hospital was, Ross had said, using the language of the group-counselling sessions, a 'wake-up call'. As was the hepatitis C he acquired from shared needles, and the HIV scare, and the methamphetamine-induced coma that he miraculously came round from. They were wake-up calls in the sense that he had woken up, and immediately gone out and scored again. In the recurrent cycle of relapse and recovery, Tamara and her mother had chosen to see recovery as Ross's default position and the relapses as a harrowing deviation from the norm. In their desperation and naivety, they had seen the syringe as half empty, rather than half full.

And still Tamara looked for signs of hope. But her brother's phone call had not given much cause for that. The doorbell of Crystal's flat was not working – a neutral indicator, Tamara decided – so she rattled the letterbox, which set off a frenzied barking and the scraping and skittering of animal claws on linoleum.

'No, Rex. Sssh. Good boy,' said a croaky-voiced woman behind the door.

Bolts were drawn back and a haggard face framed by coarse ropes of hennaed hair peered out apprehensively.

The intention was Pre-Raphaelite flower child, the effect *Night of the Living Dead*.

'Oh, right. Tam. Come in. He's expecting you.'

Crystal's hands, knuckledustered with silver rings, were gripping Rex's collar as the dog – a Border collie with one unnerving blue eye – strained to leap at Tamara.

'Don't worry. He don't mean nothing. He's really friendly.' She yanked at the collar. 'Down, Rex. Good boy.'

Tamara sidled into the hall.

'Really, he's not a problem,' said Crystal, tugging at the dog as she closed the front door. 'He'd only lick you to death.'

Noting the strings of saliva swinging from Rex's jaw, Tamara smiled and kept her distance.

Crystal forced the dog into the kitchen, slammed the door on it and turned a key in the lock.

'He's learned how to open doors. He jumps up and bites the door handles,' she said, smiling with maternal pride.

'Amazing.'

The sitting room was in darkness, lit only by an orange lava lamp and the flickering light of a TV, tuned to a children's cartoon show in which, against a soundtrack of flatulent trombones, scurrying strings, whistles and quacks, an assortment of farm animals were engaged in a high-speed chase. As Tamara's eyes got used to the gloom she saw six silhouettes sitting on the floor in a circle, like Hollywood redskins in a pow-wow. One of them called out her name and Tamara's brother took shape before her eyes – the skinny body and gaunt urchin face – as he struggled to his feet to greet her with a hug.

'Don't get up,' Tamara said.

She crouched to accept her brother's kiss and sank to the floor, crossing her legs, to join him. The flat smelled damp and rancid. In the artificial twilight, she tried to assess Ross's state. He was not shaking. He did not seem manic – no unstoppable monologues, no conspiracy tales, no tears or cackling laughter, so far. Nor was he catatonic. This was all good news. He seemed as comfortable and at ease in this squalid circle as she did at a good lunch in the Bubbles. She felt a sudden indignation; if Ross was okay, why had he dragged her all the way here, at the end of a working day, to hand over her hard-earned savings?

Someone passed Tamara a joint, damp with spittle. She handed it straight to Ross, resolving to give him the money and leave the flat as soon as possible, without touching any surfaces, or using the toilet, or breathing too deeply. But she also knew that she should not produce her purse here, in this room, flashing banknotes in front of stoned strangers. She had to get Ross outside on his own.

Crystal came in with a tray of cups.

'Herb tea?'

Tamara accepted a cracked mug bearing the slogan 'Best Mum in the World' – a present from Crystal's twins, who had been taken into care at the age of eight – and Tamara blew on the hot red liquid.

'Rosehip,' Ross said helpfully. 'Full of antioxidants. Boosts your autoimmune. Very balancing.'

When he bothered to eat, Ross was particular about his diet. It had to be organic, macrobiotic and additive-free. The only reading he seemed to do was ingredients lists on supermarket packaging and he regarded the inclusion of chemical additives, preservatives and E-numbers as evidence of a pernicious state plot to pacify and destroy him. He did not seem to apply the same scrupulousness to all the unprovenanced dope, speed, crack and heroin he ingested. Tamara blew on the tea again, determined not to put the mug to her lips.

The rest of the group were now in focus and, between lingering draws on the joint, Ross introduced them.

'Tam, this is Baz. Baz, Tam.'

A slack-jawed Goth with kohl-rimmed eyes nodded towards Tamara as effortfully as a narcoleptic roused from the pillow.

Sal, a slight West Indian girl with cornrow hair, was more forthcoming.

'All right, Tam?' she said, giving her a sleepy, welcoming smile.

'Chiggy. This is my sister, Tam.'

A trembling wino, his teeth a miniature Stonehenge, raised a bottle in salute. Goody, a Medusa-haired Rasta busy at a bong, squinted briefly in Tamara's direction before returning to the job in hand. Tamara looked around the room, a broad smile masking her unease. At least there were no needles around. A tattered poster showing two dolphins leaping through turquoise waves was pinned above the electric fire. Next to a pack of tarot cards on a wicker table were photographs of grinning twins in impeccable school uniforms, and of a defiant teenage beauty, her blonde fairy tresses crowned by a daisy chain. Dawn. Crystal's dead sister.

Tamara flexed her foot. She was getting cramp. How did those yogis manage to meditate in this position? It was then, with a shiver of astonishment, that she saw him, on the far edge of the circle: handsome and healthy in a roomful of wrecks, razoring some powder on a CD case with the graceful dexterity of a sushi chef.

'Tam, this is Dev.'

For a moment, Tamara wondered whether she was hallucinating. Could you get stoned so quickly from secondary smoke inhalation? But no. It was him. Honor Tait's lunch date and late-night visitor; her gigolo. And he had materialised here, right in front of Tamara, inches away, almost within touching distance. What a gift. And now the puzzle of the story resolved itself. It was suddenly clear; his taste for pricey mind-altering substances explained his sordid occupation. This pensioner's plaything had a habit to subsidise. He bent his lovely head to the powder, his profile almost obscured by the tangle of curls as he poked a rolled banknote up one nostril and sealed the other with his index finger. Then he threw his head back, sniffed appreciatively and offered Tamara a line of cocaine.

'No thanks. I had one before I came out,' she said.

318

Ross gave her a quizzical look then accepted the CD case himself.

'Don't mind her, Dev,' he said. 'My sister's a bit of a straight.'

Tamara reddened. Just when Ross was on the brink of being useful for the first time in his life, he was trying to sabotage her, laughing at her and inviting others to laugh at her. She could have snorted a line for form's sake, but she had so much work to do, she could not afford to write off the evening, or the following morning. Not everyone was on permanent holiday. Okay, she wanted to say, so I'm straight. How else would I come up with the odd two hundred quid, see you've got enough to eat, bail you out when you're in trouble? If this tip of a flat on this gruesome estate, and these tragic derelicts you call friends represent the non-straight, 'alternative' life-style, then give me the good old perpendicular any day.

Another joint came round, this time from Sal. Tamara hesitated. She could manage a puff in the interests of social cohesion. She took a swift hit; it was strong stuff, skunk probably, and, as she passed it to Ross, her irritation and anxiety began to dissolve. She flexed her legs and her cramp was gone.

Minutes passed and the joint was hers again. What was that music? The cartoon soundtrack seemed to have speeded up and there were new elements: percussion, like a thousand syncopated heartbeats, and a flute so high and pure it sounded like birdsong in paradise. Now she was listening attentively, the music seemed to incorporate all the magnificence and tragedy of human experience. And Crystal's insanitary flat was, on closer examination, a place of genuine warmth, infused with a benign, roseate glow. How could she have missed it before? Exhilarated by a new sensory expansiveness, Tamara felt supremely in control.

She looked again at Ross and his friends, and saw that they were, each one of them, beautiful, even noble, in their individuality, sparkling-eyed, humorous, philosophical and heroically flawed. And most beautiful of all – the old crone Tait had taste, she would give her that – was Dev, who was gazing directly at Tamara now under hooded eyes, as she was gazing at him, with naked ardour. He wanted her and she wanted him. It could not have been simpler.

'Tam? Tam? You all right?'

Ross's concern touched her.

'Of course. Look, I just wanted a quick word with you. On our own.'

They went into the corridor and stood outside the kitchen. On the other side of the door, Rex was hurling himself at the handle in a yelping frenzy. Tamara's elation began to drain away. She handed Ross the money.

'Thanks, Tam. You're brilliant. That'll help sort out a few outgoings.'

Tamara looked at him sceptically.

'Just sort out your flat. Get back there. You and Crystal, you're not good for each other. But I can't keep doing this, Ross. Bailing you out. I really can't.'

'I know, Tam. I'm sorry. I'll get myself a little job, pay you back, get myself straight.'

That word again.

He kissed her and she flinched. In the full light of the hall her brother's teeth looked cracked and rust-stained, his pitted skin had a yellow sheen, his hair was matted and his fingernails were black crescents of filth. His torn jeans were too big for him, falling in grubby folds over the tops of his soiled trainers, and the nauseating whiff of mould, she now realised, emanated not from Crystal's flat but from Ross himself.

'Don't worry about it,' she said.

'Honest, Tam. That's brilliant. I'll pay you back. Anything. I know I owe you, big time.'

'Well, listen, maybe there's one favour you might do for me. A work thing . . .'

She kept it simple. She could not rely on her brother's discretion, any more than she could rely on his honesty or self-discipline.

'Work?' Her brother raised his eyebrow playfully. 'Oh, right. You can call it whatever you like, sis. Secret's safe with me.'

'There's no secret.' She bridled. 'I just wanted to have a private word with him. Mutual advantage, sort of thing. Work-based, like I say.'

'You sly devil, Tam.' He winked. 'He's more Crystal's pal than mine. An old mate. Family stuff. But trust me, I'll sort it.'

Ross flashed his ruined teeth in an Artful Dodger smile.

*

Tamara was feeling high again. She had taken another couple of pulls on a joint before Dev announced that he was leaving and Ross had suggested, a little too chirpily maybe, that he might give his little sister a lift. And here she was, sitting in the passenger seat of his van, thrillingly adjacent to a desirable man who also happened to hold the key to the biggest story of her career.

'The tube all right for you?'

His voice was as smooth and rich as a TV voiceover – an advert for a malted bedtime drink, perhaps.

'Great.'

She watched his hands – strong and sure, with delicate fingers – resting on the steering wheel, and found herself imagining them playing across her breasts. As he stared at the road, she slyly studied his profile, taking pleasure in its perfection: his nose straight and fine, with faintly flared nostrils; the slight jut of his upper lip inviting a kiss; his chin with its dusting of stubble, abrasive proof that he was all man, not some overgrown pretty boy.

He glanced towards her, catching her stare.

'How well do you know Crystal?' he asked.

She turned her gaze to the road ahead.

'Not that well . . . She's more my brother's – Ross's – friend.'

'Right.'

'You?'

'We go way back. Practically family.'

His laugh was ironic. He must have known what an

unlikely pair he and Crystal made; he heroically hand-some and athletic, she a ghoulish wreck.

He slowed to turn a sharp corner and, as he moved the gear stick, his hand brushed against her knee and Tamara experienced an enfeebling swell of pleasure.

'Seems . . . hospitable. Crystal, I mean,' she said presently.

He laughed.

'Hospitable? You could say that . . .' He turned briefly to look at her. 'You're some kind of writer, aren't you?'

'Sort of. A bit. Here and there.' She hoped he didn't detect the tremor in her voice. 'How do you know?'

'Ross – your brother – mentioned it. He's proud of you, isn't he?'

She felt an inconvenient tug of guilt.

'How about you?' she asked. 'What do you do?'

He ran a hand through his hair.

'Me? I'm a clairvoyant.' He grinned.

'Really?' Tamara smiled back. 'So what's the future got in store for me, then?'

He narrowed his eyes.

'Mmm. I see a journey ahead. A long tunnel, dark, all the way to Hornsey.'

He was wearing some kind of exotic scent, a sweet, aromatic oil that was beginning to make her eyes smart.

'You're good!' she said. 'Except there isn't a tube station in Hornsey. You must be channelling Turnpike Lane.'

'That's it!' he said. 'I over-reached myself. There *will*

323

be a tube station in Hornsey – in a couple of decades. Mark my words.'

She laughed and looked out at the empty streets, playing for time.

'Tell me, Dev, what's your last name? Where are you from?'

'So many questions!' he mocked her lightly. 'My name is Dev, just the one name, and I'm from everywhere and nowhere.'

'Just Dev?'

'I used to have two names, like everyone else. But when I started on The Path, I jettisoned everything I didn't need. A second name was just one more worthless material possession. Dev is Sanskrit. It means follower of God. That's good enough for me.'

'Right,' Tamara said. 'One name, one syllable.'

'I like to leave a light footprint on the planet.'

Was he teasing her? They had pulled up outside the tube station. Time was short.

'Can you make a good living, as a clairvoyant?'

'I work as a healer, too.'

'Healing? In what way?' she asked.

He leaned towards her and lowered his voice.

'In *every* way.'

'You mean like the laying-on-of-hands stuff?'

He cupped his hands and held them towards her, smiling.

'Yeah. I've got healing hands.'

'So, what do you do with them?'

She had stepped into a minefield of innuendo. But if he had noticed, he let it pass.

'Aura massage, crystals, prismpuncture, spirit painting, psychic surgery . . .'

Aura massage! An unpleasant vision loomed of Honor Tait lying naked, a withered peat bog mummy, awaiting the ministrations of Dev and his healing hands.

'Prismpuncture?'

'You know acupuncture? It's like that, only instead of needles we use colours.'

Tamara strained to picture it. She had a horror of needles – unlike Ross – and, though acupuncture had been recommended as a hangover cure, she had always avoided it.

'Colours?'

'Specially treated glass vials of pure colour. You apply them to the pressure points. So, you've got kidney problems? I hold a vial of red in the second quartile of your lower back. The energy radiates the blood.'

Was her story about to shrivel away? Could this be the service Honor Tait was paying for in the restaurant? OLD WOMAN CONSULTS HIPPY QUACK would not make an arresting headline. But Tamara could not imagine Tait having much time for alternative therapies of any sort. And it would not explain the kiss, or the cash-stuffed envelope.

He continued: 'Or you're feeling jaded? I apply yellow to the third meridian just below your throat. We get fantastic results. And it's completely non-invasive.'

'Where do you do all this?'

'Clapton.'

Not so far, then.

'I hold surgeries at my flat,' he continued. 'Workshops, too – past lives, inner voices, angelology, life coaching.'

Life coaching. Was that it? She tried to imagine Honor Tait sitting attentively while this seductive huckster dispensed advice on her life, or what was left of it. Then again, Tamara thought, looking across at Dev, she could do with some life coaching herself. That and the gentle application of some healing hands.

'Wow. Brilliant,' she said. 'In fact, I'm a pretty spiritual person myself.'

'You know, I could tell. Straight away.'

He glanced at his watch then reached in his pocket to pull out a business card. It was grey and grainy, as if made from compressed oatmeal, and the words, 'Dev – Master Prismpuncture practitioner (RCPP – First Class). Aura Massage', were printed in heavy gothic script.

He took out a fountain pen and wrote down a phone number in violet ink.

'Give me a ring, Tamara. I've got a good feeling about you. You've got a beautiful aura. There's a lot of purple in there. It's the colour of truth. And gold. The colour of strength. Lots of gold.'

'Wow.'

He leaned in closer to her and she looked up, startled.

'Look, I've just had another premonition,' he said.

'What's that?'

'If you don't run, you'll miss the last tube.'

Eighteen

Honor had not heard from Ruth or Clemency, and Bobby was not responding to her messages. Inigo, still absurdly puffed up by the success of his show, had flown to New York with a girl he had picked up at his opening. Even Paul had been out of contact. Aidan had gone to France with Jorge for a week and before he left, he phoned to tell her that Paul had been seen at the National Theatre, on the arm of Martha Gellhorn. Paul was just Gellhorn's type, Honor supposed.

She stood at the window and watched a young family, a husband and wife in their early thirties, probably American, as they bumped an aerodynamically styled pushchair down the steps towards the garden. These fashionable young people were so preening in their parenthood, as if they had invented the whole arrangement. The carriage lurched towards the pavement and the toddler, muffled in blankets, hat and mittens, swayed as impassively as a Himalayan idol in a mountainside procession. There was love, Honor supposed, its invisible, indivisible chains clanking behind them.

Her eye had been drawn in that morning's paper to a story on Diogenes Syndrome. If this was an affliction of age, she thought at first glance, she would welcome it. She had been drawn to the Greek philosopher ever since she came across references to him when she was a rebellious schoolgirl, at a time when cynicism had seemed the only rational world view. Diogenes' choice of poverty and simplicity, his decision to forego all possessions and to live in a barrel, was particularly attractive to a girl whose home life was characterised by material abundance and intellectual poverty.

But now she looked more closely at the article and saw that Diogenes Syndrome was a misnomer. In fact, the condition was characterised by obsessive hoarding of rubbish and was more properly termed 'senile squalor syndrome'. Sufferers turned their homes into midden mazes, stacking piles of newspapers, rags, old tins, food wrappers, even faeces, and they often lay dead and undiscovered in their tunnels of trash for weeks.

No danger of that here. But there was still some work to do. She switched on the radio. Muslim riots shake China. IRA abandons 600 pound bomb in Strabane. Bosnian Croats open fire on Muslims in Mostar. Ramadan ends in more violence in Algeria. She walked to the window. The news from Mr Bose had not helped her mood. The colonoscopy had been inconclusive – would she care to submit to another? Outside, against the clear night sky, the moon was a neon crescent and in the garden the slender limbs of the beeches were pale as bone against the prison bar silhouette of the railings.

Her isolation had an undeniably different quality to the solitude she had once welcomed. Today it drained; then it irradiated. As a young woman, she had been filled with a purity of purpose. Work was the thing – the urge to tell, and to tell it first. And friendship and love, if not always the enemies of truth, were not its most assiduous allies. She had worked remorselessly, cultivated a stringent emotional self-sufficiency, and told the truth no matter what it cost her. But her reputation among her colleagues, distilled, in the cheap, reductive way of these things – she became the subject of two silly *roman-à-clef* novels by *Tribune* reporters – was simply for a glamorous ruthlessness. And her reputation now? She should be beyond caring. But still she worried at her work, a terrier with an old bone. She reached for the proofs of *The Unflinching Eye*.

The Moslem village of Melouza, south of Great Kabylia in the foothills of the Hodna mountains, was silent as I walked its dusty streets this week. All the men and youths – more than 300 in total – had been massacred by Algerian rebels loyal to the National Liberation Front (FLN). The women and children were too shocked to weep. Some, it is said, have been driven mad by grief.

The village was believed to be originally sympathetic to the rival nationalist group the National Algerian Movement (MNA). Despite their common hostility towards France, the two groups deployed their most

murderous tactics against each other and their respective
supporters. But since the MNA suffered heavy defeat at
the hands of the FLN in the region of Melouza, the
village seems to have turned to the French authorities
for protection.

The initials were dizzying, and the piece quite unmoving.
Her memory of the visit to Melouza had completely
vanished as, presumably, had any trace of the murdered
boys and men of the village. And if *she* found the piece
arid and unengaging, how was a reader expected to
respond? She wondered why Ruth was bothering with
this third book. Was it a form of vanity publishing, which
flattered the ego of publisher rather than writer? Then
let Ruth do the editing. Honor had no wish to look at
any of this stuff – old news from a vanished world – ever
again. But only she could revisit Goethe's Oak. Here was
a chance to put something right.

It was, in the end, the Allies who did for Goethe's Oak.
A British bombing raid the previous month, intended
for a nearby munitions factory, fell on Buchenwald camp.
A total of 316 prisoners and 80 SS officers were killed.
And there was another casualty; all that was left of
Goethe's symbolic tree was a charred stump and a heap
of smoking twigs. When the air raid was over, prisoners
and camp guards scrambled to pick up splinters of the
tree, souvenirs of a symbol of Germany's greatness, to
fascists and anti-fascists alike.

After the survivors' moving parade by the shattered trunk of the poet's tree, I walked in the forest outside the camp. I heard him before I saw him and ran to alert the American troops.

The central heating was humming away, consuming money she did not have, and she was cold to the bone. Nothing could warm her, not the blankets she had draped over herself in the chair, not alcohol, not the fake fire twinkling feebly in the grate. She had turned, like a distant relative of Lot's wife, into a pillar of ice. Was this a similar punishment for the same crime? Had they both looked back, lingering indecently, relishing the details of scenes too brutal for mortal eyes?

*

Simon was sulking. He had given up Morning Conference, he said on the phone. *Psst!* was Tania's baby now. Let her read the list, and all her other lists, and listen to everyone else's lists at all the other meetings, and try to wrest a smile from Wedderburn, and laugh at his miserable jokes.

'But you can't let her get away with it, ride roughshod over us, just like that,' Tamara said. 'We've got one more month in reader-friendly full-colour paper format before we vanish into cyberspace. We've done all the work and we deserve the credit. *Psst!* needs proper representation.'

'You go then,' was his curt reply. 'I'm still at Davina's. I'll see you at lunchtime.'

By the time Tamara had printed out the summary of this week's stories, checked the morning papers and arrived on the fourth floor, all the seats had been taken in the boardroom and she had to stand by the door, next to a couple of nervous teenage interns. She edged discreetly into a corner, a safe distance from the tea trolley.

Wedderburn, flanked by Tania and Lyra, who were busy making notes, was in a grave mood. He cleared his throat and the two women looked up sharply and put their pens aside in a synchronised move that could have been choreographed by Busby Berkeley. He moved briskly to business. This morning's *Courier* had done a spoiler on *The Monitor*'s Elite List, the painstakingly compiled pull-out supplement, planned, at great expense, to appear on Saturday week, naming the Top 100 Figures of Influence in Politics, Arts, Publishing, Business and Sport. There was a disturbing degree of confluence between *The Courier*'s Alpha List and *The Monitor*'s own, but there was one flagrant omission: Wedderburn himself had been overlooked in *The Courier*'s roll-call of Publishing and Media giants, as had Lukas Lukauskis, *The Monitor*'s leading shareholder. In their place was Neville Titmuss, Editor of *The Courier*, and Bohdan Bohdanovich, his paper's Ukrainian proprietor.

There was more: *The Monitor*'s His 'n' Hers Elite give-away had been trumped by *The Courier*'s Hers 'n' His free gifts of a faux-gold tiepin with a faux-gold necklace, both stamped with the letter A, for Alpha. The Elite pull-out had already been printed, ready to go in a fortnight, the

TV advertising campaign had been paid for, the faux-gold trinkets had been shipped from Taiwan and were waiting to be bagged-up at the printers. The promotion could not be scrapped at this stage. They would have to go ahead on Saturday 1 March, giving the impression that *The Monitor* was scrambling to follow *The Courier*, rather than the other way round.

'It is irksome in the extreme,' Wedderburn said.

Everyone, including the teenage interns, nodded grimly. Tapping the table with his pen for emphasis, the Editor stressed that the only way of salvaging the costly circulation-building campaign was to ensure that the Saturday edition for that key date would be a 'bumper issue'.

'I'd like all the Saturday editors, when reading their lists today, to also give us advance notice of their plans for the first of March issue. You need to pull out all the stops. Only the best will do.'

The post-mortem on the rest of the morning's papers was cursory; there seemed to be an unspoken pact that, for today, jokes, or attacks on the competence of one's colleagues, were not required. Wedderburn looked as if he might sack them all if he was irked any further. The Home News editor read his list – more Tory sleaze, British Oscar nominations, the postponed Kensit–Gallagher nuptials – as swiftly as a tobacco auctioneer, and the Foreign editor was a paragon of icy industriousness as she chanted today's plainsong of mayhem and murder in distant lands. Politics was not represented – Toby Gadge was attending a mass to mark the feast of St Adelaide of Bellich – and Vida, standing in for Johnny, who was attending a course on non-verbal communication, gave a subdued account of the main features planned for tomorrow's *Me2* – 'Wish You Weren't Here', a pictorial guide to the worst seaside resorts in Britain, and 'Granny I Hardly Knew You', an empowering tale of incest survival.

The Money editor seemed to be impersonating a speaking clock as he enunciated details of interest rate rises, retail price index falls and fluctuations in the exchange rate. Ricky Clegg had anticipated the sober mood of today's conference by wearing a suit and tie. Or perhaps he was going for a job interview later. He spent longer than necessary speculating about the likely performance of David Becking – or was it Beckham? – a twenty-one-year-old London-born Manchester United striker, who would be playing in tomorrow's World Cup qualifier. Tamara was reassured to see that Wedderburn – scrutinising *The Courier*'s Alpha List again, as if closer reading might yield up his name after all – seemed as little interested as she was in fledgling footballers. The Arts editor gave his account of tomorrow's lead arts story – a comparison of the poetry of Keats with the lyrics of Kylie Minogue – with an air of wounded self-importance and only a passing reference to the brutal spiking of the review of Monday's Wigmore Hall recital.

Then, so swiftly, it was the turn of the weekend sections. Tamara looked down at the printout of the *Psst!* list. She had an exclusive to announce: Pernilla Perssen was pregnant. That Tamara had got the exclusive as a result of a complaint – the model's lawyers had not been amused by *Psst!*'s interpretation of her morning sickness or her weight gain – need not be mentioned here. It was a firecracker of a story. Other papers would stampede to pick it up and speculation about the identity of the baby's father would keep the press going for weeks. Perhaps they should save the exclusive for 1 March, which was also the date of the penultimate issue of the genuine, full-fat, carbon-based *Psst!*. They would go out in a blaze of glory.

Tamara mentally rehearsed her delivery. Lofty efficiency would be the key.

Lyra was announcing this week's contributors to *S*nday* – two Booker winners and a Nobel laureate, an Elite List all of its own – with the passionate urgency of a Shakespearian actress auditioning for the part of Portia. One day soon, thought Tamara, her own name would be slipped in among The Greats in Lyra's stellar *S*nday* list. The Books' editor was speaking now, stumbling through his dull catalogue of reviews and literary non-stories – an exploration of the genius of Alexander the Great, long overdue; a global history of colonisation, and a new novel by, or perhaps about, a hard-drinking Bulgarian punk. Caspar Dyson's manner was apologetic and Austin Wedderburn's displeasure, or simple lack of interest, was obvious.

'. . . We've also got a study of nineteenth-century Portuguese verse,' added Caspar, wiping a glistening moustache of sweat that had formed on his upper lip.

Tamara looked through her own list again. Should she go with the Pernilla Perssen scoop first or save it till the end of her list? End with a bang, as it were? But Caspar had not finished.

'. . . And on March the first our lead review will be Tania Singh's four-thousand-word essay on the life and work of Honor Tait, in advance of the publication of Tait's new book, *Dispatches from a Dark Place*.'

Tamara rocked back in her chair, appalled. What was he saying? She looked across at Tania, smirking self-importantly, and at Lyra, evasively doodling on the cover of her notepad.

'You can't do that!' a voice cried out in impassioned protest.

Every head turned towards Tamara, stunned at the breach of protocol. The voice of protest, she realised, had been her own; the words had flown from her lips at the speed of thought.

Austin Wedderburn dropped his pen, which made a guillotine clatter in the silent boardroom. He looked at Tamara directly, probably for the first time since she had started work at *The Monitor*.

'Why, precisely, can't we "do that"?'

She felt a sudden tightness in her throat, which made it difficult to breathe. When she finally spoke, her voice was a strangulated whine.

'It's a spoiler,' she said.

'A spoiler?' said the Editor. '*Another* spoiler?'

He emitted a bitter laugh, granting permission for the susurration of mirthless hilarity that ricocheted round the table.

'Surely we're all for spoilers here,' he continued, 'if it means we steal a march on the opposition. Or do you have a moral objection?'

Tamara tried to ignore the slow smiles spreading across the faces of her colleagues; they knew that as long as someone else was buckling under the heat of Wedderburn's wrath, they were safe, for the moment.

'Not the opposition,' whispered Tamara. 'It isn't a spoiler against the opposition. It's S*nday's story. One of us.'

Wedderburn looked to his left at the radiantly innocent face of Tania, then to Lyra, who had resumed her note-taking.

'Lyra? Do you have any objections? This Honor Tait piece in the Books section? Does it pre-empt any plans you have for future issues?'

Lyra looked briefly at Tamara then turned back to Wedderburn.

'No,' she said, shaking her head. 'Not at all. No plans.'

This was treachery on a spectacular scale. All Tamara's hopes drained away, as suddenly as if a cistern had been flushed. She was left with nothing, humiliated.

'Glad we've got that straight,' said Wedderburn, turning to address the conference. 'One spoiler in a morning is unfortunate, two would be careless!'

His mouth crinkled tremulously then relaxed into a shallow smile and dutiful laughter eddied round the table. He gathered up his papers, signalling a move to the next item on the agenda. Only Tania was looking at Tamara now and her expression – clear-eyed, her head cocked, bird-like, to one side, with a wry twist of a smile – was of unbounded pity.

Wedderburn nodded to Xanthippe Sparks, whose appearance today – back-combed hair, flounced skirts, laced boots and torn fishnets – suggested that she had just emerged from the Nancy Sykes Refuge for Distressed Burlesque Artistes.

'This week,' she said, 'we've got "Catwalk Confidential", backstage at the shows; and "Sole Sisters", a story about sibling shoe designers. The picture-spread focus is on The New Rococo . . . Frills and Spills . . . Tiers for Souvenirs . . .'

The News editor and Foreign editor exchanged glances. At least, Tamara thought, when it was her turn to speak, she could reclaim some dignity. Compared to the Fashion schedule, the *Psst!* list would sound like Hansard.

'And for March the first, in our Menswear Special, we'll be heralding the return of Medallion Man in our picture special: Chest Hair Chic.'

Tamara looked through this week's *Psst!* list again. Should it be 'Inside Baggeley Market: Outrageous Real Life Stories Behind Top Soap' first? Or 'The Pits: Underarm Hair Horror of the Stars'?

Wedderburn looked at his watch.

'Right,' he said, raising an eyebrow, 'we need to cut this short. That's all we have time for. Tania is going to update us on interweb development. And then we've got a paper to bring out!'

There was another outbreak of approving merriment,

which drowned Tamara's bitter gasp of incredulity. Overlooked again! Had she been of a more paranoid cast of mind, she might have begun to see this as a conspiracy. Her spasm of self-pity was interrupted by the sudden intrusion in her field of vision of a white porcelain jug, which was being waved under her nose by Hazel. Bypassing the teenaged interns, the Editor's secretary had walked across the room to seek Tamara's assistance in the distribution of tea. There was no way out; Tamara accepted the task with furious zeal. She heaped three spoons of sugar in Wedderburn's cup and passed a cup to Tania, who looked up briefly and, without pausing in her dis-quisition on web traffic and page impressions, raised two fingers at Tamara. It was only by force of imagination, which filled the teaspoon with cyanide crystals rather than sugar, that Tamara was able to finish the job without blundering from the boardroom in a tearful rage.

The weeping came later, over lunch at the Bubbles. She had spent so much time fantasising about the life of excitement and ease that would follow her official eleva-tion to Lyra Moore's team that the alternative was unthink-able. Now she had to face it; her future was destined to be a dreary extension of the existing reality, a long grey corridor lit only by the distant glow of the crematorium.

Simon passed her an envelope of blanks, procured from the maître d' of a new Michelin-starred restaurant in the City.

'Could you manage to do these by the end of the week?

It would be really helpful, what with Dexter's birthday and everything.'

She took the envelope without comment and it was then that he noticed she was crying.

'You okay, Tam?'

She told him everything. He passed her tissues to staunch the flow of tears and ordered a consolatory bottle of champagne.

'It's Lyra I can't understand,' Tamara sniffed. 'I know exactly what Tania's up to. It fits in perfectly with her masterplan for world domination. But what was Lyra doing commissioning me to write the piece in the first place? And then she just walks away, leaving me stranded, just when I've cracked the story, after all the work I've done.'

Simon reached across the table and patted her hand.

'Look, Tamara, I didn't know how to tell you this but . . . you weren't meant to be doing this story in the first place.'

Tamara looked up. He had pushed her too far. His lack of faith in her abilities was evident to the point of insult.

'Simon,' she said, her lips pinched with spite, 'you're the Content editor of *Psst!.com*, not the editor of *S*nday*. Lyra Moore is. She commissioned me. Nothing to do with you. Her decision. Her choice.'

'That's the point,' he said, 'it wasn't her choice.'

What did he mean?

'It was all a mistake,' he added gently.

Tamara was gripped by a queasy dread, like the mild

seasickness she had suffered at the Features summer party on a Thames barge. She put down her glass.

'What are you saying? She sent me a message. She asked me to do it. It's there. In my computer. I'll show you later if you need proof.'

Simon spoke slowly and quietly, like a doctor breaking bad news and fearing the patient's inevitable emotional outburst.

'She sent a message, yes. She wanted a feature on Honor Tait. But she didn't want *you* to do it.'

'But it's there. In black and white. Her message. On the office system. From Lyra. To me.'

'Tamara,' he said softly, 'remember Aurora Witherspoon? Austin Wedderburn? Best fit? Lyra had started to type in a name on her computer. The predictive text program filled in your name instead. She didn't notice the error until she got your response.'

Tamara buried her head in her hands. She remembered her elation when she received Lyra's message and the gushing enthusiasm of her instant response. It was several seconds before she felt steady enough to speak.

'If it wasn't for me, that message, then who *was* it meant for?'

But she knew the answer already. Simon's sympathy was sincere.

'Tania,' he said. 'Not Tamara Sim, but the omnipotent, all-conquering Tania Singh, the Media Medea, the Queen Semiramis of the Information Age.'

Tamara sank back in silent horror as Simon went on.

341

'She'd been pestering Lyra to write for *S*nday* for months, claimed she'd read everything by Honor Tait, admired her above all else, admired Lyra even more, thought *S*nday* was the most significant publishing event since the Book of Kells, et cetera.'

Tamara groaned softly as she recalled, again, the narcotic surge of pleasure Lyra's message had given her, and her skittish, almost flirtatious response – 'I SO much admire! . . . I'm THRILLED to be part of!! . . .' – and her repeated suggestions, so pathetic in retrospect, all unanswered for what were now obvious reasons, that they might meet for lunch, or coffee, or just simply meet, to discuss the project further.

'Lyra felt pretty bad about it all,' Simon explained, 'inasmuch as she actually *has* feelings. She said you sounded so damned happy about it in your reply. Delirious, she said. She didn't have the heart to slap you down. She was avoiding the issue really. Told me that you might turn something up in your interview that she could use in a caption story.'

'A caption story?'

'You know, run glitzy photos of the old bag in her heyday with a couple of hundred words by you. And then Lyra heard that Tania was going to do a big piece for the Books pages and she felt that got her off the hook. She was really only lukewarm about the Honor Tait story anyway.'

'Then why didn't she *say*?' Tamara moaned.

'You know what she's like,' Simon said. 'She's a prima

donna who'll never admit mistakes, even to herself. She had moved on, trusting you and Tania and Caspar and all the other journalistic pygmies would go away and leave her in peace to commune with The Greats.'

'You could have put me out of my misery at least. You're supposed to be my friend. Why didn't you tell me?'

'Precisely because I'm your friend. Something could have come of it. Something has. News of the commission really boosted you – you'd been low for weeks. Don't deny it. You were in such a state over Tim, I had to send you home from the office. Remember? And when you finally found your way into the story, you rose to the challenge.'

'Great,' Tamara said with a croak of self-pity. 'Where does that leave me now?'

'It's been a blow, I know,' Simon said. 'And Lyra hasn't handled this well. Great editor, hopeless people person. But I'd say you're in a pretty good position.'

'Oh yes? Where's that? Poised outside on a high-rise ledge staring into an 80-foot drop?'

He reached across the table again and gripped her hand.

'Come on, Tam. It's not that bad. This small temporary hitch could work in your favour.'

'How's that exactly?'

He was trying to humour her now.

'Get on with your piece. You've made a terrific start. You're sitting on a brilliant story and, since *The Monitor*'s given it the brush-off, you're perfectly within your rights to take it elsewhere and make some serious money. Pursue the racy angle, the toyboy story, and the tabloids will be gagging for it. It would have been wasted on *S*nday* anyway. Forget *S*nday*. Think big. Tim would pay a lot for a yarn like that and you might even be offered a staff job on the *Sphere*. It might be time for us old-fashioned fun-loving hacks to bale out of *The Monitor* anyway.'

It was an appealing argument. But there was one problem.

'Tim?' she said. 'He dumped me, remember? And I wasn't exactly friendly to him at the Press Awards last week.'

Simon sighed, checked his pager and got to his feet. He threw a roll of notes in the saucer and put the receipt in his pocket, ready to clip it to an expenses form that afternoon.

'You've just got to put it behind you. Move on,' he said. 'I wouldn't let a little thing like that stand in the way of a good story. Time for some bridge-building.'

*

Honor picked up the day's newspaper.

Twenty-four people, including a former football star, were killed by armed groups in Algiers at the close of Algeria's bloodiest Ramadan since the Muslim insurgency began five years ago, according to official sources yesterday. Mohamed Madani, a former top footballer, aged 52, was shot dead after he left Friday prayers in a mosque in Algiers. Elsewhere, in the southern Algiers suburbs, attackers disguised as police slit the throats of fourteen civilians from three families. In the nearby neighbourhood of Beau Fraisier, another group killed a couple and their six-month-old baby.

Violence in Algiers; riots in Albania; Basque separatists bombing and bludgeoning their way to a dream of independence; famine; brutality; the slaughter of innocents. She could have read, or written, the same stories fifty years ago but Honor was still drawn to the daily deadly déjà vu of the papers. What had changed was the context in which these stories of human cruelty, greed and injustice were placed. Once, they would be given dour prominence on pages as unadorned as tombstones. Today you had to search for them in a dizzying visual vortex.

These timeless stories of injustice now bleated ineffectually, shouted down like Calvinist preachers at a carnival, by brash accounts of the private lives of royalty and popstars, actors and footballers. Political coverage, too – its trivial bellicosity, puffed-up personalities, old-fashioned sex scandals, endless worthless speculation about the date of the forthcoming election – was reduced to the parochial, a subset of show business. And then there were the columnists. Glancing at the bottomless banalities – 'Crumpet King: why cheating TV chef's wife should dump him' – of another lipsticked fool, she had wondered if it was the picture byline that had administered the *coup de grâce* to newspapers. The introduction of this simple design device, the postage-stamp-sized portrait, to brighten the appearance of pages for a public infantilised by television, had created a need for young, pretty, ideally blonde, journalists – regardless of their abilities as writers and reporters – whose winsome photographs would contrast favourably with those of the balding middle-aged men who then made up the majority of newspaper staff. Hence the prevalence of vacuous ninnies like Tara Sim.

But then, Honor reflected, her own contribution could be called into question: the banner of truth she had waved so often on the front line was a poor, tattered, bloodstained thing. The world had not necessarily been better under the old dispensation, and her failures had mattered more than the silly blunders of Tara Sim, or of all the jobbing 'journalists' today. Perhaps, Honor thought, her greatest crime had been a sin of omission. It was the story that she failed to report that lingered more vividly now than any of her breathless dispatches from the front line.

Buchenwald. 14 April 1945. Liberation Day Four. Twenty minutes later, I was walking through woods outside the camp's perimeter fence, following the route Goethe must have taken that lovely late autumn day nearly 120 years ago. Suddenly, I was startled by a noise in the undergrowth. I heard him before I saw him, and ran to alert the American troops.

Nineteen

The music, a random assault on the electrified strings of an unidentifiable Eastern instrument, was playing at police-siren pitch as Tamara made her way into the smoky twilight.

The Chakra Bar, formerly the Chequers Pub, seemed to have been designed by a committee whose members had competing memories of drugged-out gap years; Buddhist prayer flags were strung across the room like Christmas decorations, Hindu gods smiled from purple walls, hookah pipes stood on every table, their coiled lengths of tubing suggesting exotic life support machines.

The smoke – from joss sticks, cigarettes, the hookahs and, from somewhere in the corner, a fruity joint – was as thick as dry ice, and what light there was flickered from a host of votive candles.

Gradually, Tamara made out the lone figure at a corner table. As she drew nearer, she saw that he was reading from a paperback, which he had propped against a hookah and illuminated with a candle.

He looked up and smiled, his eyes creasing roguishly.

His paperback, she noticed, was called *The Book of Changes*. They ordered drinks: cocktails of vodka and kiwi fruit called The Sound of One Hand Clapping.

'So. Tamara the Writer. What do you want to know?'

'You're the clairvoyant,' she said. 'You tell me.'

He laughed and touched her hand lightly. She felt an unprofessional ripple of pleasure.

'Well, Tamara, Seeker after Truth. I'm here to help in any way I can.'

He was looking at her appreciatively. Her look this evening – spiky moussed hair, low-cut, leopard-print blouse and slinky pencil skirt – evoked Paula Yates as classy rock chick.

'I was really interested in what you said about your work,' she said. 'I thought I might write a piece about you.'

She reached for her glass. The cocktail was not bad.

'For a magazine?'

His expression was neutral.

'A magazine. Or maybe a newspaper,' she added.

'I didn't know you were that kind of writer.'

'I'm not really. I'm working on a book but I do a bit of journalism on the side. I'm the kind of writer who needs to make a living.'

He laughed again.

'Well, that makes two of us, I suppose. I'm the kind of healer who needs to make a living. How much would you pay?'

She was startled.

'For what?'

'For this piece you're going to write about me.'

'Oh, you don't get paid for this kind of story,' she said with a coquettish shake of her head. She needed to approach this gently. She mustn't scare him off. 'This is a straightforward story about your work; the healing. It's not a kiss-and-tell.'

'We'll see about that.'

He smiled and touched her hand again. This time his fingers lingered on hers. Why shouldn't she enjoy this? It was not as if she would jeopardise the story by responding. And this was her first date in weeks. Ideally, she should have fixed it for Friday, Valentine's Day, and pre-empted all those irritatingly coy questions from colleagues. But this was an emergency. Work came first, even before love. It had to be tonight.

'Tell me a bit more about aura massage.'

'Take *your* aura, for example,' he said, gazing directly at her. 'You've got a beautiful aura. Do you know that? There's a lot of red in there, the colour of sensuality. And silver. The colour of spirituality. Lots of silver.'

'What about your clients?'

'They're all sorts really. Young, old, wealthy – mostly wealthy.'

'Any famous people? Celebrities?'

He looked at her quizzically.

'Oh yes. I've had a few well-known types. Quite a few. You'd be surprised.'

'I'm sure I would,' she said.

They ordered another cocktail. Three parts grappa to one part ginseng tea, with a garnish of a single mung bean, set alight by a bored waitress dressed as a belly dancer. The cocktail was called The Art of Tantra.

*

These Augean stables had to be cleaned. More books – history, current affairs, alarmist tracts about the future of the ecosystem, American political analysis, biographies, Graham's novels, which had been another point of contention with Tad. His jealous rages, though tiresome, had never intimidated her. Sometimes, although she would never admit it to him, she had even found them comic. Despite Honor's repeated, weary assurances, he had always been inflamed by the very sight of the name of her second husband. Tad was stirred to fury whenever Bartók, with whom the tone-deaf Sandor had no link other than birthplace, was played on the wireless, and he had once disappeared in a huff for three days in Salzburg when he had seen posters advertising a performance at the Mozarteum by the violinist Tibor Varga, who, like tens of thousands of Hungarians, shared Sandor's surname.

Dead husbands, Honor supposed, had been more of a threat than extant exes or deceased divorcés, though Sandor's cardiac, presumably brought on by the carnal ministrations of Miss Monte Carlo, had beaten the divorce courts by a mere month. Spouses were usually sanctified in death, no matter how monstrous, or inadequate, they had been in life. And now it was Tad's turn for canonisation.

Candles and coasters, ridiculous hoards of pens – old felt tips, an unused Mont Blanc, countless biros, a set of fluorescent highlighters packaged like candy bars – all fell with satisfying finality into black plastic sacks. She remembered a similar operation after her mother died, though some of that detritus was destined for the ritzier auction rooms and kept her father in whisky and beaters for a few more years.

Bradley, Honor's brother-in-law, a blandly polite retired heart surgeon from Phoenix, had done the honours here for Tad, clearing his closets and drawers and disposing of the contents. Honor could not face it but she had kept back the locked trunk, telling Bradley it was hers, and a week later she asked the porter to come up and carry it to her front door. Late one night, conscious of the strange ceremonial quality of her task, she had unlocked the trunk and, one by one, sent Tad's billowing costumes on their final spree, slithering down the chute in the hall to the vast communal garbage bin behind the apartment block.

Lois's flat had to be cleared, too, before it was sold to pay for her incarceration in the residential home. Two greedy nieces had done the job, squabbling like magpies over glittering scraps.

Honor closed tonight's sacks with a decisive knot and unpeeled another bag from a roll. Someone would have to perform this posthumous task for her – Ruth, most likely, in a tumult of self-importance. This clear-out was a satisfying pre-emptive strike.

The radio would give her all the company she needed. She turned it on and listened with growing impatience. Yet more speculation about the date of the election, the Tory government faced a fresh row over sleaze, feeble analysis of a newly divorced princess's attempts to make herself useful by posing with landmine victims in Angola. No interest here to divert her. Silence was preferable. And work could no longer be avoided.

> It was in this beech forest, Buchenwald, that Goethe said 'of late I have often thought it would be the last time that I should look down hence on the kingdoms of the world, and their glories; but it has happened once again, and I hope that even this is not the last time we shall both spend a pleasant day here . . . Here man feels great and free – great and free as the scene he has before his eyes, and as he ought properly always to be.' Outside the death camp which bore the name of Goethe's epiphanic forest, on the northern flank of Ettersberg, where a century ago the poet had contemplated the glories of the world, I heard a noise, a cracking of twigs, and saw a young Nazi soldier cowering in the undergrowth. I ran to alert the Americans. The German was unarmed and surrendered immediately.

*

Tamara lay staring up at the fringed Chinese lantern suspended between the eaves in the shabby attic flat. She was basking in the warmth radiating from the sleeping form beside her, and in the prospect of professional triumph. Tim would not like this. He would not like this at all. He would certainly share her exultation once she had delivered the copy and it was laid out on two double-page spreads, with incriminating pictures and punchy headlines. But he would hate the fact that while he was stuck in his deadly marriage, reduced to pawing ambitious interns for kicks, Tamara had moved on to a younger, more agile, infinitely more attractive lover.

Memories of last night – a languorous unfolding and entwining and, what seemed like hours later, a mutual climax of raucous intensity – would keep her going for weeks. She turned on the pillow to face him. At this moment, she realised, she had become one of those people who could say with heartfelt honesty, 'I love my work.' But there was something troubling her too; recollections of the night's pleasures were interrupted by unwelcome thoughts of her new lover's recent exertions with Honor Tait. She looked at the sweet perfection of his face, at the touching groove above his lovely lips, pursed in sleep – and that was only his face. What a waste.

The principles of female prostitution were obvious. It would not be difficult to keep emotion out of the trans-action and, if the client was unsavoury, you could always focus on his wallet. But, in the case of male escorts – masseurs, gigolos – with their inevitably unappetising female clients, what Tamara could never fathom was the question of gravity; how did they manage to perform?

His back was now turned to her and his faint snores vibrated like a cat's purr. She needed to move the story on. Would now be a good time to broach it? She put an exploratory hand on the honeyed curve of his shoulder. He moaned softly and seemed to slip into a deeper sleep. Shrugging herself into him, she ran the arch of her foot down his calf. Now he was groaning, coming to life. He rolled over, stretching his arms as he yawned, glanced at her then stared up at the ceiling.

'Dev?' She stroked his arm.

'Mmm?'

'You awake?'

'I am now.'

'I really enjoyed last night.'

'Mmm.'

She slid her hand down his groin. There was not much going on there either.

'Those healing hands of yours were really something,' she said.

He took her wrist and held it firmly.

'Don't you have work to do this morning?' he asked.

She could not tell him that *this* was her work – lingering in bed, exhausted by pleasure, next to a living, breathing, sexually adept version of Michelangelo's David.

'Got the morning off,' she said, only half lying.

'Right.' He turned towards her, releasing her hand. 'Well, we can't all afford to hang around. I've got stuff to do. Clients to see.'

'Some of your famous clients?'

'Maybe.'

'Like who?'

'That would be telling.'

'Like Honor Tait?'

His smile faded.

'You know her?'

She felt a tightening in her throat. Had she blown it? Gone in too soon?

'Vaguely. Every journalist knows Honor Tait. Knows *of* her.'

He pulled back the duvet and got out of bed.

'So, how did you hear? About her and me?'

He walked towards the kitchen area – two portable gas rings on a pine table by a sink.

'Word gets round,' she said.

'What sort of word?' he asked, filling the kettle.

Tamara sat up and leaned back against the pillow in a show of calm. This was dangerous territory. Maybe he had spotted her at the charity event or in the café after all. Or outside the art gallery.

'Oh, you know, you and her, angels, prisms, auras . . . that sort of thing.'

'Camomile?' he asked.

'Great.'

'Seriously,' he said, 'how did you hear about her and me?'

'Actually, I've seen you before. At that meeting in Archway. The children's charity? I was there, sitting at the back.'

'Really?'

'Yes. I noticed you arrive late.'

He turned his back, reaching for two mugs from a rickety cupboard.

'I just wanted to check her out,' he said. 'See her in action. On duty. She's got quite a following, hasn't she?'

'Yes. I suppose she has. And then I saw you together,' Tamara continued. 'There's a café I go to in Maida Vale and I saw you outside her flat there.'

'Outside Holmbrook?'

He froze.

'Yes. I'd heard she lived there. Bit of a coincidence, really. I'd been coming to the café on and off for a while to write my book.'

He brought the tea over, got into bed and leaned over to retrieve a red velvet pouch from the floor.

'What sort of book are you writing?' he asked.

'A memoir, sort of,' she hedged.

'You write for newspapers too, don't you?'

Her heart lurched again. Had Ross told him about her work for the *Sphere*? Or had she let it out in a moment of drunken indiscretion last night? She sipped the tea and recoiled. Did anyone honestly like this stuff? It was like a microwaved urine sample.

'Now and again. Helps to pay the bills.'

He picked up a hardback – the *Tibetan Book of the Dead* – and began to roll a joint, licking the gummed edge of the cigarette papers. His tongue was pink and pointed as a sugar mouse.

'Yeah. We've all got to pay the bills. What sort of newspapers?'

356

Her heartbeat was so loud she was sure he could hear it. He was suspicious and she was absurdly vulnerable – naked and alone with him in a part of London she barely knew. This was front-line reporting.

'Oh, a few papers, and magazines. I do TV listings, that sort of thing.'

He snapped the catch on the lighter and applied the flame to the joint, narrowing his eyes as he inhaled deeply. After ten seconds, two plumes of smoke shot from his nostrils like steam from the nose of an enraged bull. When he finally spoke, his voice was a cracked squeak.

'Ever work for the Sunday tabloids?'

This was it. He must have locked the front door when they stumbled in last night, his hands kneading her breasts, hers grasping his cock. Where had he put the key?

'Once or twice. Bits and pieces.'

She checked her exit route, noting the position of her shoes and clothes, heaped where they left them when he stripped her on the sofa last night. Was this a bone fide flat? Or was it a couple of rooms in a badlands squat – the sort of place Ross used to hang around before he plunged downmarket?

'How much do they pay for stories then?'

Tamara had no memory of their journey here last night, apart from a vague recollection of stumbling upstairs past a punk girl in a plastic miniskirt.

'Not much, really. I might get sixty pounds a shift for doing the TV listings.'

He passed her the joint. She needed a clear head for

this conversation. But if she refused to smoke, he might become more suspicious.

'Not you. I wasn't asking how much *you* got,' he said. 'The people who sell stories, scandals, the dirt on ex-lovers? Don't they get a fortune?'

She applied the joint to her lips, taking small, shallow breaths. Despite her restraint the smoke unspooled slowly through her system. At least he didn't seem hostile now. Irritable, perhaps, but not openly hostile.

'They can make a packet, yes. Depends.'

'What are you talking? Five figures? Six?'

Despite his agitation, a delicious calm began to spread through her veins. She wriggled further down into the bed and passed the joint back to him. His urgency was oddly attractive.

'Sometimes six. If it's a good enough story involving a celebrity.'

'Would you call Honor Tait a celebrity?' he asked.

'Not really . . .' If she appeared too keen it would raise his price. 'She's too old to be a celebrity. She's kind of famous – but only to journalists and pointy-head writers.'

'She was on that TV arts programme,' he said. 'And they say she screwed Frank Sinatra. He's a celebrity, isn't he?'

'But he's dead. Where's the fun in that?'

He pushed his hair back from his forehead. He really was a lovely sight. She wanted to trace her finger across his lips, follow the line of his jaw, then draw her hand down his chest. But this wasn't the moment.

'There must be some mileage in her,' he insisted. 'She's been on the telly. People recognise her in the street. Her husband, Tad Challis, was a famous film director. MBE, the lot. He made *The Pleasure Seekers, Hairdressers' Honeymoon* . . . British comedy classics. There might be something on him. Everyone's heard of him.'

'Everyone over thirty with a taste for retro comedy. Besides which, he's dead. Not much of a circulation builder, stories about dead people.'

'There must be something.'

He gnawed at his thumbnail. This was her moment.

'Well, there might be some money in a story about a respectable old woman, recent subject of a TV programme, profiled in *Vogue*, darling of the chattering classes, etc, shares platforms with members of the Shadow Cabinet, if, for instance, illicit sex was involved.'

Levering himself up on the pillow, he turned to look directly into her face.

'Sex?'

'Yes. Ridiculous, I know.'

'What do you mean illicit?'

'Well, it has to be a bit out of the ordinary . . . transgressive. If she was doing it with another pensioner, there wouldn't be a story, and no one would want to read about it anyway. Kinky's good, but it mustn't be too gross. No bestiality, for instance. These are family newspapers.'

He began to roll another joint. It was agony to look at him but not to touch.

'What sort of "transgressive" sex would these family newspapers find acceptable then?'

'I suppose all sex involving the over sixties is transgressive but if, for example, she were sleeping with someone – same species, alive, obviously – younger, much younger, then that would be the sort of acceptably weird sex story they could carry.

'Hard to imagine, I know,' she added.

'And they'd pay a lot for that kind of story?'

'Yes. I think you'd find they would.'

He leaned towards her, his lips within kissing distance – she would not even have to raise her head – and passed her the joint.

'Six figures?'

'They might. Depends.'

She held the smoke in her lungs, savouring it, before exhaling slowly with a covert smile. Her job was almost done. He had taken the bait.

'Depends on what?'

'Just how much he's prepared to say,' she said hoarsely. 'Whether there are any pictures – of him with Honor Tait. No porn shots, though. No one wants to see old people with their clothes off.'

He laughed, throwing his head back.

'And you could put me in touch with these papers?'

She reached up and gently stroked his face.

'Treat me nicely and I'll see what I can do.'

*

Honor's life, as much as was possible in this spare final act, had given every outward impression of being fulfilling, or at least interesting. Old and useless as she was, she had at least mastered the illusion of purpose: work, of a kind, friends, music, theatre, an interest in world affairs. She had kept herself busy.

Travel was no longer possible and, though this had seemed the cruellest blow, she resisted bitterness, thinking of Lois, for whom an unaccompanied journey down to the foyer of the hospital, or even to the lavatory at the end of the ward, would be as hazardous, heroic and unlikely as a lone trip up the Amazon. Their world had shrunk. Accept it. And that adventurous spirit she once shared with Lois, their relish for new places, must now be turned inward. Honor was at last entering true *terra incognito*; there were no maps, no one would follow her precise route to this unknown destination and she would be making the journey alone.

Until recently, blank days in her diary could make her as panicky as a teenage wallflower. She had meted out appointments, events, dates with friends, even phone calls, spacing them carefully, luminous landmarks in the lengthening dusk. And what, truly, did all this activity amount to? Cheerful tunes, asinine music hall songs, hummed in solitude to mask the terrible silence. *My old man said, 'Follow the van, and don't dilly dally on the way.'* The van, it struck her now, must have been a hearse.

Buchenwald. 14 April 1945. Liberation Day Four. In woodland at the edge of the camp, I glimpsed a fugitive Nazi soldier hiding in the undergrowth. Minutes later American troops had captured him and dragged him into the compound. A queue of US soldiers, merry as a line outside a Saturday-night movie, formed to give that young German a savage beating. In the chaos of victory, with the stink of death around them in this terrible place, in the shadow of Goethe's Oak, the Americans were pumped up with righteous vengefulness.

Twenty

'Tim!'
'Yes?'
He sounded cautious.
'It's Tamara.'
'Tamara!'
The frisky shout down the line could not mask his wariness.
'How are you?' she asked.
'A bit the worse for wear after last week's shenanigans.'
'Oh?'
'The Press Awards. Did you hear?'
'I was there.'
'Oh, right . . .'
He had forgotten her central role in his humiliation. This was a relief as well as an insult.
'What happened?' she asked, testing his memory further.
'A minor scrap with some arsehole. One of your lot, I think, from *The Monitor*.'
'You okay?'

'Bit of a shiner, bruised pride and all that. But you should have seen the state of the other guy.'

'What was it about, your fight?'

'No idea. You know how it is. Some slapper, probably. Anyway, how are *you* doing, my darling? To what do I owe the pleasure?'

He had used her, dumped her, broken her heart and insulted her. And now he was talking to her as if they were old friends. She wished Alistair had hit him harder and inflicted some real damage. But this, she reminded herself, was business. Revenge could wait.

'It's a story. I thought you might be interested.'

'Try me . . .'

They agreed to meet in a pub five minutes from his office. The Swan was a sour-smelling pit with a neon jukebox playing Eighties dance hits. Mid-afternoon, when Tamara arrived, it was full of men in hard hats and work boots drinking their day's wages. Hacks from the *Sphere* would arrive later and then the real fun would begin. As her ex-lover walked in, she tensed herself for pain but was relieved to find she felt only a cringe of embarrassment. The comparison with Dev was stark. He looked old, puffy-faced and seedy and there was a dark raccoon circle around his right eye, giving him a piratical look. He ordered their drinks and sat down. He seemed nervous and sat on the edge of his seat, a plastic banquette scarred with a constellation of cigarette burns.

'This had better be good,' he said.

'It is.'

He was silent as she pitched the story. By the time she had finished they had both drained their glasses. There was none of the bluff flirtatiousness of this morning's phone call.

'Let's get this right,' he said with sarcastic relish. 'Some posh pensioner's been having it off with a young stud? Unhygienic, I admit. But I think you'll find that falls into the *Sphere*'s W.G.A.T. category. As in Who Gives a Toss?'

Tamara was indignant.

'But she's not just any posh pensioner. She's famous.'

'Listen, Tam,' he said, lighting a cigarette, 'she may be famous as far as the unpopulars are concerned – she might pass as a celebrity in your poncey, low-circulation broadsheets like *The Monitor* and *The Courier*. But for a mass-circulation tabloid like ourselves, the only posh pensioner we're interested in is the Queen Mum, and if she was in the sack with a good-looking gigolo, it would be a case of "God Bless You, Ma'am!"'

Tamara tried to curb the pleading note in her voice.

'But Honor Tait's different.'

'Look, I'd love to help you, Tam. For old times' sake.' He winked, then clapped his hand to his bruised eye. Alistair's handiwork was still giving him trouble. There was some satisfaction in that, anyway.

'It's really not up our street,' he continued. 'I don't know. This Honor Tait. She's not some leggy supermodel, is she? No one wants to read about some old bird like that. We don't want to put our readers off their breakfasts.'

Breakfast? It was not so long ago that this man's idea

of breakfast was a line of coke on Tamara's breasts. And now he was turning her away as if she was just another desperate freelance trying to flog a duff story.

'But she's been in all the magazines. *Vogue, Tatler* . . .'

He shook his head.

'Sorry, love. We've blown our budget on the new promotion campaign – "Slap a Paedo, Win a Twingo" – and the Pernilla Perssen story.'

'What Pernilla Perssen story?' Tamara asked in sudden panic.

Had the *Sphere* got hold of her pregnancy scoop? That would be all she needed.

'One of her exes is spilling the beans on her drug-fuelled three-in-a-bed romps,' Tim explained.

Tamara was reassured. Her exclusive was safe – any *ménages à trois* were likely to have preceded Perssen's pregnancy. This would be old news. She continued to press her claim.

'*The Monitor*'s running a four-thousand-word piece on Honor Tait in the Books section in three weeks' time. Here's your chance for another spoiler.'

'The Books section? Four thousand words? Do me a favour!' he said. 'Minority interest. Not the sort of stuff we want to be spending good money on at the *Sphere*.'

'I thought you liked to get the better of *The Monitor*. You shelled out good money to poach that snobby old windbag Bernice Bullingdon,' she said, peevishly picking at the corners of a beer mat.

'Old Bernice?' He laughed. 'Yeah, we really wound up

Wedderburn there, didn't we? Got our own back on him for doing the dirty on us with Ricky Clegg.'

Tamara stood her ground.

'This story's much more interesting than one of Bernice's screeds on early day motions and adjournment debates.'

'That wouldn't be difficult,' he said. 'Anything's more interesting than that. But don't worry. The *Sphere*'s readers have been spared. Let's just say Bernice's been redeployed – she's known as Bernie the Bin Queen these days.'

Tamara refused to be sidetracked.

'But Honor Tait *used* to be famous. More famous than Pernilla Perssen. Old-style, Hollywood-star famous.'

He glanced at his watch.

'We're shelling out for some terrific pictures of Pernilla,' he said, his eyes misting with pleasure. 'Wait till you see them . . .'

'Terrific,' Tamara said, without enthusiasm. 'But this is a whole different order of story.'

'Look, darling, your Honor Tait – she's old and she's ugly and most of our readers have never heard of her.'

'But they've heard of Frank Sinatra. Of her famous friends. Liz Taylor, Marilyn, she knew them all . . .'

He leaned towards her and patted her knee.

'Sorry, babe. Nice try. But it's not for us. One more for the road?'

She used his time at the bar to marshall her arguments.

'There was a recent TV show all about her,' she said when he returned with the drinks. 'Prime time. She's involved in all the fashionable left-wing causes. She hangs out with Labour MPs. And movie stars. Jason Kelly. And telly stars. Paul Tucker.'

At the mention of Tucker, a risible figure to Tim and his associates, he spluttered into his drink.

'Don't tell me she's shagging Tucker, too.'

'I couldn't say for certain. But she shagged everyone else. All the greats.'

Tim raised a quizzical eyebrow, forgetting last week's injury again, then flinched as the pain reminded him.

'Which greats?'

'Sinatra . . . Picasso . . . Bing Crosby . . . Bob Dylan . . . Castro . . .'

'Pictures?' He traced a finger tenderly round his eye.

'Yes. I'm sure. Most of them. Not actually in bed together. But together.'

'A goer then.'

'Yes, and that's the point. She's still at it. In her eighties and insatiable.'

'So, what's he like? Her toy boy?'

'Very fit,' Tamara said. 'Very fit indeed.' And she allowed herself a smile of dreamy satisfaction.

It could have been the next drink, or the chance to ridicule Paul Tucker, or simply the identity of Tait's third husband, that changed Tamara's fortunes.

'Not old Tad Challis? *Hairdressers' Honeymoon*? Comedy genius?' Tim said. 'Ah, good old-fashioned English smut . . . He must have had his pick of all the saucy starlets, old Tad. This Honor Tait must have been a looker then.'

'Oh, she was,' Tamara said. 'Check her out. She really was.'

'I don't know, Tam. You're really pushing me on this.'

She gave his thigh a playful pinch through the grey flannel.

'You know how important this story is to me,' she said. 'There's a lot at stake for me here.'

'Look. I don't know, girl. I'm too soft-hearted for my own good. I'll see what I can do.'

Tim called her that afternoon. He had ordered up Honor Tait's picture file.

'They had to go into the depths of the Morgue to find the early stuff but once I'd blown off the dust, it was fantastic,' he said. 'Absolutely priceless. What a corker! And she knew them all, didn't she? Sinatra, Kennedy . . . you name them, your old biddy had it away with them.'

'She was connected. I told you.'

'Recent stuff's not so bad, either. Those pictures with that young Kelly bloke. He's hot, isn't he? All the girls on the desk have been oohing and aahing over him. She looks like she'd have him for breakfast, the old bag. We'll have some fun with this.'

'How soon do you want it?'

'Can you get the goods this weekend? We'll rush it in for the Sunday after. Front-page splash and two double-page spreads?'

At the other end of the line, Tamara gave a victor's clenched-fist salute.

'What happened to the Pernilla Perssen story?' she asked.

'It's running in the *News of the World* this week.'

For an editor who had learned he was to be the victim of a spoiler, Tim sounded surprisingly cheerful.

'You lost the story?' she asked.

'The guy was a complete con man,' he said. 'Pictures were a set-up, with a bargain basement Pernilla-lookalike. We sent him over to the *News of the World*. Looks like they're going to take the bait and blow their budget for the next six months. And then there'll be their legal fees. They'll be stuffed.'

*

How many more times was she going to subject herself to this degradation, Honor asked herself; the tedious business of washing and dressing, then forcing herself out, dragging dread in every step, to be stripped back, exposed and reduced to her unappetising essence? Mutton to the slaughter. She knew she should not complain. If Lois had been offered the choice, she would have favoured daily colonoscopies and CAT scans in full possession of her intellectual faculties over perfect physical health and Alzheimer's. She might have bridled at today's doctor, however. A young privately educated swaggerer, he had an inauthentic line in sympathy. His indifference was obvious. Honor could almost hear it: 'What the hell do you expect?'

Back at her flat, she continued her labours. The maid had been shocked when she arrived this morning and asked whether there had been a break-in. When she learned the truth she was even more horrified and refused to throw away the bags of books, clothes and trinkets. She would not even take them to a charity shop. For an unnerving moment, Honor feared there might be tears, until she agreed to let the maid have the junk herself. Honor could not imagine where she would put it all in her overcrowded council flat.

There really was not much more to do. Honor took the newspaper and ripped it up, wrapping the torn pages around Tad's precious Sèvres cups, which she stuffed in a plastic bag with other breakables – Aidan's scent bottle, champagne glasses, and the vase. More junk for the maid.

She poured herself a drink and sat down in the empty gloom of the sitting room. So what, she wondered, watching her shadow rear against the bare walls, would an interviewer make of this room now? And what would it matter? It was easier to perceive error than to find truth – Goethe again – but sometimes it was impossible to discern either.

Even the astute could get it wrong. She had done so herself. Unforgivably, in the forest of Ettersberg. She could not face this now. Easier to contemplate, and with consequences no greater than private embarrassment, was her account for the *Paris Review* of the reclusive Canadian writer living alone in upstate New York in a clapboard farmhouse, his wife long-fled and their children with her. Honor had found him stooped and rheumy-eyed in that wintry house, warming his hands, metaphorically, over the fading embers of his literary fame. By the fireplace in his lonely house she had noticed an empty magnum of champagne, a dusty souvenir of that tabloid staple – happier times. He had turned his attic into a museum of his early success: walls crowded with framed reviews of his one best-selling novel, lurid posters and stills from the film adaptation (Tad had been first assistant director) and photographs of miniskirted starlets, eyes canopied by extravagant lashes, smiling in the company of a fashionable writer in a Carnaby Street suit who couldn't believe his good fortune.

He had shown Honor round, talking solely of that one book, three decades old: the writing of it, the revising of it, the publication of it, the sales figures, the filming of it. Every attempt she had made to change the subject – his other books, contemporary politics, his family, the house, the garden – had been steered back thirty years to the glory days of that one bright triumph when everyone, even the critics, had wished him well and the earlier years of disappointment and failure seemed behind him for ever. How could he have known then that, after a brief *scherzo* of success, failure would be the *leitmotif* in a lifelong symphony of loss and bitterness?

It was not until her melancholy article had been printed that she received a call from a former colleague from the

Herald Tribune, long retired and cultivating dahlias in the Chenango Valley.

'So you saw old G——? Did you get a sight of the Vestal Virgins?'

These, she learned, were the writer's twenty-year-old lovers, identical twin sisters, rosy Renoir beauties of Irish origin from a housing project in Vestal, outside Binghamton, who had exchanged their jobs behind the till in the local supermarket for a wing of the farmhouse, champagne on demand and monthly shopping sprees. Yes, you could be gulled. And well-meaning misinterpretations could be as damaging as maliciously revealed truths. It had to be faced.

Skirting woodland at the edge of the camp twenty minutes later, I spotted a fugitive German soldier hiding in the bush and hurried back to the camp to alert the American troops. Then I stood and watched as the Allies formed a high-spirited queue to give the young Nazi a savage beating. In the chaos of victory, the Americans were pumped up with righteous vengefulness over the horrors they had witnessed in the newly liberated camp. The captured German moaned softly as one GI held him by his hair, which was matted with blood, while others took turns to pummel him, shouting abuse.

'Want a turn, lady?' one soldier asked me. I declined.

Eventually, with blood streaming from his face and soaking his detested Nazi uniform, the German fell to the ground.

Twenty-one

Tamara settled on a three-star hotel in a Paddington terrace. It was not the Ritz but, while Tim had finally offered Dev £50,000, plus a generous fee of £3,500 to Tamara, he insisted that her expenses for the piece had to be modest.

'I'm already stretching my budget with this, babe,' Tim told her. 'I've had to fight to get this through our managing editor.'

Dev, who had been hoping for at least £100,000, was not impressed when Tamara phoned to tell him the news.

'If that's the best they can do, I'm not sure it's worth my while,' he said.

'But you said it yourself. This story needs to be told.'

'Once it appears, my main source of income will be gone. She won't give me any more money. Ever. That will be it. Then what do I do?'

And once he had outed Honor Tait in the tabloids, his other clients would melt away too.

'But you wanted to make a fresh start,' she argued. 'Put it all behind you.'

There was a pause. This could go either way, Tamara thought.

Finally, he spoke.

'Okay. As long as it's in cash. No cash, no deal.'

Tim handed Tamara a briefcase filled with enough banknotes, clean and crisp as counterfeits, to make a substantial down payment on a decent west London flat.

'Highly irregular,' he said, winking with his good eye. 'But I'm counting on you for some quality sleaze.'

She booked the room over the phone, negotiating a discount by implying that she would give the hotel a favourable mention in *The Monitor*'s Travel pages. She insisted on their best suite, which apparently included an 'emperor-sized' bed and a whirlpool bath.

Strangely, Tim seemed to be encouraging extra-curricular activity.

'A bit of hotel rumpy-pumpy? If that's what it takes. You go for it, girl,' he said.

Tamara was peeved by his absence of jealousy but she was looking forward to some serious pampering, some rest and recreation, as well as some rewarding work, and it would be negligent not to take advantage of the hotel facilities.

The display advert in the Yellow Pages had promised 'intimate luxury and superlative service,' but the shabby carpet in the hotel foyer and the yawning receptionist on the front desk suggested neither. It was too late to do anything about it now. Dev turned up with his backpack just as Tamara took the key. They stepped into the lift, a narrow wooden box, like a vertical coffin, which enforced an intimacy – groin brushing groin, thigh rubbing thigh – neither seemed prepared for.

He seemed almost shy, looking away when she tried to engage him with a knowing smile. She was going to have to handle the next two days with great sensitivity. He was feeling humiliated, she knew. What self-respecting man would be happy admitting to the world that he was sleeping with a geriatric? He might also be feeling guilt at betraying Honor Tait. That was, Tamara knew, one of the most pernicious aspects of abuse – victims felt responsibility for their victimisation.

'Have you got the cash?' he asked, as the lift stopped on the third floor.

'Yes. Right here.'

She patted the briefcase, accidentally brushing his crotch with her elbow.

When she unlocked the door to their suite they were met, though not welcomed, by a brassy fanfare of colour: an enormous heart-shaped arrangement of carnations barred their way into the room and, above it, like a pastel punchbag, bobbed a pink balloon bearing a Disney-style image of two kissing cupids.

'What the hell is all this about?' asked Dev, squeezing his way round the giant floral display, which was giving off a sickly fructose scent.

Pink bunting – more hearts – was pegged up around the window, which looked out on to the bleak service area at the back of the hotel. Over the bed (prince-sized rather than emperor, she would guess, and covered in pink candlewick) was a banner in jolly nursery lettering enthusing, 'Congratulations!'

'I asked for the best room in the hotel. I didn't expect all this. It must be the honeymoon suite.'

'It's an eyesore,' he said, with the pursed mouth of a spoiled child. 'I can't stay here.'

Then he saw the bottle of champagne in the ice bucket by the bed.

'Well, this will come in useful, anyway.'

'There'll be plenty more where that came from,' Tamara reassured him.

He poured himself a glass, sullenly stretched out on the bed and began channel surfing.

'Any for me?'

He passed her the bottle without averting his eyes from the TV at the foot of the bed, which was showing a children's quiz show – eager little swots vying for a worthless prize. She phoned room service for more champagne and the receptionist, now wearing a chambermaid's apron, brought in the bottles, edging carefully past the flowers. She left the tray on the table and backed out of the room, unsettling the cupids and almost toppling the carnation heart.

Dev switched to a porn channel, taking in a scene of naked mud wrestling with a connoisseur's cool eye while rolling a joint with one hand. Tamara opened a second bottle, kicked off her shoes and passed him a drink in exchange for the joint. They lay inches apart like figures on a medieval tomb, their brows creased with stoned concentration as the mud wrestling evolved into sludge sex. She reached across to stroke his arm and he sighed.

'So when do we start?' he said.

'Whenever you like,' she murmured.

'I mean this story deal.'

He seemed unaccountably tetchy.

'No pressure.'

She got up and dimmed the lights, arranged herself decoratively on the bed and opened another bottle of champagne.

'You sure you've got the money?' he asked.

'I told you. In my bag.'

'Show me.'

For forty hours they holed up in their suite, sleeping little, sedulously smoking their way through two ounces of grass, snorting the best part of a gram of cocaine, drinking a crate of champagne and talking; above all, talking. They ignored the whirlpool bath, and Tamara's hopes of a weekend sex junket were soon forgotten. They made love only once, almost by accident; he rolled on top of her to reach for a bottle, their thin hotel bathrobes parted, flesh met flesh, and they were surprised by desire. Their bodies did the work, but it was a perfunctory entanglement. As they rocked together conscientiously, to the metronome accompaniment of the bed's headboard banging against the wall, his mind was evidently elsewhere. Something had happened to her, too. He was beautiful, yes. But all she really wanted was the story.

And she got it. What a story. Once he started to talk, he could not stop, and the sordid tale unfolded in a smog of recrimination and marijuana smoke. Tamara, taking notes, propped up on pillows next to him, with her tape recorder running on the bedside table, marvelled at the transformation; the enigmatic man of few words turned out to be a monologuist. She put in more than a dozen cassettes. This would, she knew, mean a marathon transcription job later, but her notes would shortcut the process.

He was angry, and spoke with such vehemence that it seemed revenge, rather than money, propelled his confession. He was not, he insisted, a professional gigolo, nor any kind of male escort. He never had been. He had been entirely truthful when he first met Tamara; he was a qualified masseur, a healer and 'seeker after truth' with psychic gifts, but he had been groomed as a boy and then abused for years by a manipulative old woman who had lured him into her clutches and destroyed his chances of ever having a normal relationship.

'I've tried to get away, believe me,' he said. 'But she always dragged me back.' He shook his head, overcome by regret and shame. 'She drew me back in each time. I could never escape.'

Tamara looked up from her notebook.

'How young were you when it started?'

He avoided her eyes, staring straight ahead at the blank TV screen.

'Twelve? Thirteen? I don't know. What I do know is that I was a complete innocent.'

Tamara's disgust was tempered with jubilation. This was a story of boundless depravity, and she could not wait to tell it.

'Thirteen? You were a schoolboy?'

'What else would I be doing? Career opportunities for thirteen-year-olds were limited.'

She would not be deterred by his sarcasm. His real hostility was towards Honor Tait, she knew.

'How did you meet?'

'She was close to my father.'

'Were they lovers?'

He bit his lower lip. This was agony for him.

'Everyone was her lover.'

'Does your father know about you and her?'

'Not the full story, no. He died years ago.'

He closed his eyes. She reached over and stroked his hand.

'It must be hard for you. You must feel you're betraying her in some way. But you've got to fight that. You're the one who was betrayed.'

He seemed grateful for her insight.

'Maybe, by telling this, by putting it out there, I can start the healing process,' he said, rolling another joint.

They lost track of time and slept where they sat or sprawled, at odd hours in brief snatches. They called room service when they were hungry or needed more drink and the more he talked, the more aloof and distant he became. At one point, as they lay side by side on the bed, Tamara thought she had lost him altogether. It was an indelicate question but she felt it needed to be asked.

'You're young and good-looking. She isn't. How does that work?'

'How does *what* work?'

'You know. When you're together. Alone.'

He rolled over on his elbow and for a moment she saw a flicker of menace in his eyes.

'What exactly are you saying?'

There was no diplomatic way of putting this.

'You know . . .' She mimed, crooking and flexing her index finger. 'How do you get it up?'

He hit his pillow with such force that it sent up a spray of feathers.

'Use your imagination, for fuck's sake! Do I have to spell it out to you?'

It was a tricky moment. She had to work to soothe him, ordering more champagne and promising (rashly, she knew) that the *Sphere* would throw in his air fare to Goa – if that was what he wanted – on top of the agreed fee for the story.

'First class?'

'First class.'

He calmed down, reached for the Gideon Bible and began to cut a line of cocaine.

'How did it start? The abuse?' she asked in a neutral tone she fancied made her sound like a counsellor.

'How do these things usually start?'

He was behaving like a surly teenager.

'I don't know. Grooming? Inappropriate touching?' she suggested.

'Yes. Grooming,' he said with a harsh laugh. 'Grooming. Inappropriate touching. The lot. She was always at it. Holding me. Pawing me. She called me her Darling Boy.'

'And Tad, her husband? The film director? Did he know about any of this?'

She had to strain to hear his answer.

'He was in on it too.'

Tamara turned to check that her Sony was still recording.

'In what way?' she asked.

He put down the rolled banknote, licked his index finger and dabbed at the few grains of cocaine left on the Bible. He was further away than ever from her now, lost in past traumas.

'In every way,' he said, closing his eyes. 'He liked to dress up to do it. Women's clothes. Make-up. Wigs. High heels. The lot.'

'Sick,' she said. 'Sick bastards.'

'That's exactly what they were. They destroyed my past, and my future, too.'

Tamara's first reaction, after checking her tape recorder, was to reach out and console him, but he shied away and lay curled up, unreachable in his misery, on the edge of the bed, a broken man. The burden of shame was too great. She was moved by the hopelessness of his blighted life and could still appreciate his beauty, but now she had learned the full extent of his intimacy with Honor Tait, Tamara realised she was repelled not just by the old woman but by him, too. To make love to Dev now would be to experience a vicarious intimacy with a repugnant old woman. He was Tait's creature.

Tamara knew she would walk away from him once their business was done. It was important to tell this story, and she would tell it well. It was good, empowering even, to be on the side of virtue, to expose cruelty and hypocrisy. But she understood that their first night of lovemaking and its disappointing reprise in this hotel, were the beginning and end of their affair.

By Monday morning there was nothing left to say; all that remained was to set up the photographic evidence with the *Sunday Sphere* picture desk. Dev would emerge on the steps of Holmbrook in the company of Honor Tait at 5 p.m. on Wednesday. The photographer would be waiting outside the Gut and Bucket with his long lens and, once the pictures had been taken, would hand over an envelope containing the promised air fare in the pub. Tamara refrained from asking whether Dev would, before their unofficial photo call, offer himself to Tait for a final time.

They began to dress and Tamara took a furtive last look at his cock, magnificent even in repose. His face, by contrast, looked drained and spent as he walked towards her, beckoning.

'We haven't got much time left,' he said.

She leaned in for a passionate final kiss but he dodged her lips and pointed at the briefcase.

'The cash?' he reminded her.

*

It occurred to Honor, as she looked down on the bare wintry garden, that there was more warmth and life down there than up here in her flat. She felt a pang of pleasure as she turned back to the room, empty and clarifying as a tomb. She should have done this years ago.

Here at last, undistracted, she felt ready for her final act of purging. Only now could she exhume the truth she had buried for fifty years.

I stood and watched as the Allies formed a queue to give that young German a savage beating. In the chaos of victory, the Americans were pumped up with righteous vengefulness over the horrors they had witnessed in the newly liberated camp.

It was a young sergeant from Idaho, a big farm boy, who finally stopped the rout. Had he been brought to his senses by the childlike whimpering of the victim? Or was he alerted by the shouts of a freed prisoner, a German speaker, who had stumbled on the scene and heard the boy's mumbled pleas? Perhaps the sergeant was simply sickened by the blood feast. The Nazi soldier, it turned out, was a fourteen-year-old schoolboy who had never seen action. He was a prisoner himself; four days earlier he had been forced at gunpoint by retreating German officers to put on the uniform and he was drafted into a forced-labour battalion. He had been put to work digging trenches that would never be manned.

She never knew whether the boy survived the Allied lynch mob. His limp body was stretchered away by medics and she made no attempt to find out what happened to him. Nor did she ever write or speak, not even to Lois, of the scene she had witnessed, and of her complicity. There was, she knew, no moral equivalence here. On the spot where the soldiers had administered their freelance rough justice, 56,000 had recently died as a result of state-sanctioned murder. No, she could not blame the Americans. It was herself she could never forgive; the cold eye, the reporter's eye as she had liked to think of it, looking on, impartially recording. 'Want a turn, lady?' the GI had asked her. She had declined. But she had not flinched. She had seen herself as a truth machine. But there was something else happening, something animal, a worm of sadistic pleasure gnawing at her heart, as she watched the beating of that boy, willing it on.

Twenty-two

'What a sick old Doris,' said Tim, holding the photograph of Honor Tait clasping Dev's hand on the steps of Holmbrook.

She was hunched in concentration as she negotiated the stairs. He was staring directly into the lens with haunted eyes. In another picture, they were both in profile and she was smiling up at him with a look that could only be interpreted as possessive triumph.

'Look at that! The love-light in her eyes . . .' Tim was clapping with delight.

'Come on. This is practically child abuse. It's not funny,' Tamara said.

'Where's your sense of humour, girl? Just a bit of harmless fun.'

He shuffled the remaining prints until he found the one he was looking for.

'That's it. The bull picture. The clincher,' he said, waving it towards Tamara.

'Hold still. Let me see.'

He dropped the photograph on the desk and Tamara

blenched. It was hideous. Dev was leaning over the old woman and his hands, those delicate fingers, were gently cradling her upturned face. They were kissing. Honor Tait's eyes were closed, caught in a moment of deep, forbidden pleasure. His eyes were shut too, but Tamara knew that, behind his closed lids, they burned with hatred and self-disgust. The Judas kiss.

'Blimey,' said Tim. 'So that's your latest fancy-boy, Tam? And she's your eighty-year-old love rival?'

Tamara was too furious to reply. Still chuckling, Tim gathered the pictures into a pile, with the Kiss uppermost.

'There's just one thing I want to know, Tam,' he asked.

'What's that?'

'How the hell does he get it up?'

'Oh, use your imagination, for fuck's sake.'

*

He had phoned again. At last. A farewell visit, he said. For as long as they had known each other, even in the best of days, it had been one long farewell. He arrived within the hour, looked briefly round her empty flat but made no comment. He was swift and to the point. There was no pretence on either side. Honor signed the cheque and gave it to him. They went down in the lift and walked together to the cash dispenser outside the supermarket. He kissed her twice; once with unexpected tenderness, on the steps of Holmbrook as they made their way to the shopping parade. After he pocketed the banknotes, his parting kiss was more peremptory. He hurried away and she stood watching him fade into the distance. She knew that he would not be back. It was like watching her last sunset.

*

They needed a quote from Honor Tait to complete the package and a News desk veteran, Perry Gifford-Jones, was enlisted. A former actor in provincial rep who went on to become the sharpest re-write man on Fleet Street, he was now a casual headline sub, occasional leader writer – *Sphere Sez* – and recidivist alcoholic. He was also Tim's wife's first cousin and consequently the *Sphere* had a tolerant attitude towards his occasional lapses.

Gifford-Jones called Honor Tait just before midnight on Friday, judging that she would be at her most unguarded and candid then, after a nightcap and just before bed. She answered after two rings.

'Hello?' Her voice quavered expectantly.

'Hello. Miss Tait? Miss Honor Tait?'

Years of whisky and cigars had given his Rada-trained voice, with its camp, over-enunciated Home Counties accent, an authoritative basalt rumble.

'Yes. Who is this?'

'Perry Gifford-Jones, the *Sunday Sphere*. Just wanted to ask you a couple of questions.'

There was a beat of silence before she spoke.

'Do you realise what time it is?'

'I'm very sorry, Miss Tait. Couldn't reach you before, News desk deadlines being what they are. I'm sure you understand.'

'I'm not sure I do.'

'I'm a tremendous admirer of your work, Miss Tait,' he said, with treacly insinuation. 'I just wanted to ask your advice about a story we have here at the *Sunday Sphere*?'

What possible advice could she give a squalid tabloid like the *Sphere*? she wondered. They were unlikely to be making a foray into respectable investigative journalism, or trying their hand at serious foreign coverage.

'We're doing a feature on exploitation,' he continued. 'Sexual exploitation. I understand you know something about that.'

She was baffled. Was this something to do with Clemency's puerile outfit?

'If you want information about the Twisk charity, you should call their office at a civilised hour.'

'No, no,' said Gifford-Jones. 'It's quite definitely you we want to speak to. You're the expert on the subject.'

She resisted the pull of flattery, though it occurred to her that if the millions who read the *Sphere* were to be made aware of these issues, that would be no bad thing. It was all very well remaining a *Guardian* purist, but it might be more effective to preach to the unconverted.

'I did write about the street children of Calcutta and Rio, and the child prostitutes of Thailand,' she conceded. 'I also wrote about the trafficking of children from the former Soviet Union and Africa.'

'You know your stuff.'

She did not like his pandering tone.

'This was all a long time ago. I'm rather out of date.'

'On the contrary. That's not what I hear. You're very up-to-the-minute, Miss Tait.'

'I haven't been able to travel much over the last few years. You need to try a younger hand on the subject, someone who's done some recent groundwork.' It pained her to admit it.

He was unfazed.

'More recently, and closer to home, I was wondering what you thought of young men selling sex for money in West London.'

Was he drunk?

'I've no idea what you're talking about. I really must go now.'

'It's a serious problem,' he insisted, 'male prostitution in your neighbourhood. We're running a story on it on Sunday.'

She was exasperated by the man's bone-headedness. 'Are there any more male prostitutes in West London than in any other part of the city? Or in any equivalent district of any other capital in the world? In global terms, it could be argued that they have more choice, and they're certainly less exploited than the child sex workers of the Far East.'

'Sex tourism? You know something about that, too.'

'Yes, but as I say, I haven't been able to travel for some years. My first-hand knowledge is limited. You're really talking to the wrong person.' It was instinctive, this reluctance to turn down a commission, even from a paper as despicable as the *Sphere*. The *Statesman*'s rejection still stung. Who knew when the next editor would call?

'What about the male brothels in your neighbourhood? Maida Vale, isn't it?'

Who *was* this imbecile?

'*Are* there any male brothels in Maida Vale? If there are, I haven't seen any. Look, I really don't think I can help you.'

He might, it occurred to her, be a crank, a loopy fan who had got her number and caught her off guard by calling so late. She was about to put down the phone. Then came the question that sent her reeling.

'What do you know of a man called Dev?'

Her breath faltered and she struggled to compose herself.

'Miss Tait? Miss Tait? Are you there, Miss Tait?'

'What exactly do you want?'

'Do you deny that you know him?'

'I may have met someone of that name. I can't be sure.'

'You can't be sure? We have the photographs, Miss Tait.'

'Photographs?'

She could not stifle the panic in her voice.

'You and him. Dev. Outside your flat. This week. Wednesday. After one of your assignations.'

She took the phone from her ear and looked at it, horrified, as if the unctuous voice issued not from a seedy journalist in an office five miles across the capital, but from the device itself, croaking in her hand like a malevolent toad. Shaking, she returned the receiver to her ear.

'What on earth are you implying?'

'So you don't deny that you know him? Dev?'

She replaced the receiver, closed her eyes and leaned against the wall. Her heart was racing and she felt dangerously light-headed. Resting her cheek against the cool plaster, she waited for the dizziness to pass.

She made her way into the kitchen and poured a drink. Her hands were trembling and she saw that she had been gripping the phone so tightly there were red marks, stigmata, on her right palm. It rang again and she recoiled. Let it ring. After several seconds it switched to the answering machine. It was him again. The man from the *Sphere*.

'Just wanted to ask a few questions . . . We're going to publish anyway . . . Just wanted to get your side of the story . . .'

She froze until the machine whirred and clicked into silence again. The *Sunday Sphere*, that squalid scandal sheet specialising in spite and gleeful bullying. What were they planning? What public ignominy was she about to endure? And what about him? Was he safe? Could she reach him to warn him? They had three days before the paper came out; three days before their fragile world would implode.

Twenty-three

The front-page headline, over the snatched photograph, a twisted parody of Doisneau's *Kiss*, was in white type framed by a black box: TOYBOY LOVER SHAME OF SINATRA'S EX, 80.

Under it, next to a close-up detail of their clasped hands – hers pitifully scrawny, his marble smooth and strong – were the words: *Telly granny's afternoon romps with mystery hunk.*

Over four pages inside, there were photographs of Honor as a succulent young woman, sitting with Frank Sinatra at dinner and in a lively group with Marilyn Monroe outside a restaurant. There was a hand-tinted portrait of Bing Crosby smoking a pipe in a cable-knit sweater (the caption read *BababaBing – another Tait conquest*), although, despite an extensive search, the *Sphere* had been unable to find an incriminating picture, or indeed any picture at all, of Tait in Crosby's company. But the rest of the evidence was damning enough. Tad Challis, 'director of much-loved British comedies', was photographed 'sharing a joke' on set with Diana Dors, under the headline, KINKY SEX GAMES: FAMOUS HUSBAND, FRIEND OF STARS, WAS SECRET TRANSVESTITE.

In Tait's middle years she was pictured in a perky business suit, next to Elizabeth Taylor, whose floor-length beaded gown suggested that at least one of them had misread the dress code for the event. More recent photographs showed Tait stooped and desiccated, at a West End first night on the arm of 'Sexy *Faraway Tree* Star' Jason Kelly, at a 'perverted art show' with 'telly newsman Tucker', at a 'kiddies' charity event' next to the toadying member of the Shadow Cabinet and, at the recent Press Awards dinner, with 'top telly comic Jimmy Whipple CBE', whose body language – one arm matily draped round Honor Tait's shoulder, the other outstretched in a chirpy thumbs-up to camera – now seemed grotesquely ill-judged. Tim's picture library had done well. SECRET LOVE TRYSTS read the headline on page three. And under a close-up picture of Dev, a firm-jawed avenging angel, was the killer quote: *She groomed me as a schoolboy. It was child abuse.*

Tamara had felt a heady pride as she walked to her local newsagent in the rain that morning to pick up the *Sunday Sphere*. Her step was lighter, she could not stop smiling, and when the clouds parted, sending a shaft of sunlight sweeping along the wet street and sprinkling dusty hedges with sparkling crystal, she had laughed aloud – it felt like a corny Hollywood moment, signalling good times after bad.

But outside the shop, when she saw the paper displayed on a rack, her mood suddenly changed to helpless rage. Where was her byline? The story bore the name of Perry Gifford-Jones. Tim had betrayed her again.

Over coffee in her basement flat, she read and reread the paper. Was there any sight more satisfying for a young journalist than this: to see your story, the subject that you had lived and breathed and dreamed of, the work that you had agonised over for weeks, made flesh? It made a spectacular spread. But it had been stolen from her, passed off as someone else's property. This was outrageous theft. Wait till she got hold of Tim. She left an incensed message on his office answering machine.

With the paper still spread out before her, and another cup of coffee, she began to calm down. Though her contribution was unacknowledged, her cheque was already in her building society account – Tim could not renege on that part of the deal – and on her third reading, she found herself grudgingly admiring the professionalism of the presentation, and Gifford-Jones's economic use of his brief telephone interview to round off her piece. There were lessons here.

In an exclusive interview with the Sunday Sphere *at her Maida Vale home, the sick octogenarian, friend of stars and politicians and liberal darling of the chattering classes, was unrepentant, saying, 'I'm an expert in sexual exploitation.'*

She refused to be drawn on her relationship with the

mystery stud, but brazenly asked our reporter: 'Are there any more male prostitutes in West London?'

She admitted that she had indulged in sex tourism in the past — 'You need to try a younger hand,' she said — but old age had put paid to her perverted trips abroad and now she trawls the streets of the upmarket neighbourhood round her £275,000 luxury flat, seeking to satisfy her unnatural lust. She defended her regular paid-for sex sessions with dishy masseur Dev, and other gigolos, saying, 'They have a choice,' and the insatiable pensioner, on the lookout for more young victims, asked us, 'Are there any male brothels in Maida Vale?'

A friend close to the couple said: 'Dev has been very hurt by all this. His life has been destroyed. He feels cynically used and thinks it is time to speak out as a warning to other vulnerable boys and their parents.'

The last quote was from Tamara herself. Her missing byline still rankled but, she reminded herself, one particular satisfaction would not escape her — Tania Singh's long, drearily respectful article on the now discredited Honor Tait would have to be spiked. Not even the Books pages would run a fawning piece about the sordid old child abuser now.

An hour later, the phone rang. It was Tim, and he was exultant.

'It's a cracker. This is global. We've had loads of interest. TV, too.'

'What about my byline, you double-crossing bastard?'

'I meant to talk to you about that.'

'What happened?' She was shrill with anger. 'You promised!'

'I know, I know. Old Perry kicked up a fuss. I owed him.'

'You owe me, too. Remember?'

'Look, our financial arrangement still stands and the fact that your byline didn't appear could work to your advantage. You're not implicated. How about doing a follow-up for next week, setting up a face-to-face with the old woman, getting the dope on her spicy life with the stars?'

Tamara hesitated.

'Money?' she asked.

'Shed loads, darling.'

'Byline?'

'Picture byline.'

'Guaranteed?'

'Guaranteed.'

'Staff job?'

'I'll see what I can do. Honest. This story's going to run and run, and if you can get the follow-up, you'll be able to walk into any job in Fleet Street.'

'But I can't really see Honor Tait agreeing to an interview with anyone from the *Sphere*. Especially after today.'

'Did anyone mention the *Sphere*? Don't you work for *The Monitor*? For now, anyway.'

The Gut and Bucket was enjoying an unexpected surge in business. Across the road, outside Holmbrook Mansions, the jostling photographers, reporters and TV camera crews, waiting since dawn for an appearance from the 'randy gran', were using the pub as their catering unit. The News desks from every paper, from the most scapegrace tabloid pranksters to the broadsheet upholders of all that was decent in British civil society, were represented in the jostling scrum. The broadsheets were there not to cover the story itself but to report on the antics of the tabloid underclass, with the haughtiness of anthropologists observing the sacrificial rites of a Stone Age tribe, but their supercilious accounts would also serve the useful purpose of providing sophisticated readers with the saltiest details of the Honor Tait story.

From a safe distance across the street, Tamara spotted Bucknell gloomily fingering a roll-up on the edge of the crowd. Tom O'Brien was in a huddle with the show business reporter from the *Star* and the *Sphere* photographer Tamara had worked with on the story about the policeman's drug-using son. Milly Hall-Westmacott was handing out polystyrene cups of coffee. Tamara crossed the road, slipped past them unnoticed and dodged into a cobbled mews heaped with damp litter.

She was not entirely alone. A stout middle-aged woman, dressed in muted tweeds as if for a pheasant shoot, was standing on tiptoes, rummaging through the large metal bins beside the service entrance of the mansion block. It was Bernice Bullingdon. She was wearing yellow rubber gloves and open at her feet lay a large wheeled suitcase, into which she was dropping damp gouts of garbage. Hearing Tamara's footsteps she glanced up with the toothy alertness of a startled meerkat. No words were exchanged. Bernice Bullingdon did not recognise Tamara from *The Monitor* – the younger journalist had been too lowly to merit attention – but she swiftly deduced that the girl was no threat and turned back to her task, sifting through another suppurating mound of old newspapers and kitchen waste. What was she looking for? Honor Tait's discarded love letters? Her credit card statements revealing details of trysts in Paris or Rome?

It was Tamara's story that had generated all this industry, that had summoned up the restless, good-humoured crowd outside the flats and set Bernice Bullingdon rag picking. Uplifted by an unfamiliar sense of power, Tamara walked on to the service entrance and pushed the buzzer. Ruth Lavenham had arranged for the doorman to meet her there and he grinned as he beckoned Tamara in. He was enjoying the subterfuge.

'Haven't had anything like this since the time they said one of the Beatles spent a night here with an Iranian princess. Pack of lies, of course. But we couldn't get rid of them. They were out there for days.'

She followed him down to the basement, a fetid concrete bunker housing a vast and ancient boiler.

'They've tried all sorts,' he said, leading her into the shabby service lift. 'Dressed as bike messengers with urgent packages for her, pretended to be florists delivering bloody great bouquets to her. They even got a window cleaner's cradle from somewhere. Went up the outside of the building with mops and buckets. I noticed the cameras just in time. I threatened to cut the cables.'

He got out at the ground floor and, smiling conspiratorially, extended his stubby hand. Tamara shook it vigorously but a look of displeasure clouded his face as the doors closed between them. Only then did she realise she had been meant to tip him. Never mind; she was unlikely to be back here for another visit. She continued up to the fourth floor alone. The building was silent, apart from the creak and wheeze of the lift doors and Tamara's own footsteps, which rang out ominously as she walked along the corridor. Where was everyone? Were they *all* hiding from the press?

She rang the doorbell. Minutes passed, marked by the scrape of bolts and jangle of keys, before the door was finally opened a couple of inches, secured by a brass chain, giving Honor Tait a full-length crack through which she could safely satisfy herself that Tara Sim was entirely alone. The chain was unfastened and Tamara was admitted in silence.

This time, the old woman had made no attempt to smarten herself up for the interview. Her hair was unkempt, wisps of it coming astray from hastily fastened hairgrips, and her dress – probably the same black dress she had worn for their first meeting – was stained and creased. She looked appropriately haggard, this seedy corrupter of boys and defiler of young men, as she led Tamara into the sitting room. This too had changed. The room was shockingly empty. The place had been stripped.

The old woman sat down, breathing heavily, and placed her hand across her bony chest to calm her heart.

'What is it you want?' she said eventually.

'I thought it was you who wanted me,' Tamara replied, briskly laying out her tape recorder and notebook.

Honor looked across at her, taking her in properly for what seemed like the first time – a gift-wrapped package of ignorance and greed. Was that twist in the girl's mouth a simper of satisfaction?

'I've agreed to give a further interview for your magazine, *S*nday*,' Honor said. 'I'd be grateful if you could make this as brief as possible.'

'I won't be long,' Tamara said, pressing the record button. 'I just need to fill in a few gaps. You talked a lot about your work last time but I wanted to ask a few more questions about your life.'

Honor sighed.

'What you don't seem to understand is that my work *is* my life. There is . . . has been . . . nothing else.'

'It's not your work *they're* interested in, is it?' Tamara said, indicating the front door with a nod. 'That lot out there.'

Honor leaned forward, her hands kneading the arms of her chair, and spoke quietly, as if to herself.

'It's been ghastly. A complete nightmare.'

'I suppose in one way it shows just what a respected figure you are,' Tamara offered, anxious to get the interview moving. 'That people are still so keen to read stories about you. You're a cultural icon.'

Honor's laugh was like a howl of pain.

'You've read these "stories", I take it?'

'I've seen a few things in the press, yes.'

'A "few things"? It's everywhere, impossible to escape. On the wireless, too. And the television.'

'Really?' Tamara felt another flush of pride.

She had watched a fusty academic, T.P. Kettering, being wheeled out on several TV news programmes to give his considered views on Honor Tait's 'tempestuous love life'. Kettering's biography of the old woman, previously remaindered, was being rushed into print again with a new chapter taking in the recent revelations.

'I'm the Monster of Maida Vale to the tabloids,' Honor continued, 'and a vain old fool to the liberal press. An object of loathing and a national laughing stock.'

International, too. Under Gifford-Jones's byline, Tamara's story had gone out on the wires and been sold round the world. The *Sphere*'s usually becalmed syndication department had to get in extra temporary staff to deal with the frenzy of enquiries. Tamara would get 30 per cent of the fees but the money seemed almost superfluous now; the real reward was the transcendent euphoria of generating the biggest story of the day. *El Pais*, *Le Monde*, *Frankfurter Allgemeine Zeitung*, *Izvestia*, *Kathimerini*, *O Globo*, *La Prensa*, *The Times of India* – they had all bought it and, in the case of those papers without the funds or inclination to buy the piece from the *Sphere*, simply lifted it, gratis, and rushed to publish it before their rivals, generating a planetary pandemic of spoilers.

All of them, those papers that had paid for it and those that had pilfered it, claimed the story as their own and, with the exception of the *New York Times*, had labelled it as 'exclusive'.

In the US, newspapers and magazines had focused on Honor Tait's Hollywood connections and her anti-Vietnam War stance. TV stations were running the story with old film footage unearthed of a charity event she had attended with Bing Crosby and Bob Hope, though Tait was not actually caught on camera with either of them.

VETERAN WAR REPORTER, 80, IN BRITISH TABLOID SEX SCANDAL, was the *New York Times* headline. It used the picture with Sinatra, and a recent photograph of Tait taken at a theatre first-night party with a dashing left-wing playwright and the actor Jason Kelly, but the paper refrained from printing the *Sphere*'s snatched photographs with Dev. *El Pais*, similarly reticent, focused on Tait's role in the Spanish Civil War and chose the Franco shot to illustrate its story. For *Le Monde* it was an opportunity to air respectful accounts of her *amitie* with Cocteau and Picasso in its news pages, and for its commentators to shake their heads over Britain's unsophisticated attitude to sex. In the UK, however, there was homogeneity in approach if not in presentation; newspapers, broadsheet and tabloid, were unanimous in their condemnation of Honor Tait – the hypocritical champion of the weak, the Kids' Crusader, who had, all along, been abusing the vulnerable in the most evil way imaginable.

As the veteran war reporter buried her head in her hands, Tamara wondered if she should rummage in her bag for a tissue and present it with a cocked head and an understanding smile? But Tait had paid no heed to Dev's tears. She was at the end of a long life of boundless privilege and had never been called to account for her crimes until now. A few years of public disgrace at the end of her days – tears before bedtime – were the only price she would have to pay. He was a young man with years ahead of him and he had been robbed of any chance of happiness and a normal life. She had got off lightly.

The old woman looked up and clenched her frail fist at an invisible adversary.

'Almost worse than the howling lynch mobs and the sneerers,' she said at last, 'are the feminists, the Isadora Talbots, who have spoken out – for a reasonable fee, presumably – solemnly defending what they call the "unsung sexuality of the post-menopausal woman".'

'It'll blow over,' Tamara said.

'Blow over?' Tait's voice cracked. 'Like a tropical hurricane, I suppose. Leaving devastated towns and countless corpses.'

Tamara glanced at her tape recorder and wondered how much more humouring she was going to have to do here.

'Your publisher agreed that this was the best hope of setting the record straight – a long and sympathetic profile, reminding people of your achievements, the other aspects of your life. Your legacy.'

Honor rallied.

'Ah yes. "Setting the record straight." You mean giving me the opportunity to damn myself further for the idle pleasure of your readers?'

Honor had set several records straight herself over the years, duping conceited fools into greater indiscretions. But she had run out of options. Ruth and Aidan had tried to persuade her to sue the *Sphere*, and Clemency, after a period of sulky evasiveness – the story had generated some unhelpful publicity for her new charity – had offered to fund her costs. But Honor had refused to take legal action.

'Do you really think I want to spend weeks in court, paying expensive libel lawyers, entertaining this pernicious nonsense?'

Bobby volunteered to run a piece in *Zeitgeist*. It would, he had insisted, be entirely about Honor's work, and would make no reference to the tabloid storm. But Ruth had been dismissive.

'*Zeitgeist* has no real heft. It's full of lightweight reviews of bestsellers and blockbusters and has no international profile.'

Besides, she said, Bobby had no influence on the rest of the paper and any *Zeitgeist* piece on Honor, no matter how sanitised, would be trumpeted on *The Courier*'s front page, providing its News desk with an excuse to air, all over again, every last lubricious detail of the original tabloid story.

'Your only hope is some high-minded hagiography,'

Ruth had continued. '*S*nday* magazine – see the girl from *The Monitor* again.'

So here it was. Today, in her own home, with the bawds and the titillators baying outside, Honor was entrusting her reputation, her legacy, to this little booby and her fatuous magazine.

'Did he ever sing to you?' Tara Sim was asking.

'I'm sorry?' Honor was perplexed. 'Sing? Who?'

'Sinatra!' The girl's tone was sardonic. She was frustrated by the old woman's failure to keep up. 'When you were alone together. Private . . . intimate . . . moments. You know, "Strangers in the Night"? "Fly Me to the Moon"?'

Honor shook her head.

'Look, I really didn't know him . . .'

'But the pictures!'

'I sat next to him at dinner once,' Honor said wearily. 'We were photographed together. I didn't know him. I barely talked to him. I couldn't abide his music.'

Tamara leaned towards her with a complacent smile.

'Bing then. Tell me about Bing Crosby.'

What was the girl talking about?

'Never met him.'

'But you *danced* with him. You told me.'

Honor drew herself up and laughed, remembering.

'Ah yes. Our first interview. When you were leaving. Don't you know when your leg is being pulled?'

Tamara stiffened. So the old woman was now claiming it had been a joke. Too bad. She had said it. On the record. And Bing was not around to deny it.

'Marilyn,' said Tamara. 'Did she ever confide in you?'

'Marilyn?'

'Monroe. Did she strike you as the suicidal type?'

'For goodness' sake, I think I met her once and barely exchanged a word with her.'

Even in defeat, the old woman was stubborn. Tamara pressed on. She would return to Marilyn and Bing later.

'And Liz Taylor. How close were you – you and Tad – to Liz?'

This was prurience of an eclectic kind, thought Honor.

'Close? We weren't close. I think Tad worked with her once. On a picture.'

'What about those wild Hollywood parties?'

This line of questioning puzzled Honor.

'Tad could be sociable, certainly.'

Tamara's eyes widened to an inquisitor's stare.

'How sociable? Was he sociable in the bedroom, too?'

'What on earth do you mean?'

Was this the broadsheet alternative to tabloid bile? Was the narrative of her life to be reduced to a tepid gush of name-dropping and innuendo?

'Even the most serious stories need some pep and human interest,' Tamara said, with open condescension.

The old woman's reply was a reflexive snap: 'I need no lessons in basic journalism from you.'

'Well, perhaps that's exactly where you're going wrong. When did you last write for a newspaper? I mean, actually write a story? How many decades ago? Things have changed. The world has changed. You might benefit from a little instruction in late-twentieth-century journalism.'

Tamara was enjoying this. But the old woman, too, seemed suddenly roused.

'*Journalism*? Really? What do you know about it? You and your kind have the same relationship to journalism as lavatory graffiti to the Sistine Chapel.'

'I don't see what makes you so superior.'

Honor shook her head. It was a pointless squandering of diminishing resources to pursue this further. To blame a witless shop girl, who by some accident of fate had ended up typing titbits in a magazine instead of scanning barcodes at a supermarket check-out, was to give her an importance she did not merit. It was the culture that was at fault, not her.

'Look,' Honor said more gently, 'it's not about you. It's about the time you're living in. You're a pawn, an innocent, the end result of a process of decline which has elevated nonentities, moved the bedroom into the bazaar and conflated fame with virtue.'

Her conciliatory tone did not soften the insult.

'You weren't so very high and mighty then, were you?' Tamara replied. 'In the good old glory days? Hob-nobbing with the stars, thinking you were something of a star yourself, photographed with a Spanish dictator in your hot pants. Do you think that picture would have gone anywhere if you hadn't been glamorous and scantily clad? At least I've generally managed to keep my clothes on in the course of an interview. You played the game. You put yourself about – all that "high IQ in a low-cut gown" stuff. Nobody's fooled by your intellectual *grande dame* act.'

The silence that followed was prolonged and intense. Honor could hear her breath roaring like a stiff north wind in her ears. Tamara was staring fiercely at her notes, wondering whether she had finally gone too far. Tim had been very keen on this second interview, she reminded herself, and there was a good deal at stake here. Suddenly, as clamorous in the quiet of the room as a fire alarm, the telephone rang. Honor rose from her chair and walked stiffly into the hall.

'Hello . . . Who is this? . . . How did you get this number? . . . No. I have nothing to say . . . The whole thing is ridiculous . . . Who gave you this number? . . . I just want to be left in peace . . . Of course it's untrue . . . No. I have nothing to say . . .'

She dropped the receiver as if it had scalded her hand and walked back into the room with cautious steps. Tamara watched Honor – still lying, still in denial – shut her eyes and tense her body against pain as she lowered herself into the chair.

'You need me more than I need you,' the young woman said.

Honor's eyes flashed open.

'Don't you think I have been mocked and humiliated enough? What exactly do you want from me? Should I howl and sob into your tape recorder? Is that it? Go into the street and weep for the photographers?' She pointed a shaking finger at Tamara. 'What your generation doesn't seem to understand is that there are such things as private matters; that to some people, no amount of money or promise of advantage would induce them to talk about these matters. It's a question of integrity. And the vulgar publicity, the public exposure, brought to them by airing family business, private affairs, in confessional memoirs or newspaper articles would be completely abhorrent, unthinkable.'

'Very noble, I'm sure,' Tamara said with a slow smile, her triumph nearly complete. 'But they're out there now, your "private affairs", aren't they?'

Honor shrank back in her chair.

'This is preposterous.'

'You can be as snooty as you like about it, but when more than one person is involved in "your affairs", you can't guarantee they subscribe to the same moral code. Not everyone can afford to be that principled – or perverted.'

Honor Tait's face hardened into a mask of such ferocity that, for a moment, Tamara feared she might be capable of violence.

'Just what are you implying?'

Tamara paused. Honor Tait was barely able to stand unaided, much less strike out with any force. She was clearly not, at this stage, going to spill any beans on her celebrity friends, but if she could be provoked into an angry quote, admitting her guilt over Dev, perhaps attempting to defend her actions, then that would give a new angle and extend the story's life. Every paper would run it.

'Your "boyfriend", companion, whatever you call him, he obviously felt he stood to gain more by telling your story than by continuing your "arrangement". Maybe you just didn't pay him enough. Maybe, rather than being an active supporter of worthy causes – Kids' Crusader! – defender of the underprivileged, scourge of injustice, you are actually a callous, hypocritical exploiter, a vile child abuser.'

Honor felt the blood drain from her face and she was seized by a sudden weakness, as if her bones and sinews were melting away. All she could do was sit, silent and horrified, as the girl continued her senseless rant.

'You had all the power – the money, the reputation – and he was a kid, an innocent boy. Was this what you meant by "championing the weak" and "shining a search-light in the darkest corners of human experience"?'

Honor closed her eyes and her hands balled into fists in her lap. When she spoke at last, her voice was so faint and tremulous that Tamara had to strain to hear it.

'At seventy-nine years of age, after a long life, rich and interesting by any standards, with a respected body of work behind me, devoted to the pursuit of truth and exposure of injustice, it seems this absurd lie is what I'll be remembered for.'

'This *lie*?'

'I will be seen forever as a vain and foolish old woman, a grotesque object of ridicule, a byword for deluded and distasteful lust. A female Malvolio, cross-gartered in her dotage.'

Tamara was losing patience.

'This lie?'

The old woman shot Tamara a whiplash look.

'Yes. This lie, which will stay in the press cuttings, along with all those other lies, distortions, misrepresentations, and will be endlessly repeated. Like nuclear waste, these lies will have an infinite half-life. They will never entirely disappear.'

Tamara was not going to be thrown by her bluff.

'Don't try to deny it. We have the evidence. Dev told us everything, in minute detail.'

We? Us? She had given too much away. But the old woman did not seem to notice.

'In some cultures,' Honor said, 'your *naïveté* might be seen as charming.'

Her voice was returning to her, regaining some of its strength.

'But the facts were all laid out: the times and dates of your meetings . . .' Tamara said.

'The facts? This isn't fact. It's a crass contemporary fantasy for the lowest common denominator. You people are only interested in simple-minded archetypes. Bad people. Good people. Fairy-tale endings. Cruel comeuppances. Imbecilic morality tales for an amoral age.'

Tamara was not going to be harangued by a repulsive old paedophile.

'Now wait a moment. This was a serious investigation,

with a strong public interest element. You're an influential figure. You've published pronouncements on moral issues, talked endlessly about truth. What you say, how you live, matters.'

'A simple, lurid lie will always be more attractive to people like you than dull, complicated truth.'

'Don't give me "people like me". It's people like you who are the problem here. How complicated can it be? You have been seeing him regularly, your "aura masseur". Your gigolo.'

'Aura masseur? One of his many skills. And gigolo, too? A true Renaissance man.'

'This isn't the time for sarcasm. He's been coming to you for private sessions.'

'A lie.'

'You were photographed with him!'

Honor sighed and shook her head.

'Yes. I was photographed with him.'

Tamara felt a thrill of righteousness. She knew how this went; she had seen the prosecuting barrister's merciless routine in countless TV soaps.

'You were holding hands.'

The old woman, the defendant, bowed her head, and was about to change her plea to guilty.

'Yes.'

'Kissing.'

Tait lowered her head further. Telling the truth, Tamara could see, was costing her a great deal.

'Yes.'

'Like lovers.'

At this, Tait lifted her head. She was nodding now. An admission of guilt. Tamara had her at last.

But when it came, the old woman's answer was a vehement denial.

'No! No! Not like lovers.'

Tamara was exasperated, but she was not going to give up. One more push.

'So, you agree you *do* know him. He did come to see you. And you held his hand and you kissed him, just as you'd done since he was a boy.'

The next 'yes' was a whisper.

'Your lover,' pressed Tamara. 'Your paid-for lover.'

Honor extended a wavering hand and gripped the arm of the chair, using it to lever herself to her feet. She was agitated, trembling all over now, and walked slowly to the fireplace where she clutched the edge of the mantelpiece for support.

'He was a . . . friend. A close friend. I've barely seen him in the past seven years.'

This was procedural, a distraction. Tamara refused to be deflected.

'Never mind times and dates. Let's deal with the truth here. You kissed him.'

'Yes, I kissed him,' said the old woman wearily, unwinding the green worry beads coiled around the base of the clock.

'You were lovers,' Tamara said, elated by her adversarial mantra. 'You kissed him, like a lover, not like a friend.'

'Not like a friend. Not like a lover,' Honor repeated faintly, twisting the circle of jade in her hand.

'We've seen the photographs. How exactly were you kissing him then?'

Tamara had her now.

A sudden sound, like a hailstorm rattling against a window, broke the silence as the thread snapped in Honor Tait's fingers and the beads fell in a sudden stream, bouncing and scattering across the parquet. The old woman did not move.

'Like a mother,' she said quietly.

Tamara had a sudden swooping sensation of weight-lessness.

'What are you saying?'

'I kissed him,' Honor Tait said in a voice ringing with anger, 'not like a friend, or a lover. I kissed him like a mother. A mother kissing her son.'

Tamara reeled back in her chair.

'Dev is your son? But you never mentioned a son.'

Honor sat down again and Tamara stared as the old woman absently sifted the few remaining beads, like grains in an hourglass, through her gnarled hands.

'He was – is – my only son: Daniel, Danny, Hari, Asgar, Dev – whatever name he's calling himself at the moment. He's my son. My adopted son.'

She was lying. She must be. What else could she do? It was the reckless act of a cornered woman, a practised manipulator. She had succeeded in throwing Tamara off course, but only temporarily. Tamara checked her recorder

– still plenty of tape left – and picked up her notepad. She needed to get the facts absolutely straight.

'There was no mention of a son in any of the cuttings I read.'

Honor answered in a mocking drawl.

'Well, if it's not in the cuttings file . . .'

Tamara sat, silent and tense, trying to recall Dev's accusations – his exact words – as Honor continued.

'Daniel Edmund Tait, or Varga as he preferred, went – fled – to New Zealand in 1990 at the age of twenty-three. He bought enough land to set up a commune on the South Island with a bunch of like-minded crackpots. It all fell apart, of course. Then he went to Hong Kong, and blew the rest of his money there before moving to northern India, then Spain, then on.'

'You're lying.'

Honor stiffened.

'If it's lies that interest you, Daniel could run master-classes. He always had a taste for invention and reinvention. During a brief period of teenaged gentrification, when he swaggered about Chelsea in a waxed jacket like a country landowner at a point-to-point, he insisted we called him by his middle name, Edmund. When the drugs first took hold, he changed that to Ed.'

'Dev and Daniel are the same person?'

Honor tilted her chin and smiled with false pity.

'In his early teens he insisted on using the last name Varga, the name of my second husband, whom he'd never even met. It was a deliberate insult to Tad, and to me, of

416

course. At that time – we learned from Daniel's school later – he was affecting an aristocratic Hungarian past.'

'So you're telling me,' Tamara said, picking her words carefully, for the record, so there could be no mistake, 'the young man in the photograph, Dev, the man you were seen kissing, is your son?'

'I am telling you,' the old woman said, jaw clenched, 'my son, my adopted son, Daniel, was – is – a dangerous fantasist and a pathological liar.'

She let the beads drop in her lap. Daniel's *komboloi*, his worry beads, an affectation he had acquired after a month living in a Greek island cave with fellow hedonists. They were 'finding themselves'. That was the trope. First he had found himself, and then he was lost for ever.

Now Honor was no longer parrying the dumb girl's questions. She was telling the story because she had to. Because she never had. She was enjoying the young woman's discomfort. And there was nothing to be gained from concealment now, no one to protect. Least of all herself.

'He was there, in Glenbuidhe, the night of the fire. He'd taken a key and gone up there without our consent after we refused to give him more money. He bought a plane ticket with our final payment and left for New Zealand the next day.'

'I don't understand.'

'Of course you don't. You don't understand anything. Why should you?'

It was a double curse: confidence and ignorance, Honor

thought. Was this the burden of Tamara's generation, affluent children born in an unprecedented time of peace and privilege? Daniel, not much older than this girl, had been similarly afflicted. By the time he had reached the age to be curious about the world, there were no hidden frontiers that had not been meticulously annotated by backpackers' guidebooks; the only uncharted journey was interior. And what a disappointment that must have proved. Daniel's psyche had not turned out to be a transcendent range of virgin peaks and hidden valleys, nor a candlelit pleasure palace. No amount of mind-altering drugs could change the fact: Daniel's mental landscape, his inner life – or his soul, as he liked to characterise it – was a commonplace shopping mall, a kitsch temple dedicated to envy and greed.

'Why?' Tamara asked, lost in a pained replay of the most intimate moments of that first night in Clapton, and their last in the Paddington hotel.

'As the adopted child of moderately well-known parents, he had some scope for storytelling – and for the nursing of resentments, real and imagined. In that, at least, he excelled.'

The revelation that the story departed so much from the tabloid version had, Honor noted with satisfaction, wiped the smile from the girl's face. Tamara sat crushed and silent as the old woman resumed her story unprompted.

She had been nearly fifty when her second marriage had come to an end.

'I was between lovers, too. The child was a project, the

suggestion of a childless friend who thought the thing that she most yearned for, a baby, would give me the profound happiness it would have given her. I went along with it. Motherhood was an experience I had not had, and this lack, I stupidly thought, defined my distance from other women. By becoming a mother I would join the stream of humanity, instead of just looking on. I wanted to feel that love, to give it and to receive it.' The old woman closed her eyes. 'Selfish folly, I realised later. I wasn't cut out for motherhood, just as he wasn't cut out for the filial role.'

Her voice trailed away again as she lapsed into thought. The womanly stuff, the wise wound and the aching womb, the call of biological destiny, had always seemed bogus to her and she had sometimes wondered, when she first gathered the vulnerable baby into her arms in that orphanage in the shadow of Ettersberg, if it had been an act of contrition rather than love.

The silence in the room was crystalline. As Tamara turned to check her cassette, her notebook slipped from her lap and hit the floor with a slap, jolting Honor out of her thoughts and back into her spoken confession.

'I had visited the orphanage in Weimar, covering a story about post-war adoption in Germany – thousands of girls who'd had liaisons with occupying soldiers had abandoned their babies. The boy's decorative quality – his fair putti prettiness – drew me in. We looked good together, that little fellow and me.'

She had sent him to the best schools, furnished him with all the toys, tools and gadgets he required.

'Later, Tad came into our lives and did his best as a stepfather. Together, during school holidays, we escorted Daniel round the museums and monuments of Europe's greatest cities, and introduced him to some of the most interesting men and women of the age. I took his silent watchfulness for awe, but some years on I learned I had been badly mistaken.'

It was when he reached his teens that her beautiful son, newly expressive, disclosed that, far from appreciating all she had done for him, he had been harbouring resentments for years.

'He was a difficult adolescent: lazy, surly, with little aptitude or interest in anything apart from self-pleasuring and comic books.'

Lois, dear Lois, had tried to help, true to her word, taking Daniel into her home when Honor was away working, sometimes for months on end during school holidays. At first, Honor had resented Lois's closeness to the boy and felt her attempts to help were interference. Lois had always been better at that sort of thing. People. Friendship. Children. Love. Later, though, Honor came to feel relief at her friend's intervention. She was welcome to him. Adoption had been a mistake. Honor had been a fool to think she had anything to offer a child. Daniel had repaid Lois's kindness by stealing from her – cash, jewellery, antiques, pictures – but she refused to go to the police and, with stubborn patience, had continued to offer him affection and hospitality as if nothing had happened.

When he finally completed his schooling without further serious trouble and got a place at art college it seemed, to Honor's private chagrin, that Lois's faith had been rewarded. But the Slade had proved a short-lived diversion and Honor's scepticism was vindicated. It soon became clear that Daniel preferred girls and drugs to life classes and printmaking. He ran up catastrophic debts, acquired a circle of semi-criminal friends and began his involvement with a succession of cults.

'He was on a spiritual path, he said, salaaming unscrupulous gurus and affecting a vegan diet, while popping handfuls of pills and haunting squats with tramps and sociopaths.'

Honor rolled the worry beads in her palm. 'The trouble with the Darling Boy,' Tad had once said, 'is that he doesn't worry *enough*.'

There were spells in rehabilitation centres, costlier than five-star hotels – Lois had helped to pay the fees – then there was the Hari Krishna phase, followed by a stretch as a cerulean-robed devotee of Alandra, The Blue Goddess. For a while he was a sanctimoniously jocular adherent of the Sacred Laughter Fellowship, then he spent two months as a sandalled zealot of the New Jesus Militia. But he was always drawn back to his sordid milieu, to his derelicts' circle in grim North London flats, to his addict girlfriends and his own ruinous drug habits.

'It was Tad,' Honor told Tamara, 'who finally insisted: no more money to fund this fecklessness.'

Lois would have gone on shelling out but her money

simply ran out and the anxiety over her proxy son seemed to trigger her mental decline.

'And that was when I first saw Daniel's vicious side,' Honor continued. 'He stumbled across evidence of Tad's sexual peccadilloes – "occasional cross-dressing", as they call it now.'

She saw the girl stir and reach with automatic swiftness for her pencil and notepad again; but what was the point of dissembling any more? Didn't people boast about this sort of mild eccentricity these days?

'He tried to blackmail us,' Honor went on.

Looking for something valuable he might sell, he had prised open the tin trunk. He had mocked and raged at his stepfather, stormed at his mother for tolerating 'life with a drag queen' and threatened to go to the tabloids, which would have gone into ecstacies of disapproval at news of the private urges of a well-known film director.

Tamara was scratching away at her notebook like an industrious schoolgirl.

'I was repelled by his ruthlessness, his venality,' Honor said. 'I didn't want anything more to do with him. I gave him what he asked for but said it would be our last contact. Severance payment.'

And so, a week later, in their London flat, Tad had answered a call at 4 a.m. from the police in Inverness-shire. Glenbuidhe was in flames.

'Local police initially suspected arson. There had been rumours of attacks on second homes by nationalist hotheads. There were also uncomfortable questions about our relationship with Daniel, about his state of mind – the day before the fire, he had been seen in a local pub, insensible with drink – and about his underclass connections. But their curiosity faded when forensics revealed a fault in the wiring, which hadn't been renewed since the Twenties. The case was closed and Daniel was, by then, setting up his doomed utopia on an abandoned farm on the Abel Tasman peninsula. I never expected to see him again.'

'But how . . . ? Where . . . ?'

Honor dismissed Tamara's questions with a wave and continued. Five years ago she heard reports from one of his old girlfriends, just out of a rehabilitation clinic and looking for money, that Daniel had been sighted at an Indian monastery in Uttar Pradesh.

'She probably thought she was telling me, a mother, what I most wanted to hear. I put the phone down on her.'

Weeks later the girl called again with news of a rumour that he had been asked to leave by the monks, who accused him of abusing their hospitality.

'That's when I knew it was him,' Honor said. 'It's his trademark. He's been abusing hospitality all his life.'

Honor had kept the news from Tad, and from everyone else, and silenced the girlfriend with a pay-off, 'sufficiently large to fund a fatal overdose of heroin'.

Outside Holmbrook Mansions, late afternoon had ceded to evening and the glow from the streetlights gave a jaundiced cast to the flats opposite. Tamara thought of her colleagues standing outside as night fell, waiting for a glimpse of the old woman. There would be laughter, gossip and a comradely sharing of drinks and smokes. Someone would be nominated to go to the pub for bottles of spirits to liven up the coffee and keep off the chill. Night was descending in the flat, too. But there was no warmth or conviviality here. Tamara could barely make out her own handwriting. But Honor Tait did not seem to mind the dark. It suited her.

'So, when exactly did he come back into your life? Daniel?'

'He phoned just after Tad died, two years ago.'

After that call, Honor had been uncertain whether the chief cause of her anguish was Tad's death or Daniel's resurrection. Her son had expressed no sorrow about his stepfather's death, no sympathy for Honor, no curiosity about Lois, who could no longer be of use to him, nor any remorse about the blackmail or the fire. But still she had wanted to see him.

'I was lured back in, suckered. What mother wouldn't be? Even a mother as inadequate as me. My own guilt played a part, obviously. But in the end it came down to money. That was all he ever wanted. I know that now. I sent banker's drafts to aliases in Goa and Almora, arranged payments to American Express offices in Ibiza, Athens, Marrakesh . . . Friendship, kinship, love – it was always a financial transaction with him. You listened for a heartbeat and heard the click of an abacus.'

The shock had subsided and Tamara knew she had to regain control of the interview.

'When did you first see him again?'

'Before Christmas, there were a number of silent phone calls – I guessed it was him – then a taunting postcard. He finally phoned a few weeks ago. We agreed to meet. He said he was staying with friends.'

'In Clapton?'

'He wouldn't tell me where he lived. He seemed to move around a lot.'

'But everything he told . . . said about you, in the *Sphere*?'

Tamara knew the answer but needed to hear it baldly stated.

'Lies. Ludicrous, self-aggrandising untruths. And greed. He would have received a large cheque from that repugnant tabloid, I don't doubt.'

Tamara held her breath, hoping the gloom concealed her blush. The streetlights outside seemed to grow brighter as the edges and outlines in the flat – the mantelpiece and shelves, the fireplace, the squat, solid furniture and the insubstantial shape of Honor Tait herself – gradually dissolved in the darkness. The old woman talked on regardless, her voice disembodied, as if emanating from a ghost.

'But he can't just have invented it all,' Tamara said.

She could just make out Honor Tait's silhouette as she shifted in her chair and leaned across to switch on the table lamp. The light it threw on her was brutal, giving her face a greenish lustre and making a grotesque woodcut of its folds and shadows.

425

'You're not simply a ninny, are you? You're a dangerous ninny.'

She looked at Tamara with the detachment of a sphinx.

'I just want to get this right. What happened . . .' Tamara said.

Wincing, the old woman rose from her chair and walked to the fireplace again. She gripped the mantelpiece, bent to turn a lever and the flames of the gas fire flared up, casting shadows against the room's bare walls.

'I came to write another piece altogether,' the young woman continued. 'I really don't know where to start with this.'

'You expect my sympathy?'

'Of course not. But this really is a chance to set the record straight.'

Honor Tait slowly returned to her chair. She was nodding now. Compliant at last, thought Tamara, restraining a self-congratulatory smile. She wondered how she might approach this new angle. It would not be for the *Sphere*, obviously. No paper wants to trash its own story and Tim would be apoplectic when he learned they'd been taken for an expensive ride. The *Mail on Sunday* might welcome the chance to knock a rival's story: EVIL LIES OF JUNKIE SON IN GIGOLO BLACKMAIL SCANDAL. Maybe the broadsheets would take it: *The Times* or even the *Independent*. The tone would be loftier and might be more to Honor Tait's liking: BETRAYED BY THE SON I LOVED. SHAMED PULITZER PRIZE-WINNING JOURNALIST SPEAKS OUT.

'No.' Honor Tait brought down her hand on the table with a force that made the photograph of her last husband rock precariously. It was, Tamara realised now, the only photograph left in the room. 'That's it. There'll be no more stories.'

'But there will be. You know that. This story will run for years, decades, as long as there are papers to print it and people to read it. Unless we put a stop to it now. Publish the truth.'

'We?' Honor shrank back into her chair. 'Don't, for a moment, assume that you and I have anything – even a shared humanity – in common. I have no need for you or your kind. I withdraw my cooperation from this or any other story. It's finished. The whole damned charade is over.'

'But why?' Tamara asked, her voice hoarse with indignation.

'That is quite the most stupid question you've asked all afternoon,' Honor said. 'Now get out.'

As she walked towards the door Tamara turned to look back at the small seated figure, dwarfed by the room's leaping shadows. In the lamplight, Honor Tait's face was set in a grimace of mad defiance, her head thrown back, her eyes blazing: an ancient Joan of Arc at the stake.

Twenty-four

By the time Tamara arrived outside the Clapton flat, the flames were under control. The fire, onlookers said, had been mostly confined to the attic. Tamara saw the punk girl, barefoot in the cold, wearing only a sweatshirt and leggings, drinking tea with a couple of firemen. No one was hurt, they said, but there was some serious structural damage.

Tamara had tried phoning him from a call box as soon as she left Holmbrook Mansions, but she had known, even as she dialled, that his number would be disconnected.

She walked over to the girl whose face was streaked with black tears – mascara, or smoke.

'You missed him,' she told Tamara, wiping her eyes with the back of her hand. 'He left this morning. Said he was heading east, and he didn't mean Canning Town. The vibe round here was bad, he said. Too much negative energy.' She gave a wry laugh. 'And there will be, when the landlord finds out he's gone. On top of all this,' she gestured at the attic, the broken, blackened windows and the caved-in roof, 'he owed three months' rent.'

*

Honor had all she needed for this journey on her bedside table: a jug of water and a glass, her cache of pills. The wireless was tuned to Radio Three. Schubert Lieder. 'Erlkönig'.

'My father, my father, oh do you not hear/What the Erl-king whispers into my ear?'

She picked up her notebook – the habit of work was hardest to break – and looked again at her latest revisions.

Then I stood by, watching as the Allied soldiers took turns with fists and boots until that young German, an innocent schoolboy and victim twice over, sprawled bloody and unconscious by the blasted stump of Goethe's mighty oak. It was in this spot that the poet had written, 'Here man feels great and free – great and free as the scene before him, and as he ought properly always to be.'

She flinched as she remembered the jubilant blows and the boy's stare as he went down. His eyes, nursery blue in the ruin of his face, found hers. And then he cried out: *'Mutti! Mutti!'* Mother! Mother! His last words. The notebook slipped from Honor's hand and fell to the floor.

The day before she had been to her GP, leaving and returning by the rear entrance of the mansion block. She had complained of angina. Heart pains. Half true, though the pains were not, in the main, physical. But the recent visit to her doctor would mean there would be no fuss, no need for an inquest. She had shaken her stockpiled tablets into a cup and thrown the bottles down the chute. Back in her bedroom, she emptied the pills into her palm and swallowed them, two handfuls, with the water, in four bitter mouthfuls. All her remaining strength was needed to suppress the urge to vomit. This was to be her last fight.

She drew the blankets up around her throat. She had completed her flat clearance. Her photographs of Tad and Daniel had been thrown down the chute with the last of her books and papers. All that remained was the final notebook, lying face down on the floor. She had unplugged the phone and disconnected the doorbell. The maid was not due until next week. The doorman had agreed to post the letter – simple, evasive, no blame or recriminations – to her publisher, second-class. By the time she received it and hurried over to let herself into the flat with Bobby's key, it would be finished, and self-important Ruth could be trusted to keep Honor's final secret. Death from natural causes would be the story.

Ruth was to be executor of her will. The flat would be sold, debts paid and any residue to be given to an Alzheimer's charity. There was no point in leaving it to Lois herself. And as for Daniel, he had had his final payment. She settled back on her pillows and closed her eyes, trying to still her mind and shut out this terrible sense of failure. Had Daniel been born bad? Or had she, the most unnatural of mothers, an observer of life rather than a participant, made him so?

Honor had often wondered what her last thoughts would be. Work, whatever role it had played in her life, was not a matter for the deathbed. It would be people – memories of friends, family, lovers, enemies – who would provide the final torment or consolation. Would it be a slow fade, a gradual extinguishing of the lights? Or would she die in anguish, howling her regrets? She could not shake it, this sense of misdeeds returned to haunt her. The whimpering boy in that place of beauty and horror. And her own ruthless curiosity.

'My father, my father, he's gripping me fast!/The Erl-king is hurting! Help me, I'm lost!'

She reached across the bed and switched off the radio.

Gradually, the black void, vast as the universe, dissolved behind her closed eyes to a restless blue – Loch Buidhe, shimmering in its amphitheatre of soft green hills, and in the distance Ben Firinn, its peak shining with snow, rearing over its sister mountains. Not Ettersberg, then, and its sinister beech forests. This was an unexpected benediction. The hills and mountains around Glenbuidhe were, in world terms, topographical pygmies. But they were her own pure and lovely Himalayas. And there was her childhood home in the distance, restored to her, its granite bulk softened by evening light, a place of peace, perhaps for the first time. No sign of her parents. At peace she hoped, also for the first time.

Here by the lodge at the water's edge, gazing up at the mountains, she is not alone. By her side a small boy, solemn and trusting, reaches up and entwines his fingers in hers. They stand there silently, hand in hand, watching the light shifting on the mountains. Soon, the sun will set, showering golden embers on the loch, and they will go inside, prepare supper and light the fire against the cold night to come.

*

How ironic that it should have been Ross, who had never been good at beginnings or endings, or much else in between, who was to provide the story's conclusion; Ross and crazy Crystal, whose sister Dawn's tragic fate had been sealed eight years ago, the day she had met Danny Varga, also known as Dev, with whom she had shared an interest in New Age beliefs and old-style substance abuse. But this was not for publication. As Honor Tait had said, there were such things as private matters, and no amount of money or promise of advantage would induce Tamara to talk about them. It was a question of integrity. Besides, another story had to be written.

It was a small victory, but a victory nonetheless, when Tamara's piece on Honor Tait's life and work finally appeared in *The Monitor*. Her hours of research, the interviews and her tireless legwork had not gone to waste, and there was the additional satisfaction in the thought of her new boss, currently in California for a technology conference, opening the paper and seeing Tamara's name on a story that she, pompous, power-hungry Tania Singh, would have claimed as her own.

Some fudging of facts was necessary. But, Tamara reckoned, this was only fair. She owed it to the old woman. The piece was a good deal shorter than Tamara had anticipated and unimaginative sub editors had cut many of her best lines, deleting the reference to T.S. Eliot's West End musical and the mention of Tait's close friendship with Lord Byron. They changed 'transgressive' to 'improper', excised 'hermeneutic' and refused to give way on 'chthonic', and the tone of the printed piece departed from that of her original drafts. But in the circumstances, this was only to be expected. There was no point in being precious; adaptability was one of Tamara's professional strengths, after all. *The Monitor*'s Obituaries page was not *S*nday*, but neither was it *Psst!* or the *Sphere*.

Tim's job offer never materialised, and now it never would – he had been sacked, along with Gifford-Jones, after Tamara's follow-up news story appeared in *The Monitor* and revealed the extent of Dev's deception. A PACK OF LIES – TAIT'S JUNKIE SON DUPES TABLOID was the headline, and the picture byline beneath it was Tamara's. They had used the *Sphere*'s photograph of the kiss, now revealed as an image of selfless maternal affection and a son's betrayal, as well as Bucknell's snap, furtively acquired from the bedside table during her first interview, of an angelic-looking boy holding Honor Tait's hand outside the family home in Scotland. Johnny had sent Tamara a herogram, telling her that Wedderburn, delighted by the chance to expose the gullibility of other newspapers, and overlooking the fact that *The Monitor* had initially been taken in too, singled out her news story for praise in Morning Conference. Such a pity that Honor Tait, who had slipped into a coma as the presses rolled, never lived to see her name cleared so emphatically.

The story of tabloid folly and filial greed had ricocheted round the world's press, on the day Tamara's cheque from the *Sphere* for the original story had been cleared and she sent Ross £2,000 to settle his debts. He could make a fresh start – or not – just as she was making a fresh start, with the obituary marking her second appearance in a week in the serious pages of *The Monitor*'s main paper. Her erstwhile protector, Simon, was no longer there, alas – a discrepancy over expenses had come to light, finally giving the management the excuse they had been looking for to sack him. So he was jobless as well as homeless. Jan, who had found out about Lucinda, and Davina, and all the rest, had kicked him out and taken up with the party planner who had organised their son's eighteenth birthday celebration.

'A "party planner"! The guy's sixteen years younger than her! Sleeping with my wife! In my bed! In my house! Can you believe it?' Simon said when he rang. 'What am I supposed to do?'

'Get a grip, Simon,' Tamara said. 'You've just got to move on.'

Just as she had moved on. Johnny, newly promoted as

434

the paper's deputy editor and tipped for Wedderburn's job, had invited her to lunch at the Bubbles next week. She'd even been given a company mobile phone and Simon, before his untimely departure, had passed her a list of celebrity phone numbers and taught her a few useful tricks. She had already managed to access Pernilla Perssen's voicemail. Pure journalistic gold. And now there was talk of a staff job on Features. She was on her way up. No question.

Honor Tait – Veteran Journalist, Friend of the Stars
Born Edinburgh, 2 April 1917
Died London, 25 February 1997

Honor Tait, the Pulitzer Prize-winning journalist with a colourful private life, died alone of natural causes aged 80 in her West London flat. Born in Edinburgh into a hermetic world of wealth and privilege she was educated by governesses on the family estate near Inverness, a Belgian convent and Swiss finishing school, before defying convention, abandoning her studies and moving to Paris. There she worked as a secretary for a press agency and partied with some of the most celebrated artists and bohemians of the day, before persuading the Editor of the Herald Tribune *to try her out as a reporter. She never looked back. On the many papers and news magazines she worked for, she was known for her great beauty and her insatiable hunger for a scoop. She wasn't afraid to use the former in pursuit of the latter. Among the many stories she covered were the Spanish Civil War,* the D-Day landings and the Vietnam War. Her mission, she said, was 'to champion the weak and to shine a searchlight in the darkest corners of human experience'.

In Los Angeles, she was a close friend of Hollywood royalty, including Marilyn Monroe (pictured, above right) and Liz Taylor (pictured, bottom left). Her name was linked to many famous men, including Frank Sinatra, Fidel Castro, Bob Dylan, Pablo Picasso, T.S. Eliot and Bing Crosby (pictured, centre left), of whom she said in a recent exclusive interview with The Monitor: 'He had marvellous feet. Whenever he held me, I felt like a gossip columnist.'

She married three times, firstly, in 1941, to the Belgian theatre impresario Marquis Maxime de Cantal. The union ended in divorce two years later. After several well-publicised romances, she married Sandor Varga, the Hungarian-born publisher, in 1957, who subsequently left her for the actress Bebe Blondell, (pictured below, right), star of the Sixties French film hits Après Vous! and Pardonnez Moi!. In 1967, at the age of 50, Honor Tait visited a German orphanage in the course of her work and adopted a three-month-old baby, whom she named Daniel. She moved with him to Los Angeles. There she met Tad Challis, the transvestite American-born director of much-loved British comedy film classics, including The Pleasure Seekers and Hairdressers' Honeymoon. They married in 1970.

She relocated to London with Challis but retained a shooting lodge on her family's former estate in Inverness-

shire, which she visited regularly. Seven years ago the lodge was destroyed in a fire.

In later years, following the death of Challis in 1995, Tait devoted herself to good causes and lived quietly alone in London, in a crepuscular flat full of her collection of valuable antiques and old master paintings, occasionally entertaining a few close friends and becoming something of a recluse. A devotee of plastic surgery, she had recently undergone a further cosmetic procedure in the weeks before she died of a heart condition. She recently found herself the subject of unwelcome publicity when a tabloid newspaper claimed that she had been engaged in an improper relationship with a young man. The claims were unfounded and the young man proved to be her adopted son, as revealed exclusively in The Monitor *this week. The Editor of the offending newspaper has since been sacked.*

Tait's funeral will be held next Thursday at West London Crematorium.

Tamara's fee for the obituary was disappointingly small but, as a mark of respect and by way of recompense, she spent it on a large wreath of Honor Tait's favourite pink lilies, to be placed on her coffin. The card pinned to the wreath read simply: 'To the doyenne of journalists. From your greatest admirer.'

Acknowledgements

The research for this book gave me a pleasurable pretext to read, or reread, the work and memoirs of many distinguished women journalists, none of whom bear any resemblance to my fictional war correspondent, Honor Tait. Only Marguerite Higgins, the courageous and beautiful American reporter whose career path would have crossed Honor's, might legitimately raise an eyebrow. Higgins' description of an incident after the liberation of Buchenwald has some parallels with my story, but the details of her account, her response and the outcome, are markedly different. I am, however, indebted to Higgins' memoirs, *News is a Singular Thing* and *War in Korea*, and to her biography, *Witness to War*, by Antoinette May. Thanks are also due to Isabel Fonseca and Jane Maud, who read my early drafts and were generous and perspicacious in their suggestions, to my editor Rebecca Carter, and above all to Ian McEwan for his unfailing support and loving counsel.

www.vintage-books.co.uk